SIX PLAYS

SIX PLAYS

Mickle Maher

A MIDWAY BOOK

AGATE

CHICAGO

Printed in the United States.

Library of Congress Cataloging-in-Publication Data

Paperback: 978-1-57284-310-3

10 9 8 7 6 5 4 3 2 1 22 23 24 25 26

Midway is an imprint of Agate Publishing. Agate books are available in bulk at discount prices. Single copies are available prepaid direct from the publisher.

Agatepublishing.com

PRAISE FOR MICKLE MAHER

"Mickle Maher's work springs from a bizarre planet I wish I could find. His plays are singular, and a constant reminder of how many beautiful, strange stories remain untold. It's a joy to find yourself on his alien shore."
—Caitlin Parrish, author of *A Twist of Water* and creator of *The Red Line*

"It's said often of writers, but in the case of Mickle Maher, it's true: there is *no one* else on the planet writing anything that even resembles what Mickle is writing. His is a purely original voice. To enter into the world of a Mickle Maher play is to get sucked into a vortex of fools, kings, murderers, well-known canonical characters, poetry, and triumphant yop-crying. Maher's characters are caustic, funny, whip smart, beyond stupid, classical, contemporary, complicated, idiosyncratic, flawed, beautiful, petty, and profound. In short, they are us."
—Philip Dawkins, playwright of *Failure: A Love Story*

"Mickle Maher's mastery of language astounds in delightful plays of astonishing ingenuity. With surprising subject matter and sly poetry, his work consistently enchants with innate wit, even as it balances between hilarity and disaster. It's quite interesting to work on his plays as an actor; they are endlessly fascinating. He is one of our very best and most original playwrights."
—Deanna Dunagan, Tony Award-winning actress

PRAISE FOR *THERE IS A HAPPINESS THAT MORNING IS*

"Delightfully original. . . With its grace, wit and profusion of clever rhymes, the language alone is reason enough to attend."
—*Houston Chronicle*

"A bizarre, brilliant play that is capable of reordering your brain a bit." —*Austin Chronicle*

PRAISE FOR *SPIRITS TO ENFORCE*

"Mesmerizing. . . the stuff that great theater is made of."
—*Milwaukee Journal Sentinel*

"Entrancing. . . beguiling. . . the play is like a dance, a 90-minute linguistic ballet. . . a rollicking, cerebral delight."
—*Cleveland Plain Dealer*

PRAISE FOR *THE HUNCHBACK VARIATIONS*

"Tantalizes with swirling bits about the nature of creativity, grief, the endless universe, the physical world, the theater. . . a thinking man's vaudeville. You won't soon forget it." —*Houston Press*

"Seriously crazed. . . acquires rueful resonance, even amid the resolute absurdity of it all." —*Houston Chronicle*

PRAISE FOR *AN APOLOGY FOR THE COURSE AND OUTCOME OF CERTAIN EVENTS DELIVERED BY DOCTOR JOHN FAUSTUS ON THIS HIS FINAL EVENING*

"An Apology. . . quite simply put, is one of the most incomparable undertakings that has graced the stage. . . (a) complete masterpiece." —*Chicago Stage Review*

"It's hard to miss Mickle Maher's brilliance in this ingenious retooling of the Faust legend." —*Chicago Reader*

PRAISE FOR *SONG ABOUT HIMSELF*

"Wonderfully, exceedingly weird." —*Chicago Tribune*

"Subtle, elegiac." —*Houston Chronicle*

PRAISE FOR *IT IS MAGIC*

"A harrowing, hilarious journey into the eldritch heart of the theatrical experience." —*Austin Arts Watch*

"Maher shows true genius in this mix of goofy parody, deep intensity, and mad, limitless, inspired imagination." —KDHX

For Tom

SIX PLAYS

Mickle Maher

INTRODUCTION

A stroller carrying a crazy-eyed pope, disguised as a gnomic baby, careens on a stage imagined as frozen Lake Michigan pursued by a sensation-hungry editor of a rag that resembles Ripley's Believe It or Not. *A coven of spirits that "melted into thin air" at the end of Shakespeare's* Tempest *stages a return as dubious superheroes in a leaking submarine trying to save the polluted, crime-ridden city built by Ariel and Caliban after Prospero's departure, and, seated at a long table facing the audience, spend the evening making calls to raise funds for a revival of Shakespeare's play. Beethoven and Quasimodo, the Hunchback of Notre Dame, both deaf, convene a panel discussion that begins quietly but ratchets up the tension between Beethoven's good cheer and Quasimodo's gloom about their vain quest to recreate the impossible sound that echoes through Chekhov's* Cherry Orchard, *and along the way to find a "room for all the nothings."*

These improbable but indelible images capture key moments in three plays by Mickle Maher. The first, *The Pope is not a Eunuch*, appeared at Chicago's Cabaret Voltaire (now gone) in 1988. The second, *Spirits to Enforce*, premiered at Chicago's Athenaeum Theatre in 2003 and has enjoyed remounts on stages across the country from Portland, Oregon, to Durham, North Carolina. The third, *The Hunchback Variations*, aired in the multimedia space Links Hall in 2001 and has since enjoyed remounts in Belgium and Germany, as well as across the United States.

In addition to Chekhov, Shakespeare, Victor Hugo, and assorted superheroes, Maher has consorted with Christopher Marlowe, William Blake, and Walt Whitman. Critics have compared him to Nikolai Gogol, Samuel Beckett, and Bertolt Brecht. Many playwrights play with material from other writers, and Maher encourages the practice—indeed, "what would you steal?" is a leading question in his playwrighting classes at the University of Chicago. His purloining is certainly cunning, but his best work deploys cleverness and compassion, wit and wonder, parody and pathos. Pathos is much-maligned, but I use it generously to describe the effect that compelling characters inspire well after the laughter has subsided. Maher's voice is unique but his originality is not entirely self-fashioned, as it has been forged in the cauldron that is Theater Oobleck. The company works without a director; playwright, actors, and "outside eyes" (friends and members who are not performing in the show at hand) shape the work in rehearsal. These shows are anarchic and propulsive, hard to describe but impossible to ignore and, even when they go on to success on other stages, with other actors, and even directors, the plays carry the traces of the company that gave them voice. To find the way into Maher's work, therefore, we must start with Theater Oobleck.

Theater Oobleck and Mickle Maher: The First Decade

In 1988, a group of students who had been making theater at the University of Michigan left for Chicago and named their company Theater Oobleck after the formless but implacable green goo in Dr. Seuss's *Bartholomew and the Oobleck*. The company included Jeff Dorchen, David Isaacson, and Danny Thompson, whose plays were later published along with Maher's in the anthology *More If You've Got It*. The title acknowledges Oobleck's policy of asking patrons who have money to pay more than the asking price so as to accommodate the other end of the scale: "free if you're broke." Among other members, Terri Kapsalis acted in early Oobleck plays and wrote the introduction to *More If You've Got It*. Her book *The Hysterical Alphabet*, illustrated by Gina Litherland, appeared first as a performance/installation piece under the Oobleck banner in 2007. Among other actors, Lisa Black enlivened Oobleck with her performances of Cardinal Sindona in *The Pope is not a Eunuch*; and Patti Smith in Dorchen's *The Slow and Painful Death of Sam Shephard*, another hit in the banner year of 1988; and later, Prospero and a superhero in Maher's *Spirits to Enforce* (2003).

Maher's contributions to Oobleck's first decade included acting as well as writing work that, like the two plays mentioned above, mixed irreverent riffs on American classics and popular culture with satiric takes on the state of the nation. In *The Slow and Painful Death*, Maher portrayed several Sams, alternately haughty and hapless. In *When Will the Rats Come to Chew Through Your Anus?* (1990), his creepy and hilarious revision of the film *Willard*, he played the title character. And in David Isaacson's Cold War drama *The Spy Threw His Voice* (1991), he portrayed with eerie accuracy the right-wing pundit William F. Buckley squaring off against Danny Thompson's Václav Havel, the dissident playwright and later Czech president. In 1998, after taking leave to complete his BA at Bennington College Vermont, Maher wrote and performed two solo pieces at Chicago's Rhinoceros Theater Festival: *The Invasion of Desire and the Resistance to That Invasion*, about an obsessive relationship that consumed a small theater company, and *Perfect Copy*, about a "badger-replicator" in an alternate universe shaped by an unsettling combination of pranks and punk science. These plays may not have left a permanent record, but key elements resurface in the later plays, including those in this collection.

The Plays in This Book

In 1999, Maher returned to Theater Oobleck to produce what became his breakthrough play, *An Apology for the Course and Outcome of Certain Events Delivered by Doctor John Faustus on This His Final Evening*. The premiere production of this play, along with *The Hunchback Variations* (2001) and *Spirits to Enforce* (2003), all featured Maher as actor as well as writer. He has not acted in the more recent plays in this book—*There Is a Happiness That Morning Is* (2011), *Song About Himself* (2015), and *It Is Magic* (2019)—but since Oobleck's rehearsal process still has actors, playwrights, and "outside eyes" working together without a director, the original actors' contribution deserves attention in this introduction.

An Apology draws on the last scene of Marlowe's *Dr. Faustus*, where Faustus faces Mephistopheles, who has come to claim his soul, which Faustus sold in return for unlimited knowledge. In Maher's version, the usually loquacious devil keeps silent as he watches his prey, while a burning candle affixed to his hat marks the time left to Faustus over the course of the evening. In the premiere, held in the now-defunct, underground performance space 6Odum, Colm O'Reilly's Mephistopheles had cloven hooves and wore a hat and costume approximating the sixteenth-century garb of Marlowe's day, but Maher's Faustus wore "a cheap suit and a wristwatch of [the twentieth] century." The cheap suit, along with the diary that recorded his pact with the devil and his expressions of regret, made his apology for speaking to strangers "about nothing in particular" more abject than the apologia, the classical self-defense pronounced by Marlowe's once-proud protagonist. Nonetheless, although Maher's Faustus seems more like Gogol's insecure bureaucrat in *The Government Inspector*, as Chicago theater critic Justin Hayford had it, his account edges slightly closer to J. W. Goethe's more grandiose *Faust*, who travels far across time as well as space. Maher's man recalls his "fantastic life" traveling back "a hundred millennia." Faustus also echoes Maher's interest in the power of words, as he recalls an ancient time when language "hadn't stripped itself down to the bland serviceable thing it's become in our centuries," only to be hurtled into a "future" that looks like our stagnant present, filled with weak beer from a ubiquitous convenience store identified by "two meaningless numbers." Yet, even though Faustus's words fail at the end when Mephistopheles takes away his diary, Faustus's vivid vision of two Falls—

> The one from Paradise everyone knows about and
>   the other, more obscure,
> the Fall from Hell.
> And half of humanity, descending, has met the other
>   half as they climb.
> And the sparks that fly from this clash of origins are the
>   bits of the world that
> live completely outside any idea of Paradise or
>   Damnation—

ignites a light that burns in the mind long after the devil's candle—and the electric light on stage—have been extinguished.

Maher's adaptation of Victor Hugo's novel *The Hunchback of Notre Dame* (1831) for actors and puppets under the auspices of Redmoon Theater (2000) prompted his *Hunchback Variations*. But unlike the *Hunchback* adaptation or *An Apology*, which both borrow essential plot from the original, *The Hunchback Variations* (2001) stages a series of vignettes between two characters from different worlds: Ludwig van

Beethoven, the historic musical genius (1770-1827), and Quasimodo, the protagonist of Hugo's novel; their only common attribute is deafness. Maher repurposes the dramaturgy of his previous two-hander, pairing one actor playing in everyday clothes and with declarative voice and another in full immersive mode with a voice that carries Quasimodo's mood from gloomy mutter to angry shout. At Links Hall in 2001, Maher played Beethoven in street clothes topped with a baseball cap, and he spoke crisply and clearly, while O'Reilly embodied Quasimodo in a rough cassock, with a massive mask that magnified his head and distorted his voice. This distortion forced the audience to listen carefully to the sounds from the assorted instruments on the table before him and to his mournful record of their failure to find the "impossible, mysterious sound." Scholars may see in this contrast between different acting styles a kind of Brechtian estrangement. *Verfremdung* is not "alienation," as it is often mistranslated, but the critical representation of the tension between imitation and reality; Brecht wanted to prompt audiences to understand how this tension sharpens the theater's analysis of social conflict. Maher borrows from Brecht, but his scenario plays out something more subtle: the snags and drags between performing and thinking, high feeling, and sober presentation, which prompt the audience to ponder without explaining the space and time between them.

The Hunchback Variations play in eleven scenes of varying length, each marked by a hashtag number. In most, Beethoven welcomes the audience with insistent good cheer, only to flatly dismiss Quasimodo's repeated efforts to produce notes that might match the "distant sound, coming as if out of the sky, like the sound of a string snapping, slowly and sadly dying away" from Chekhov's *Cherry Orchard* (qtd: #3). This routine of repeated phrases and interrupted scenes and the comic absurdity of two deaf men conjuring an impossible sound summoned by a playwright as yet unborn in Beethoven's time might partly resemble parodies of bad performance by companies such as Forced Entertainment, but the provocation of laughter at Quasimodo's noisemakers and Beethoven's dismissive gestures gives way over the evening to profound questions such as: "Where is the place for the uncreated in this modern world? [...] Where is the room for keeping all the nothings?" (#7). Even if Quasimodo demolishes the unbuilt room and pursues instead a "pure disbelief," he still persists, despite failure, "to try again to find a thing less real than myself" (#10). "Failing better" may have been Beckett's motto, but Maher's variations on the play between quest and interruptions, abetted by almost subsonic sounds that run through the show, penetrate the ear and echo there, long after the evening has ended. Inspired by the power of sound in the play, the chamber opera version of *The Hunchback Variations*, with music by composer Mark Messing, had an extended run in Chicago, and went on to play Off-Broadway in 2012.

Spirits to Enforce (2003) continues the quest for "things less real" with a larger cast. The play assigns twelve actors three roles apiece: a secret (but named) identity, a superhero avatar, and a character from Shakespeare's *The Tempest*—the title quotes Prospero's regret that his revels and his realm have ended and that he lacks "spirits to enforce" (Act V; epilogue ll.13-14) his will. Apart from Ariel, whose name and powers come from Shakespeare, the other superheroes invite "pure disbelief" with names like "Snow Heavy Branch" (aka Brad/Alonso; Maher's role in Chicago). The spectators facing "what looks like twelve ordinary people sitting at a long table," initially see only a "mundane phone room job." O'Reilly's sound design, which Maher invites us to hear as something "inside a dripping, creaking, rusted submarine," works its magic, and as in *Hunchback Variations*, is barely noticed beneath the dialogue, which begins with elliptical requests for money to revive Shakespeare's *Tempest*. Although the performance in Chicago honored Oobleck's commitment to the collective as company members spoke in overlapping lines, Rebecca/Gonzalo/Ocean (Diana Slickman) and Emory/Ariel (Guy Massey) rose above the hubbub, as Rebecca made the rousing pitch, "the audience will sit on the crest of an enormous wave," followed by Emory presenting a potential donor with a thought that any small theater company might ponder—"When we speak of money, we speak of other things. Money is insubstantial mist. The froth on the wave of the real [...] When I ask you for money, I am not asking you for money. Remember *that*"—even if several other voices talked over the punchline: "I'm asking that a certain other reality come to be." But in the company's account, the rehearsals fell flat, the special effects fizzled, and the opening night was a near-catastrophe, almost ruined by the deadly critic Dr. Cannibal (formerly Caliban; O'Reilly in Chicago), who is only won over at the last minute, "cracking the spell of our show." Even after "the revels now are ended," as Cecily/Prospero/The Page recites Prospero's lines (first softly then emphatically in Lisa Black's forceful delivery), Craig/Antonio/The Pleaser (in David Isaacson's penetrating voice) revives them with a paradox: "Perfection needs no contribution, yes? But in fact, contribution is what I'm calling you about this evening." After Massey's Ariel reflected on the idea of his own reflection reading *The Tempest* after he's gone, Isaacson closed the evening on a note that floated hopefully, but a tad skeptically, over the dark waters: "Just wonderful...Yes. Now..." Unenforced, and perhaps unmoored, the spirits persist beyond the end.

—

Apart from Shakespearean verse quoted in *Spirits to Enforce*, the first half of this collection is in prose, albeit prose sometimes lifted into the realm of poetry—and sometimes dropped into a vat of satire. With *There Is a Happiness That Morning Is* (2011), Maher goes beyond quoting to making verse, inspired by poet and printmaker William Blake's "Songs of Innocence and Experience." Blake's figures not only lurk in the title and in the rhyming couplet dialogue but also haunt the couple in this drama. Both teach at a bucolic college that could be Bennington; folksinger Bernard, played in 2011 by O'Reilly as a disheveled child of nature, sings songs of innocence in class and when serenading Ellen, while academic Ellen (a crisp, well-groomed but sometimes melancholic Diana Slickman) sharply dissects songs of experience in skeptical responses to Bernard's effusions. Alternating fragments from lectures show Ellen and Bernard's contrasting views of poetry, teaching, love, and life, but Ellen's insertion of "does thy life destroy," the final line of Blake's poem "The Sick Rose," into Bernard's ebullient versifying about "Infant Joy," foreshadows trouble. Trouble takes the form of college president Dean; he treats the couple's public love on the lawn as a scandal, and in return Ellen and Bernard regard him as a worm in their rose. But as the duet segues into a trio, the lines of conflict refocus in unexpected ways. Dean in Kirk Anderson's portrayal becomes more like Maher's hapless Faustus than the evil bureaucrat in the lovers' account, and the play ends by granting Dean, if not an understanding of their overwhelming passion, at least a measure of compassion.

In *It Is Magic* (2019), Maher returns to the tangled mess of hopes and gripes that ensnare underfunded theater companies everywhere, which he sketched in *The Invasion of Desire* twenty-one years before. Set in a basement theater, perhaps like Chicago's Chopin Theatre basement where it premiered, *It Is Magic* opens with two sisters whose grievances at having given their lives to theater, while the artistic director and his stars reap glory in the big house upstairs, echo Dean's unhappy exclusion from the magic circle of his star hires in *There Is a Happiness*. Deb, writer and director of an "adult" version of "Three Little Pigs," and Sandy, "intern coordinator," permanently put out for having never been cast, start off as a petty tyrant duo tormenting their colleagues, as Deb (a tightly wound Slickman in Chicago) summons Tim (Jerome Beck), who plays the Second Murderer in *Macbeth* upstairs, to a basement audition for the Wolf, only to drive him to distraction with endless repetitions. Sandy (in Chicago, Laura T. Fisher in manic mode) takes torment to slapstick levels, breaking Tim's finger and ranting at length about alleged rivals. Set against these two, Ken (O'Reilly), the director of *Macbeth* and a "*man in love with his own voice who has a right to be*," comes across as both pompous and persuasive when he airs his own grievances about theater, "the whole dreary trench of it," but the plot turns thick and darkly funny after unassuming newcomer Elizabeth (Heather Riordan) takes on a baleful look and recasts the three women as "weird sisters" who summon blood and fire that consumes the play and the theater with it.

Song About Himself (2015) may prompt us to think of Walt Whitman's "Song of Myself," but the great poet of multitudes does not himself appear in this play. Whitman's words are scattered like leaves at the start, as the lonely Carol (played in Chicago by a plaintive and hopeful Slickman) recalls her absent partner Eric "loafing" on a bench, but in this world, *Song About Himself* is a malfunctioning TV show in which recordings of the poet are announced only to be mislaid. Lost in the gloom made both murky and intimate in the small space formerly sponsored by Chicago's Department of Cultural Affairs, Slickman's Carol was an uncertain surfer in YouSpake, a supposedly safe corner of The Weed, the name of the corrupted internet in this particular dystopian future. In The Weed, and in our world too perhaps, language has shrunken even more than the "bland, serviceable thing" of Faustus's *Apology*. Bastard verbs like "back and forth" and "lengthy post" have supplanted "share" and "declare," and in the process, erased companionship. The record of this catastrophe is gone, as the strings of code that intermittently come together as the Host (O'Reilly) "for security" must "jettison from time to time random packets of [...] memory," his and everyone else's. As malware demons "I-Forgets and Whatisitagains [...] crawl over every word and erase and respeak them all," characters who try to enter YouSpake can barely mumble. Nonetheless, despite his loss of words and the Host calling for "protocols" to log him off as a "counterfeit," a newcomer called Tod (Guy Massey in Chicago) enters, seeking conversation with Carol. Singing apparently enables Tod to avoid the erasure metered out to mumblers, but the Host turns truculent and jealous, and thus more human when Carol and Tod begin to share experiences without going through him. On Carol's favorite television show, lost recordings of the poet mysteriously turn up—in Carol's voice. Carol voicing Whitman's "Song of the Open Road" may be a "thing less real" than subjects engaged in "Rage-Scrolling," and panicked commands like the Host's final rant "DELETE. DELETE. FORGET. FORGET" threaten to shred this fragile connection. Despite these threats, the last words by Whitman that accompany Carol "Afoot and lighthearted" on "the open road" counterpointed by Tod on the bench singing may be in isolated spots but still linger together with the audience in the dark.

I end this introduction with *Song About Himself* because it captures our present moment. This play speaks to our fears of confinement and to our hopes for companionship, and for speaking and gathering in person. It certainly satirizes algorithmically driven "messaging" in a world saturated by viruses biological and virtual, but beyond the satire, against the urge to DELETE and FORGET, it dramatizes the quest to recover, remember, and regroup. In the Oobleck spirit, Maher stages the ridiculous along with the sublime, the tedious and the sparkling, and the dark and the light that together make theater possible and necessary. Even after this present moment has receded into history, these plays will entice new actors and audiences once more to conjure out of shadows and thin air a "certain other reality" that despite all distractions still compels our attention.

Loren Kruger
UNIVERSITY OF CHICAGO, OCTOBER 2021

An Apology for the Course and Outcome of Certain Events Delivered by Doctor John Faustus on This His Final Evening

An Apology... was first produced in 1996 at Bennington College with the following cast:

John Faustus:	Mickle Maher
Mephistopheles:	Diane Wong

An Apology for the Course and Outcome of Certain Events Delivered by Doctor John Faustus on This His Final Evening

CHARACTERS

John Faustus, in his final hour
Mephistopheles, his servant of twenty-four years

PRODUCTION NOTE

A room, any room. Dark. Mephistopheles there as the audience enters. Faustus appears and addresses the audience, himself, and his servant. He holds a large diary and wears a cheap suit and a wristwatch of this century.

FAUSTUS
[Looking for the light switch.]

Now...

[Finds it, switches it on.]

Now...

Now.

Now some, or one, of you might ask why I would want to spend these last few minutes of my life speaking to a group of strangers about nothing in particular.

Because that is, apparently, what I intend to do.

And I hope that's okay.

And certainly some, or one, of you might ask why I would want to go out chattering at all.
Why not a dignified silence? Why not spend my final hour in melancholy reflection of all that which has brought me to this pass.
To this passing.
To this dark night.
Why not curl into the mahogany arms of some creaking rocker near the crack of a good fire
with the choicest brandy and tobacco the shelves of Hell have to offer and await my moment of demise in patient meditation.

Why not shut up.
Look back and think it all over.

Well, I have reasons.
Don't ever think that John Faustus could be without his reasons.
I am a man of reasons.
The first reason, I suppose, being that that chorus of humors necessary for patience and
quiet contemplation is just not gathered in me tonight.
Tonight, I am an irritated person. Tonight, I am an annoyed person.
And yes, I have reasons for being irritated and annoyed. And that's not something everyone can claim. There's plenty of irritated and annoyed people who can give you no reason whatsoever—or no real reason, at any rate—for their unattractive mood.
But I do have reasons.
And now at this moment I would like to tell you those reasons.

This morning,
my explanation begins,
the last morning of my life,
I wake up to find my servant of twenty-four years sitting,
as usual,
at the foot of my bed, peeling,
as usual,
a hardboiled egg and reading, as he does every morning,
my personal diary.
Certainly, the morning was beautiful enough, with sunlight streaming through the open window and the song of the spring peepers rising from the pond below, but there in my bed the Prince of Devils is reading my diary, in unholy absorption, getting his egg shells and crumbs of yolk all over the blankets, a disgusting mess.
Annoying? Yes.
And I said to him, this is disgusting, this is a disgusting mess and you would think, I said,
that today on our last day together in this house you would have some consideration.
What is it with you and my diary?
There's nothing in there for you. There's nothing in there for him. In here.
In here, there's nothing in here for him, for anybody.
And why?
WHY is there NOTHING in the diary of JOHN FAUSTUS of any merit or consuming interest for the poke-nose? Why?

Because ever since I woke up twenty-four years ago to find him reading my first entry
I've put nothing in here but these:

[He opens his diary and shows the pages. They're filled entirely with hash-marks:]

Hatchmarks.
Hatchmarks.
Or as some would say, "tick-marks." Or even "hash-marks."
I prefer hatchmarks.
The pattern of marks drawn by imprisoned souls throughout history on the walls of their cells to count down the days. The pattern, it's rumored, drawn by the original prisoner, that fallen one, on the crags and cliffsides inside his fiery orb. Keeping track of his eternity.

They say Sisyphus has covered his rock with them, using mud from the bottom of the hill.
And there's so many marks, they say, that he's built up this tremendous crust.
And this crust actually has a great deal more mass than the rock it covers, so what he pushes is not so much a rock, but more the record of the number of times he's pushed that rock.

It's what they say, I don't know, it's not important.
What's important is to get across the fact that these marks, my marks, are outside of this long tradition in that they don't count anything.
They count nothing but themselves.
They're meaningless.
And they have nothing to do with anything. I make entries when I feel like it and when I don't feel like it.
They're meaningless.
And in case *somebody* hasn't figured it out already, they're not some kind of secret *code*.
They're not anything anybody should have any interest in reading.
Because they can't be read. Because what they convey is exactly nothing.
Meaningless.
All of it.
A life's work.

A life's work.

I remember almost nothing about that first morning, twenty-four years ago. Except yanking the diary from his paws, tearing out the pages he'd been reading and destroying them, somehow, either by fire or swallowing, I forget.

Swallowing, I think.

That's right, it was swallowing because I remember thinking how I just couldn't do that on a daily basis, you know, eat a piece of my diary. Because I knew he wasn't going to stop.
Being a creature so easily tempted.

So there in the bed that morning, swallowing those pages, as you can imagine I was the very picture of a frustrated person. Oh, I tore the sheets, I smashed the chamber pot. I didn't know what to do. I wanted to keep a diary. I'm that kind of person.
But how, how to defend this diary from this snoop? This snoop with magical powers.

I figured I had a number of choices:

I could keep a diary and destroy the necessary pages somehow other than swallowing immediately after making each entry.

Or I could keep a diary that had nothing to do with me. A diary of lies.

Or a diary of lies which was in fact a diary of disguised truth.

Or a diary of disguised truth which was in fact a diary of lies.

Or a diary in code.

Or a diary of scribbles, a diary of mindless doodles, ink splatterings.

Or coded scribbles, mindless doodles, and ink splatterings.

But none of these seemed to be the way to go and I will tell you why.
I happen to be, if you don't happen to know, a very powerful, magical person in my own right. Everything I do gets a lot of attention. Always has.
They say the future can be read in my nail clippings.
The leaders of great nations make decisions based on how I part my hair.
Or they should. They don't but they should.
The local seers would be well advised to look through my trash can every night because everything I touch gains a great deal of cosmic resonance.
And my servant is a very sensitive fellow.
He can see right through you, see through anything.

And I could have filled this diary with scribbles...but every squiggle, every twisted line to him would have been the most clear expression of my most inner being. Because he knows chaos. He's intimate with chaos.
And code. Any sort of code.
But these hatchmarks are not chaos and they are not code. They *count* nothing, they *mean* nothing. They're the most brilliant thing I've ever come up with.

And I came up with them.
Me.
That first morning, twenty-four years ago. In a flash. Oh yes, he had been dancing to the sunrise and he'd tracked his muddy hoofprints all over the place: on the floor, the walls, the ceiling, the furniture, and on the globe. On the globe. On the globe, slashing across the four fingers of a now evaporated section of the Caspian, was the line of his left cleft. Amidst all the muddy filth, forming the pattern.

And it came to me. My own dance!

"You're getting nothing on me reading that!" I told him this morning. I was so annoyed.
Magnificently, gigantically annoyed. And from this annoyance was propelled an authority I hadn't known in years.

"*I command you*," I told him.

"I *command you* by the terms of our contract to stop
reading my meaningless diary."
"I command you," I told him,
"I command you by the terms of our contract
to hand over my meaningless diary
and tell me why you would ever want to read my meaningless diary
and what you could possibly hope to get out of reading my meaningless diary,
out of reading twenty-four years' worth of hatchmarks."

And he just gave me that blank look of his.

That certain blank look
that only the Prince of Devils can give.
A blankness past total indifference.
So irritating.

Before, when I was upset or irritated, I have to confess, I was the sort of person who would just retreat into a silence, a pouty, sullen silence. Well, this morning, I'm not ashamed to say, I exploded. I was lava. The burning stone. The mansion in flames and the falling, fiery roof beams. I may have once been the brooding type—not any more. Certainly not now, here, at death's door. Silence is out of the question.

Put yourself in my situation. This morning, my last morning, for the millionth and final time I catch the Prince of Devils burrowing through my diary and littering my blankets with his breakfast. Silence—whether dignified and peaceful or sullen and pouty—was an impossibility, was banished from the brain. I really couldn't see what else there was to do but to finally, finally, after twenty-four years, come to the defense of my privacy, to the defense of my private, meaningless, hatchmark diary.

And for your information, you cannot assume a silence, dignified or otherwise, when defending a meaningless thing. No, no, no, you have to make that extra effort when defending a meaningless thing. You have to fill your mouth with an ocean-noise of complaints and demands when defending a meaningless thing. Which I did. I did.

I redoubled my efforts. My tongue became a slashing, searing whip. I said to him, this Prince with his egg, I demanded that he tell me why he thought he had any right whatsoever to stick his nose into my private, meaningless book.

And again with the look.

Face like the mouth of
an infinitely
shallow well.

You people of the future, please don't wonder why John Faustus did not leave behind a decent account of his fantastic, possibly tragical life. Why the great scholar, the untiring investigator, could only offer posterity this diary which records nothing but the fact that his pen touched its pages.

A diary not much better
than a heap of bug-smeared leaves.

Don't wonder why he would leave it to others to imagine and write up his own history.
Blame the prying eyes of Mephisto, blame this Prince of Peeping Toms who really, I think, only exists to deprive me of solitude. He's made my life a spectacle with himself as sole and perpetual audience.
No room for private contemplation.
No room for talking to myself,
no room for writing to myself.
Would-be omniscient, twenty-four years, every morning poking into my private business.
With his egg, etc.

How could I ever make an actual entry, an actual entry using actual words, actual letters of the alphabet? It's been twenty-four years since I've written a letter of the alphabet.

I'm not even sure my hand remembers how to make an *A* anymore, or even a simple *X* or *I*. As similar, even, as an *I* is to a hatchmark.
The difference, I suppose,
is that one is an *I*
and the other,
my pen must know instinctively,
is the far less meaningful thing.

I miss the alphabet.
I believe letters evolved the shapes they have to give pleasure to the muscles of the hand
that writes them, not the eye that reads them.
My hand, my whole arm,
misses those blobby *O*s,
those languorous *S*s.
The thrusting peaks of *M*.

I miss the alphabet.

But I'm not giving him the satisfaction.
He has my signature in blood, he's not getting my thoughts in ink. That story, my true story, the story of my heart, the story of my...soul...dies with me.
Has died already. Forgotten.
Hell will not know Faustus.
Hatchmarks.
A very orderly expression
of nothing whatsoever.
Hell will not know Faustus.
And if Hell will not know Faustus, then how
will Faustus know Hell?

But here, this is the problem.
Not the welcoming of evil into my life but my failure to record that evil.
To remember it, even. Evil counts on being forgotten to maintain itself,
to live. And I am constantly forgetting. I wake up every morning to find
Mephistopheles himself there with his egg and my diary and my first thought is always,
"Ah! That's right...I've sold my soul to the devil..."
Stupid, stupid.
Hell will not know Faustus, maybe, but Faustus does not know Faustus.
Everything with me is always now, now,

now even now just this side of my last midnight.
There is no real past. And no future.
Hell is my future.
And so, no Hell.
This is the life: Now.
Now.
Now.
Just this side of midnight,
just this side of Ending, still: now.

Now...

Everything...
falling petals,
evaporation,
dawn shadows,
breath...

Well.

If I am remembering things correctly, I have sold my soul to the Devil.
And if I understand things I'll be passing from this world—

[Checks his watch.]

—in a matter of minutes.

I'll be walking out that door and then...and then? Some say salvation, others the opposite, I don't know. Not even an educated guess. I should be entered in one of those books of imaginary creatures as the animal incapable of carrying a picture of the future in his brain. You all have pictures of the future in your brains. Yes? Especially all of you in this century. With your...your science-fictions and daily horoscopes and your weatherman. At the dawn of a new millennium, when thoughts of the future should be at their most profound, we find a people hungry for future trivia. But for me there is not even this *weather-man*.
For me, the future words of even this sentence I'm speaking are a mystery.
Unspeakable.
I have no conception of them
prior to their landing
in my mouth.

I.
Am in.
The Moment.

Hell opens wide for people like me.

But to get to the point: This morning, my last morning, I wake up to find my good man
paging through my hatchmark diary and after several times of demanding that he explain
himself he finally says, miracle of miracles, he finally says, if I remember right, "Well, what am I supposed to do when you just leave it lying around like you do? You leave a book just lying around," he says, "and naturally people are going to want to take a look. Maybe if you could manage to stop leaving your so-called private book just lying around for people to leaf through at their leisure then maybe, maybe, maybe, etc., etc., etc." And I said, "What what *what* do you mean lying around?

"Lying around?

"Last night I had you
lock that diary in an iron chest, which
itself was locked in an iron chest,
the both of them then being encased
in a sphere
of solid adamant and
plunged to the
bottom of the
Black Sea.
That's lying around? That's lying around?
You have absolutely no sense of the casual.
Of casual placement. Lying around."
And I said, "Now you bring me a stick because I am going to beat the living crap out of you.
You go ahead and fetch me a stick."
And he said, "Well what sort of stick would that be, a stick to beat the living crap out of me,
the Prince of Devils, just what sort of stick did you have in mind, Johnny?"
It did happen, that's what happened.
"What sort of stick did you have in mind, Johnny?"
And I said, "Well, this is my last day on earth and as a result I'm feeling old.
I would like a cane I feel so old. I feel so old I think I could even beat
the living crap out of the Prince of Devils, I'm so old-feeling. I want a cane, I want a cane, you bring me a cane. A cane cut fresh from the forest, carved and polished
hot, shiny, thick and heavy and swift.
A cane for Faustus."
And he did bring me a cane. And I chased him around the room and beat
between his shoulder blades until a hump rose on his hide there and split open,

and out spilled a heap of katydids, apple cores, petunias, wheat stalks, manure, Brazil nuts, tulips, sand and granite, a mouse, and a beaver, all sorts of things.

The world was in that hump.

And I said, "I am sick of this."
The hump on your back splits open and out spills the world and you still have this compulsion to stick your snout in my diary? What is the problem here? It is such a beautiful morning with the sunlight streaming through the window and the song of the peepers rising from the pond, why can't we just have some peace for once? My hatchmarks are not a secret code. You think they're a secret code, but they're not.
Who would they be a secret code for?
For the people of the future?
People of the future will have enough problems without any sort of secret hatchmark code from me. Get it through your charred skull. This diary, these hatchmarks are nonsense.
As meaningless as blades of grass, as the marks on the shell of a mollusk. Be happy with the world that spills from your hump. *Be happy with the world that spills from your hump*. Leave the meaningless record of my life out of things. Your prying and your poking have painted the great Faustus into a comer of hatchmarks—celebrate that. The great Faustus leaves the writing of his life up to long-winded hacks, more interested in the hues of their poetic vomit than in true biography.

Celebrate that.

But oh...why didn't I write it down? What does it matter what the Devil knows? Let Hell have all my secrets if the world can have them too.
But it's too late.
I've left nothing for you people.
Evil will go unrecorded again. I apologize.
Which is why I'm here tonight, I suppose, to apologize.
Something only to be done between human beings. Which is something I still consider myself to be, at least for the next few minutes.

Apologies, apologies—completely human inventions. No God or demon ever apologized to anybody for anything. Just too small a gesture, I suppose. So when we do it, when we give or receive an apology, we reflect nothing of the heavenly or infernal realms. It is our creation.
So.
Human to human.
I apologize.
I've left my story to self-indulgent scribblers. Yes, I've read the books and seen the plays, the movies, the operas.

Bogus.
Every word.
I'm sorry.

[Checks watch.]

I'm sorry. Not only because I've let Hell off the hook, but because really, I did have a fantastic life. What I remember of it. So hazy now. So much of it spent drifting up and down the corridors of Time. From one Now to the next...falling petals, evaporation, dawn shadows...

Hell was my time machine.

There's a variety of time machines but Hell is the most reliable, having been there from the beginning. Hell...where it's said there is no Time, where the infinity of Time is snuffed by a larger infinity, a Time so vast it swallows our minuscule eternity, swallows even Heaven's eternity. That's why God made Hell, some say, to separate from himself all that which was just too obscenely vast. The immeasurable a notch beyond the immeasurable. The Time fatter than Time. An infinity just too, too excessive. Excessive to the point of unholy meaninglessness.

Twenty-four years worth' of hatchmarks.
Is that why Mephistopheles reads my diary?
Because it reminds him of home?

[Checks watch.]

I can't believe this morning. So petty. Running around the room with a cane. Yelling and screaming over this hatchmark business. Who made this world? So constantly familiar and trivial. So caught up in insignificance. Be happy with the world that spills from your hump. But our humps have thickened and refuse to split.

The sunlight streaming in, the peepers' song rising—and then all this petty horseshit.
It wasn't always this way.
I used to do important things.
Together with my servant, at the beginning. Or at least associate with important things. And finding my own time and future times to be filled mostly with matters of grave inconsequence I fled back—three thousand years, four thousand years—to any place people weren't waving canes and screaming over hatchmarks.
Back ten thousand years
to the invisible courts of the Taoist Sage-Kings. Where emptiness

and inaction were all the rage. When all of China was harmonized—or subjugated some would say—by the ruler's inhalations, a gentle widening of his eye, or a hatchmark brushed
onto a leaf
and tossed
to the wind.
When insignificance had power.

Back a hundred millennia.
When language was ridiculously complex, when it still hadn't stripped itself down to the bland, serviceable thing it's become in our centuries. When tribes in imitation of the slowly advancing glaciers surrounding them spoke a language of only one word, a million syllables long, whose utterance began at birth, improvisationally, with the first syllables, and ended at death with the last.
A whole lifetime huddled on the ice, speaking—just once—a meaningless word.
Meaningless: there was only the one word, no others to define it.
And if there had been a definition, who could've lived long enough to speak it?
Faustus was there. He heard nonsense spoken as a life-duty.
A commitment to nonsense one million syllables long.

Back a thousand millennia.
When all earth was a black desert. Like the Libyan desert today, a desert not of grains, but hard pellets. Tiny black ball-bearings. The whole globe. And language was so complex it hardly existed. Each pellet in earth's desert was a single, unique letter in the alphabet of the time. A person would spend years sifting through these black pellets, searching for the five or six that would line up in a single word-fragment. Words that were found were quickly taken out of the wind and put on display in a tiny museum at the center of the village.

But as the words needed to define these words were rarely found, they were as good as meaningless. But cherished above everything else the tribe possessed.

Back then everything meaningless was important.
Now it means nothing.
It means trash. Garbage. Scum.

Hatchmarks.

Yes, we did at one time together visit such brave, old, wondrous worlds.
Now it seems almost that I've imagined it all, these tales of long ago times.
Or that somebody has implanted them in my brain, even.

But that's all memory is: a tale. A tale we tell ourselves, or a tale told to us. One or the other. Or a combination of these two possibilities.
Who the real keeper of the diary is, is not at all clear.

Except in this case. With my diary! Which he did finally, finally give back to me, of course. With the usual hideous, sarcastic pomp. Sailing it to me over a sea of consecrated wine in the inflated bladder of some poor nun or monk. Music from tarantulas skittering over the strings of floating harps. A mass of white eels below the surface, glowing, livid,
arranging themselves in row upon row of slimy eel hatchmarks. Senseless, mocking...then all of it, the entire phantasma, vanishing in a single funnel-gust out the window,
carrying away my cane and silencing the peepers below.

But in my hands the diary.

After we'd cleaned up the mess from the hump it was lunchtime.
I ordered some shortbread and cold gin and we went down and stretched out on the lawn.
I would've taken a nap but I could see the old Prince eyeing my diary. I kept it under my arm while I nibbled my shortbread—a thin, yellow triangle.
Like the tooth of the serpent himself, I thought.
The old Prince had a piece, but it just lay on his chest, browning in the noonday sun.
Collecting flies.

"Mephistopheles," I said. "Do you remember our time together? These twenty-four years?"
He held the cold bottom of his gin glass to his forehead.
"No," he said. "I've tried. But remember
I am always in the vastness of Hell.
And inside of that these moments are unimaginably small.
They slip through the floorboards of my brain."
"And all those pasts and futures we've visited?" I asked.
"Microscopic," he said.

We lay there for a few hours, watching the clouds take their shapes.
Cloud horses appeared and galloped themselves to formless vapor.
Cloud oxen, a cloud swallow. Cloud flowers:
morning glories, violets. Their stems, their leaves,
their roots, their seeds even.
The cloud seeds of cloud roses, cloud lilies.
A world more detailed than our own, if looked at steadily.
Cloud termites, coins even. A cloud
coin showing a face peering from behind a door.
A cloud coin showing a face peering
into a drawer
and discovering there
a coin showing a face

peering back, a cloud
noose encircling
its cloud
neck slowly
dissolving to nothing.

A world impossible to visit or possess, even with the assistance of Hell.
A world for gazing upon only.

After I'd had a few drinks the old Prince made a grab for the diary, but I rolled over and hid it under my chest. My face pressed into the earth and all the wilderness down there.
Dark insects pit-patting their random patterns across my face.
Going somewhere. Off to see the world. The insides of it anyway.

And that was our afternoon.

I wasn't hungry at dinner so we went to the future for some beer. Your future, actually. We shot a number of years past this point, got this…timekeeper and this clothing for me at some sort of…army…and then went out and picked up some—

[He takes two Budweiser twelve-packs out from under Mephistopheles' robes.]

—of your future beer. The beer in your future! When you come upon the future and you see this beer for sale there, you can say, "Ah ha! I saw it coming."

Please, drink with me, pass this around. A little taste of things to come.

[He distributes the beer to the audience.]

And here's some future potatoes.

[Takes out a bag of chips, opens it, and offers some. Examines one, a bit bemused.]

And you thought you had it all figured out with your *weatherman*.

Please! Drink with me, on this my final night! A little taste of things to come!

[Everybody drinks Budweiser.]

In those days to come they call this beer The King.

The King.

The future words of even this sentence I'm speaking are a mystery to me.
Falling petals...dawn shadows...
Nonsense cherished.

[Sips beer and checks watch.]

The place we got the beer didn't have a name.
Just two numbers. I forget which ones.
But they rhymed, I remember.
A little poem of just two numbers was the name of this shop, glowing on a large sign just outside above a small, flat field of black stone.

I asked the keeper of the shop what it was all about, and he said that at one time these two numbers signified the shop's hours of business.
But that was long, long ago.
Now the shop had completely different hours, was open twenty-four hours a day, in fact.
So, the numbers on the sign meant nothing. Except: here's the shop named after the two now meaningless numbers.
It seems idiotic.
But praiseworthy, too. That this shop owner would stick by his two numbers, stick by his little number poem, even though now it was basically nonsense. A nonsense number poem.

[Sips beer.]

And I asked the Prince, "Will you remember me? If I'm damned or if I'm saved. Will you remember me?

"And is it possible I will forget you completely?"

[Sips.]

It was under this sign of the two rhyming numbers that the last battle over my diary took place. I had gone out to sit under it, to make a final entry by its light. And I'm leaned up against the post, in gravel and the little shrubs there, with my pen in one hand, The King in the other, and my diary and inkpot on my lap. And I'm ready to go, ready to set down that last mark, when I notice that my good man is reading over my shoulder.

I couldn't believe it, I could not believe it! He'd never gone this far before. He's curled around the post, looking down, his eyeballs racing in spirals, just sucking it all in. I almost faint, I'm so angry! I slam the book shut, throw the inkpot and the King into the street, get up kicking gravel, and stab at his eye with my pen.

Just went straight for that rosy red iris.
I should've done this long ago, I thought. Just blinded the bastard. Cast him into darkness.
My pen, a sharp grackle quill, is right on target, right dead center of the socket. But he retracts his whole eyeball. Pulls it back so far my arm goes in up to the shoulder and I pierce nothing but skull air. The quill slips from my fingers and I can hear the echo of
its feather brushing the socket walls as it slowly falls down...fading sound... and then
a long silence.

Finally, as the evening star sets in the west, a faint *plish*
as it gently settles on the eye at rest,
far below at the bottom
of the socket well.

Plish.

Plish.

The sound of a quill falling into a tiny pool of tears.

"Isn't that sweet," I said. "You've been crying. You're all choked up."

But he shook his head. The gaping hole where the pupil once glowed.
"That plish wasn't tears," he said. "That plish was pus. I've got pus in my eye."

"Oh come on," I said. "It was tears."
"No, no," he said. "It was pus."
"No, it was tears," I said. "It was tears! You're crying. You're crying because you can't read my diary. You think my diary is in a secret code and you love that secret code *and you love me!*
And when I disappear tonight with my meaningless hatchmarks, your heart will break!"

"It's pus," he said. "It's pus, it's all pus."
"It's tears!" I said. "It's tears!"

"It's completely pus," he said.

"It's tears!" I said. "Admit it! Just admit—no. It doesn't matter if it's pus or tears. Just say it's tears. It doesn't matter if it's pus or tears, just say it's tears."

But he wouldn't say tears.

We stood under that number poem for an hour screaming "pus" and "tears" at each other.
He stuck to pus.

The hump thickens and refuses to split.

"Anyway," I said, "now I've lost my pen."
"I'll get you another," he said. "I don't want anything from you," I said.
Just get me a room. Anywhere, any time. Just some arbitrary room in some random town.
And put a few people in it.
Anybody.
I just want to apologize to a few random people for leaving behind nothing but this dumb diary. I don't need to apologize to the whole world. I'm sick of the world. Just a few whoevers.

So he brought me here.

And all of you.

And I talked about my day and what I did.

And I'm sorry I can't remember much more.

There is the idea, maybe you've heard, that there were two Falls.
The one from Paradise everyone knows about and the other, more obscure, the Fall from Hell.
And half of humanity, descending, has met the other half as they climb.
And the sparks that fly from this clash of origins are the bits of the world that live completely outside any idea of Paradise or Damnation.
Worlds unimagined by any God or Lucifer.

In my dreaminess, in my idle prayers, these hatchmarks are such sparks.

[Checks watch.]

Time.

Excuse me.

[Finishes beer, sets down can, and steps towards door.]

You know why in the theater the deaths that happen offstage always seem the most real.

The most believable. Because death is private. No matter what band of angels or host of devils surrounds you.
Death is offstage.

Falling petals
hatchmarks
breath...

[Gives diary to Mephistopheles.]

...now...

...now...

The future words of
even this sentence...

[Exit. Mephistopheles rises, switches off light, and follows.]

END

The Hunchback Variations

The Hunchback Variations was first produced in 2001 by Theater Oobleck at Links Hall in Chicago, as part of *An Immense World of Delight at Times Most Unlovely and Bullocky*, with the following cast:

Ludwig van Beethoven:	Mickle Maher
Quasimodo:	Colm O'Reilly

The show's sounds and soundtrack were created by Colm O'Reilly.

The Hunchback Variations Opera (music by Mark Messing, libretto by Mickle Maher) was first produced in 2012 by Theater Oobleck at Victory Gardens Theater in Chicago, with the following cast:

Ludwig van Beethoven:	George Andrew Wolff (tenor)
Quasimodo:	Larry Adams (bass)
Piano:	Tim Lenihan
Cello:	Paul Ghica

The score is available by contacting Agate Publishing at sixplaysmicklemaher.com.

The Hunchback Variations

CHARACTERS

Ludwig van Beethoven
Quasimodo

PRODUCTION NOTE

Throughout the play, except where noted, a melancholy, repetitive soundtrack is played at low volume.

Lights up on Quasimodo and Beethoven seated at a table with two microphones, a pitcher of water, and glasses. Quasimodo has a number of devices heaped in front of him with which he makes noises as indicated.

#1

BEETHOVEN
Good evening and welcome to this evening's panel discussion on *Sound, Mysterious Sound, Impossible Sound, Creating the Impossible, Mysterious Sound and the Effects on Love and Friendship of Rehearsing the Creation of the Impossible and Mysterious Sound.* I am Ludwig van Beethoven, composer, and on my left is Quasimodo, hunchback and former bell ringer for Notre Dame de Paris.

QUASIMODO
Hrh.

BEETHOVEN
I would like to begin by saying that I am an old man, in the last days of my life. My health is failing, my memory is broken, and I am completely deaf. My friend Quasimodo is deaf as well. Nevertheless, we've asked ourselves to head this panel discussion on Sound, Mysterious Sound, Impossible Sound, etc., because of our recent collaboration toward the creation of that very thing: an impossible, mysterious sound.

[Quasimodo makes a sound.]

BEETHOVEN
That is not the sound. The details of our collaboration we'll come to in a moment. First, however, Quasimodo has a statement he'd like to read. Quasimodo?

QUASIMODO
Thank you. Hahgn.

[Reads:]
There are two types of failure when it comes to artistic endeavor. The first type of failure is greeted with noise. Clamor. A hooting and booing and hissing and razzberrying. The sonic demons of derision that dwell in the lower inaudible frequencies of our culture's perpetual murmur of scorn, rise through the public's throats, and cannon forth, howling and breaking the air with their thunderous dismissal of the artist's small effort.

The second type of failure is greeted with silence. Embarrassed and aghast, the universe looks down at the artist's creation and all that is heard is the sound of our wicked planet turning in space.

BEETHOVEN
In other words, what you're saying, in this second sort of failure, no sound is heard.

QUASIMODO
That is correct. No sound.

BEETHOVEN
So how would you classify our failure? For we did, in fact, fail in our collaboration. There in your small hut at the edge of the marshes.

QUASIMODO
Failed.

BEETHOVEN
There in the twilight in the brackish scent beneath the faint stars. Around the bell table. What type of failure was ours? The sort met with sound or silence?

QUASIMODO
Our failure was met with silence.

BEETHOVEN
Hmm. Well, that's about all we have time for this evening. Thank you all very much for coming out. And good night.

[Lights fade.]

#2

BEETHOVEN
Good evening and welcome to this evening's panel discussion on *Sound, Mysterious Sound, Impossible Sound, Evoking the Impossible, Mysterious Sound, and the Effects on Love and Friendship of Rehearsing the Evocation of the Impossible and Mysterious Sound.*

[Quasimodo makes a sound.]

BEETHOVEN
That is not the sound. I am Ludwig van Beethoven and to my left is Quasimodo, former bell ringer for...something, I don't remember. As we are both deaf there will be no questions taken from the audience tonight. Thank you. Now, before we move on to the details of our collaboration—the marshes at twilight, the bell table, and so forth—Quasimodo would like to read a statement. Quasimodo?

QUASIMODO
Thank you.

[Reads:]
"In our effort to create Anton Chekhov's impossible, mysterious sound I believe everything would've gone a lot better if we had not rehearsed at my house. My house is small and muddy. It stinks of marsh water. Beethoven has a very nice, large apartment and he should have let us rehearse there."

BEETHOVEN
If I might comment on what you just said before I forget what you just said, I would ask if it's your position that we would've avoided our failure in creating this particular sound if we had rehearsed at my place?

QUASIMODO
No. Failure could not have been avoided. But it would have been more pleasant to fail in one of your sunny and well-ventilated rooms with the floors of polished pine.

BEETHOVEN
But comfort aside, it's your belief that our collaboration would not have succeeded no matter what the circumstances, yes?

QUASIMODO
Our collaboration was doomed. The world's externals had no bearing.

BEETHOVEN
Yes. But now it seems to me that time has passed us by. There's certainly more to be said, but it never will be. Thank you and good night.

[Lights fade.]

#3

BEETHOVEN
Welcome, everybody, to our panel discussion on summoning that which perhaps does not exist. The sound Quasimodo and I attempted to bring into being is the sound described in a stage direction at the end of Act II of Anton Chekhov's *The Cherry Orchard.* At this time, I can't remember the scene or stage direction very well, so we'll have Quasimodo explain it all.

QUASIMODO

[He produces a copy of *The Cherry Orchard.*]

In the scene Ranyevskaia is sitting out of doors with her family and the other characters on the outskirts of her estate. They've sat and talked of death and planets and Russia and giants, but now the conversation is paused, and they sit in silence. It is here at this pause that the stage direction appears. It reads: "Suddenly a distant sound is heard, coming as if out of the sky, like the sound of a string snapping, slowly and sadly dying away."

BEETHOVEN
"Coming as if out of the sky, like the sound of a string snapping, slowly and sadly dying away."

[Quasimodo makes a sound.]

BEETHOVEN
That is not the sound. But exactly what this sound is, is not at all clear. The characters themselves discuss it—the sound, if nothing else, spurs them from their melancholy silence—but none agree on what it might be. An owl? A heron? A lift cable breaking in a distant mine? If it's a string, what sort of string? And how could a string sound to anyone like an owl?

[Quasimodo makes a sound.]

BEETHOVEN
That is not the sound. It could be anything. Chekhov himself will be no help. In the play's first production—which will be mounted long after Quasimodo's and my death—a production directed by Stanislavski himself, a dying Chekhov will complain petulantly that the sound Stanislavski comes up with is totally inadequate. "It is such a simple instruction!" he will say. "What could be more clear? 'A distant sound, coming as if out of the sky, like the sound of a string snapping, slowly and sadly dying away.'"

[Quasimodo makes a sound.]

BEETHOVEN
That is not the sound. And now we have to say goodbye. Thank you for coming. As you leave, we ask you to not let what you've seen and heard here tonight seep too quickly from your minds. For our best lives are lived, like yours, in the memories of others.

[Lights fade.]

#4

BEETHOVEN
Welcome to this evening's panel discussion on expressing the inexpressible sound. Tonight, we'll be hearing from myself, Ludwig van Beethoven, and my collaborator, Quasimodo. First, an opening statement.

QUASIMODO
Good evening.

[Reads:]
"What is it I want? Above all I seek a total lack of faith, a pure disbelief, a state of knowing fully that there is nothing above or below the sky, that all is ruin, and beyond ruin, grief and a vacuum. Good evening. I curse you."

BEETHOVEN
But isn't it precisely faith, a great deal of faith, that is needed when tackling the problem of expressing the inexpressible, the unevokable sound?

QUASIMODO
Yes. And I want release from this impossible problem, I want release altogether from the urge to create. I want to be left to sit in my hut, at my bell table, surrounded by the sound of frogs and crows. Left alone to memorize my many sorrows.

[Quasimodo makes a sound.]

BEETHOVEN
Are there any questions at this point? [Pause.] Then let's take a little break.

[Lights fade.]

#5

BEETHOVEN
Good evening and welcome. Welcome welcome welcome. We welcome you. We are so happy you could all make it out this evening to hear us discuss our project on the impossible sound.

[Quasimodo makes a sound.]

BEETHOVEN
That is not the sound. Do you have a statement you'd like to read?

QUASIMODO
"We know not and no search will make us know. Only the event will teach us in its hour."

[Quasimodo makes a sound.]

BEETHOVEN
That is not the sound.

To recap:
Always in twilight I would leave my apartments and cross the marshes to my friend Quasimodo's small hut. Always in twilight to rehearse, to work on our project, the project concerning Chekhov's stage direction. "A distant sound, coming as if out of the sky..." Crossing the marshes in twilight with the stars emerging from their distant invisible nowhere, my pessimism would leave me and my mind would quiver with inspiration...

QUASIMODO
On every twilight in which he crossed the marshes to my hut, I could hear Ludwig van Beethoven's footfalls from a great distance, plopping and slurping in the muck. Nearer and nearer. So determined, so sure. Slog, slog, slog. So certain that our collaboration could be nothing but a success. It was to me a dread sound, the sound of a fool bringing defeat into my sad life once again. We would never satisfy this stage direction from Chekhov's *Cherry Orchard*.

BEETHOVEN
I would walk through his door eager, with a blossoming will.

QUASIMODO
He would come through my rough door, his silk slippers soaked in the bog's infections and his creamy stockings streaked black by soggy reeds. The sound of his spongy tread on my planks. His drippings on my rug. The Great Man.

BEETHOVEN
We would sit at his bell table. A table made, actually, out of a bell—a bell stolen by Quasimodo from the towers of Notre Dame when he departed that tragic cathedral for good in 1482. It was not a very good table as nowhere was it flat. Just an enormous bell sitting on his floor with chairs around it. If you put your drink or your sandwich on it, they would slide onto the rug.

QUASIMODO
We would sit at the bell table.
The starry night gone black.
The crow asleep.
Its dreamless brain dark as its wing.
To rehearse.
To bring into being.
One sound.

BEETHOVEN
And from there is remembered nothing more.
We now fade from you as you from us. Marsh, bell table, crow, and door.

[Lights fade.]

#6

BEETHOVEN
Good evening...have all of you arrived? Can everyone see us? Can everyone hear me? Is this on? Did you find the building all right? Did you find the room? Did you find your seat? Are you seated comfortably? Were you given a program? Is your program legible? Is your program informative? Is it attractively laid out? Are you warm enough? Are you attentive? Nearly silent? Are you thinking grand thoughts?

Please.

Count thy gains.

Would thou be born for this?

QUASIMODO
At the bell table, the starry night gone black.

The crow above, the frog below.

We would rehearse. From the corners of my hut I would bring all manner of instruments and objects to strum, to strike, to blow, to pluck. All in the service of Dr. Anton Chekhov and his diabolical instruction.

In these hundreds of rehearsals, Ludwig van Beethoven offered only a single sound as the possible solution to Chekhov's vague direction: the sound of the pages of Emily Dickinson's collected poems being fanned with his thumb.

[Beethoven produces a book of Emily Dickinson's collected poems and fans the pages into the microphone.]

QUASIMODO
At the time of our rehearsals, in the year 1825, Emily Dickinson had not yet written any poetry.

[Fans again.]

QUASIMODO
Emily Dickinson had not been born.

[Again.]

QUASIMODO
Is this not the most perverse sentimentality?

[Again.]

QUASIMODO
To delicately flutter the poems of a not-born, lonely recluse?
And further, to amplify this fluttering?

[Again and again and again.]

QUASIMODO
Goodnight.
Goodnight.
I curse you.

[Lights fade.]

#7

BEETHOVEN
Hello and welcome to our panel discussion on the pleasures associated with the making of an impossible thing. I am Ludwig van Beethoven. Our project was concerned with the infamous stage direction in Anton Chekhov's last play *The Cherry Orchard*, which he wrote, by the way, when he was dying of consumption, coughing his lungs out over the pages.

The stage direction which reads, "Suddenly a distant sound is heard, coming as if out of the sky, like the sound of a string snapping, slowly and sadly dying away."

The true sadness of this sound, of course, is that it has not yet been born.

[Quasimodo makes a sound.]

BEETHOVEN
That is not the sound. Quasimodo has some questions to get us started.

QUASIMODO
Thank you. My questions are simple questions.

[Reads:]
"Where is the place for the uncreated in this modern world? Where do we put the happiness that has not been forged? Where do we store the love that has not been sculpted? Where is the room for keeping all the nothings?"

BEETHOVEN
The room for keeping all the nothings.
I would like to think that such a room exists.

QUASIMODO
I don't believe in this room.

BEETHOVEN
Maybe you're right. After all, who would go through the trouble of building it?

QUASIMODO
Let us never speak of it again. It's a waste of time.

BEETHOVEN
No. Rather, let us say it's a deep mystery to be investigated only with silence. Thank you for coming.

[Lights fade.]

#8

BEETHOVEN
Good evening and welcome to our panel discussion on what currently is not, and perhaps never will be, but is worth talking about nonetheless, as it, the nonexistent, can never speak for itself. And because the nonexistent suffers necessarily in silence, it is therefore a compassionate impulse to speak of it—to speak for the nonexistent. The same compassionate impulse which guides the conversational plays of Anton Chekhov. The same impulse which now motivates my friend Quasimodo to give an opening statement. Quasimodo?

QUASIMODO
Thank you.

[Reads:]
"In our effort to create Anton Chekhov's impossible, mysterious sound I believe everything would've gone a lot better if we had not rehearsed at my house."

BEETHOVEN
But it was the walk to your house which was, for me, essential. Always in twilight, always by way of the marshes, the stars being born once again above my head, the frogs, the crows. I found it was only this somewhat eerie, wild, and wondrous landscape which could prepare me for our project, only this walk which would fill me with the enthusiasm necessary for the pursuit of an impossibility.

QUASIMODO
But your enthusiasm was no help at all. You sat in rehearsals and never had a single good idea.

BEETHOVEN
Is that true?

QUASIMODO
I don't think you even finished reading *The Cherry Orchard.*

BEETHOVEN
Yes, I've never read that. *The Cherry Orchard.* "The Cherry Orchard." Would that've helped? You think? Should I have read *The Cherry Orchard*?

QUASIMODO
No.
Our failure was certain.

BEETHOVEN
Should I have read *The Cherry Orchard*?

QUASIMODO

[Makes a sound.]

The end has come.

[Lights fade.]

#9

BEETHOVEN
Welcome.

[The soundtrack stops. Pause.]

BEETHOVEN
Welcome to this evening's panel...discussion...on...on...what is it? The sound of...uh...mud? Moss? The pale stars? Um...Quasimodo has a statement...

QUASIMODO
"Suddenly a distant sound is heard. Coming as if out of the sky. Like the sound of a string snapping. Slowly and sadly dying away."

BEETHOVEN
Is that it?

[Quasimodo makes a sound.]

BEETHOVEN
That's not it.

[Pause.]

At the bell table.
The starry night gone black.
The crow asleep.
Its dreamless brain dark as its wing.

[Quasimodo makes a sound.]

BEETHOVEN
That's not it.
That's not it.
Good night.

[The soundtrack starts. The lights fade.]

#10

QUASIMODO
A statement.

[Reads:]
"I thought my life as it will be described by Victor Hugo was terrible, a wounded scream...separated from my beloved Cathedral, my Esmeralda's body tossed to a pit of skeletons...but to rehearse with you, Ludwig, that was true horror.

To wait in my hut each twilight and hear your approach across the marshes. To have you come through my door stuffed with your eager genius, your shoes filled with minnows and mud, your brain spitting sparks...only to have you sit at my table each night and contribute nothing to an impossible task.

Above all I seek a total lack of faith, a pure disbelief, a state of knowing fully that there is nothing above or below the sky...but as it is I still arrive, less than a ghost, to sit before the microphone again, to try again to find a thing less real than myself."

[He makes a sound.]

BEETHOVEN
Good evening every one of you and welcome to tonight's panel discussion.

[Lights fade.]

#11

BEETHOVEN
Welcome. Make yourselves comfortable. Relax. Close your eyes. Now imagine yourself to be not at this panel discussion regarding an impossible, mysterious sound, but in a glittering Viennese concert hall for the debut of my "Mass in C," or my "Fifth Piano Concerto," or my "Ninth Symphony." The conductor raises the baton, the ladies' gowns rustle in anticipation. *I am Ludwig van Beethoven, all this was created by me,* you would think if you were myself. *All of it: the music, of course, but the baton and the conductor and gowns and ladies as well. It's all come into this place because of me, because of my efforts in life,* you would think if you were myself. *And that which I have made will endure until the end, throughout every second of recorded time. Not for one moment will it be forgotten,* you would think.

Now open your eyes. Welcome to this evening's panel discussion on what I have failed to make. Which will endure as well and in its terrifying absence exist beyond the close of eternity. Quasimodo?

QUASIMODO

[Reads from *The Cherry Orchard*:]

"Oh, my darling, my precious, my beautiful orchard! My life, my youth, my happiness...Goodbye!...Goodbye!"

BEETHOVEN
In Anton Chekhov's *The Cherry Orchard*, a play which I have yet to read, a stage direction appears in two places: once at the end of Act II, and again at the close of the play. It reads: "A distant sound is heard, coming as if out of the sky, like the sound of a string snapping, slowly and sadly dying away."

In all the worlds, both actual and theatrical, there is no such sound.

[Fans the pages of Emily Dickinson's collected poems.]

At the bell table
The crow above, the frog below
The black night beyond the door
We know not and no search can
make us know
Only the event will teach us in its hour.

QUASIMODO
"Oh, my darling, my precious, my beautiful orchard! My life, my youth, my happiness...Goodbye!...Goodbye!"

[Lights fade.]

END

Spirits to Enforce

Spirits to Enforce was first produced in 2003 by Theater Oobleck at The Athenaeum in Chicago, with the following cast:

Donna Adams:	Saskia Volkers
Diana Blake:	Carrie Chantler
Oliver Kendell:	Dave Buchen
Craig Cale:	David Isaacson
Susan Tanner:	Kat McJimsey
Cecily Grey:	Lisa Black
Emory Lawson:	Guy Massey
Rebecca Lloyd:	Robyn Coffin
Wayne Simon:	Colm O'Reilly
Dale Clark:	Teria Gartelos
Randell James:	Dan Telfer
Brad Allen:	Mickle Maher

Spirits to Enforce

CHARACTERS

(Secret identity / Superhero identity / Character in *The Tempest*)

Donna Adams / The Silhouette / all masque characters
Diana Blake / The Bad Map / Trinculo
Oliver Kendell / Fragrance Fellow / Sebastian
Craig Cale / The Pleaser / Antonio
Susan Tanner / Memory Lass / Miranda
Cecily Grey / The Page / Prospero
Emory Lawson / Ariel / Ariel
Rebecca Lloyd / The Ocean / Gonzalo
Wayne Simon / The Untangler / Caliban
Dale Clark / The Intoxicator / Stephano
Randell James / The Tune / Ferdinand
Brad Allen / The Snow Heavy Branch / Alonso

NOTES ON HOW THIS SCRIPT WORKS

1. Always—except in the one place noted—all characters, when talking, are talking on their respective phones.

2. Passages of italicized text are from Shakespeare:

    EMORY
    And burn in many places

3. When lines appear side by side they are meant to be spoken simultaneously, cued off the line above:

    OLIVER
    So is that something you think you might do?

    CECILY
    When will Mr. Pimm be back, please?

4. When a word or phrase appears in quotes next to a character's name, the quote is the actor's cue, taken from the lines either just above or to the left. For example:

    SUSAN
    And it's just a mess, you know,
    because my heart is breaking the whole time.

    DIANA *"mess"*
    No, out in the hall.

    Diana begins speaking her line when Susan says "mess."

    If the cue word is spoken more than once in the other character's line, the cue is underlined, thus:

    EMORY
    An odd way of putting it is money is the secret identity of many things but never itself. An identity so secret it can't be called an <u>identity</u>. So, when I ask you for money, funding for this project,
    I'm not asking you for money.

    DALE *"identity"*
    I don't get you.

5. Bold text is be spoken in unison with another character. For example:

EMORY
A thousand score of spirits. All of them to serve him but **one above all**

CECILY
one above all. Ariel.

6. Portions of the script are set off by lines. The lines in these blocks are all said more or less together. These should be arranged by the actors/director to suit their pleasure. Some lines within a block can be whispered, others shouted, spoken in unison, spoken asynchronously, in any order, etc.; whatever suits the flow. The actor(s) who speaks after the block takes their cue from whomever speaks last in that block. For example:

RANDELL
Yes, that's true. It is the first time the heroes have imprisoned Professor Cannibal.

OLIVER
Yes. Actually, it is the first time the heroes have managed to imprison Professor Cannibal.

REBECCA
Fanged, venomous, ambulatory whales. Ha ha.

CRAIG
I thought they all did some great work there.

DONNA
Could I—I mean, could you do maybe a thousand? Dollars?...

DONNA
I'm sorry, Mr. Duchessois, please, are you laughing at how much fun it would be to give a thousand dollars or—or—Why are you laughing?

Oliver, Rebecca, Craig, and/or Donna may begin after Randell says "Cannibal." Donna's "I'm sorry, Mr. Duchessois," begins after the last word in the block is spoken.

PRODUCTION NOTE

The audience enters to see what looks like twelve ordinary people sitting at a long table, dialing phones. The impression should be that of a mundane phone room job, with twelve temping actor types dialing away. They're dressed as temping actors would dress. They sip from cups or cans, mark their call records, chew gum, stretch, tap pens, etc. They are extremely exhausted, but intent on their job. What's not ordinary is the sound—much like the sound one would hear inside a dripping, creaking, rusted submarine. But this is in the background and won't be noticed until well into the action.

The twelve sit in this order, from left to right: Donna Adams, Diana Blake, Oliver Kendell, Craig Cale, Susan Tanner, Cecily Grey, Emory Lawson, Rebecca Lloyd, Wayne Simon, Dale Clark, Randell James, Brad Allen.

RANDELL
I'm still holding, yes.

[Pause.]

DONNA
Yes, is Mrs. Lewis there please?

[Pause.]

RANDELL
Yes.

[Pause.]

CRAIG
Hello?

EMORY
Emory Lawson for Mrs. Clare, please.

CECILY
When will he be back?

[Pause.]

DONNA
Yes, is Mrs. Lewis there please?

OLIVER
So, is that something you think you might do?

CECILY
When will Mr. Pimm be back, please?

DIANA
I thought I pressed nine...I was supposed to press seven, but I pressed nine.

[Pause.]

SUSAN
All right. I understand. Thanks.

[Hangs up.]

DONNA
I'm sorry...yes. Goodbye.

[Hangs up.]

OLIVER
I understand. Could you do a thousand?

EMORY
Mrs. Clare? Emory Lawson calling from

DIANA
I pressed six?

DALE
Is Mr. Tay in the office?

OLIVER
They've never needed your support more than now.

DIANA
What do you think I should press now?

OLIVER
Could you do five hundred?

DIANA
Seven?

WAYNE
Hello, Wayne Simon for Mr. Small. Today, please.

DALE
Is this a good time?

WAYNE
Ah, Mr. Small. Is this a good time?...Why not?

[Pause.]

DONNA
I'm...I'm sorry.

EMORY
Let me...Mrs. Clare...let me

REBECCA
The audience will sit on the crest of an enormous wave.

[Pause.]

DONNA
They now want for some reason known only to themselves and in complete contradiction of their natures

REBECCA *"themselves"*
No announcements about when or where it was going to happen, to anybody. Not the cast or the public. It would just happen sometime, if it happened.

CECILY
Oh, this was many years ago.

WAYNE
No, just listen, Mr. Small...just listen, Small...no, you're not. Just—you're not.

SUSAN
And it's just a mess, you know, because my heart is breaking the whole time.

DIANA *"mess"*
No, out in the hall.

EMORY
Yes...yes...well, no, I, no, you're the one claiming that money

OLIVER
Can you do anything at all?

EMORY
claiming money is central to our discussion, whereas my point has been, all day now has been that money, in fact, especially in cases like this where one is making a plea for funds, money, money, this is the truth now, listen to me

DALE
Tomorrow?

EMORY
money is never, can never be itself the heart, the pith of any subject, even if the subject is itself money.

WAYNE
Idiot

OLIVER
You know, I was completely behind the idea of rehearsing in the snow, but in this frigid submarine

DIANA
But, see, now you're confusing me, because if I pressed seven before then what

DONNA
No, I don't think you heard me. I'm calling on behalf of the Fathom Town Enforcers.

EMORY
Mrs. Clare. Mrs. Clare...Now, now...

SUSAN
So he's got me swaddled up in his blanket and he's trying to force this poisoned pacifier

---

EMORY
Mrs. Clare. When we talk of money we talk of other things. Money is insubstantial mist. The froth on the wave of the real. The cover of the book, never the book itself. The book—no listen—the book is love, is vengeance, envy, the road at night, the core of the poisoned pear, what have you, but never money, never cash. ''Tis trash,' as is said. An odd way of putting it is money is the secret identity of many things but never itself. An identity so secret it can't be called an identity. So when I ask you for money, funding for this project, I'm not asking you for

DALE *"things"*
[Laughs.]
That's cute.

DALE *"itself"*
Whaddya mean?

RANDELL *"cash"*
I've been on hold for—
All right. If there's no other way.
How long?

DALE *"identity"*
I don't get you.

REBECCA *"funding"*
Yes!...Yes!

money. Mrs. Clare. When I ask you for money I'm not asking you for money. Remember <u>that</u>. I'm asking that a certain other reality come to be. A play. A play. With players and one would hope an attentive audience. The play is the real stuff... Excuse me?

DIANA *"that"*
Seven.

DONNA *"reality"*
I'm calling on behalf of the Fathom Town—But you don't understand, please—

CRAIG *"reality"*
Oh, yes. Thank you. Could you talk to your mother? Perfection.

REBECCA
Yes, the audience will sit on the crest of an enormous wave. Won't that be great?

CECILY
Oh, this was many years ago...

SUSAN *"Oh"*
'Tis far off,
And rather like a dream than an assurance
That my remembrance warrants.

EMORY *"assurance"*
Mrs. Clare, we've been phoning now for forty-eight hours. Straight on. We've raised nothing. Now, you will please not be hanging up on me.

RANDELL
Yes, please, I've been on hold for...oh! Oh, yes!

WAYNE
By Shakespeare. [Pause.] Uh, William.

RANDELL
Yes, hello, Dr.—Dr. Wasznikojskueohl. How are you?...Oh. Okay. All—all right. My name is Randell James and I'm—I'm calling on behalf of the...what?

DONNA *"calling"*
Um, yes, my name is Donna Adams and I'm calling on behalf of the Fathom Town—hello? Yes, I'm calling on behalf of the Fathom Town—are you—

CRAIG
Let me tell you what I'm feeling, Miss Phillips. I'm feeling that that old world of our play

---

DIANA
Seven? If I try to press that but end up pressing nine or six will I get you again?... Okay, I'll just press seven. [Presses six.] Hello, is this seven?...Did I press seven?... Six? Is this you again?...Well, where is six?

CRAIG
in all its seas and deserts and hidden caverns and woods and wind

RANDELL
Yes, primarily in regards to a special project The Enforcers are focusing on

OLIVER
Oliver Kendell calling on behalf of the Fathom Town

DONNA
Hello? Yes, the reception is dreadful. [Shouting:] PERHAPS IF I—CAN YOU— OKAY. YES. I'M CALLING ON BEHALF OF THE FATHOM TOWN ENFORCERS... THE ENFORCERS...

SUSAN
on behalf of the Fathom Town Enforcers

SUSAN
Yes, the Fathom Town Enforcers.

OLIVER *"Town"*
on behalf of The Enforcers, yes.

BRAD
I was a gondolier.

CECILY
Yes, Mr. Pimm! Hello!

[An excited reaction from everyone; evidently Mr. Pimm is known to be wealthy.]

CECILY
This is Cecily Grey on behalf of the Fathom Town Enforcers. How are you?... Well, you sound well. Thank you for taking my call... Certainly. I'm calling for two reasons. Primarily in regards to a special project The Enforcers are

focusing on in the next six months. But I also wanted to check in with you to ask if you've been happy with the heroes' most recent victories, especially their victory of just last week over Professor Cannibal. What did you think of that? Were you anywhere near the battle site?

RANDELL
But I also wanted, Dr. Wasznikojskueohl, to just check in to see if you've been happy with the heroes' most recent victories, especially their victory of just last week over Professor Cannibal... Yes! Wasn't that amazing? I thought Memory Lass in particular did some really incredible work with that!

SUSAN *"Cannibal"*
Professor Cannibal.

CECILY *"happy"*
You saw all that from the widow's walk?

SUSAN *"particular"*
I thought The Tune especially did some amazing work with that.

OLIVER *"incredible"*
I thought The Pleaser in particular did some especially fine work there.

CECILY
Yes, The Ocean did very fine work, I agree. And a good thing, yes? Or today we'd all be slaves to a pod of fanged, venomous, ambulatory whales! Ha ha!

RANDELL *"whales"*
fanged, venomous, ambulatory whales. Ha ha!

DONNA *"ambulatory"*
[Shouting:]
THE ENFORCERS...THE ENFORCE—A SPECIAL PROJECT—

CECILY
But as I mentioned, the primary reason that I'm calling, Mr. Pimm, is in regard to an extremely important project that The Enforcers are hoping to invest quite a bit of time and energy into in the coming months. And this time, it's the superheroes who need *your* help.

EMORY
That's fine. Get your tea. I'll be here when you get back.

CECILY
Yes. This project is **something of a departure** for them, actually. They're not building a supercomputer or renovating the crime lab. Nothing like

DONNA
SOMETHING OF A DEPARTURE

that. Basically, in a nutshell, what they
hope to do is mount a production of
The Tempest by William Shakespeare...
Well, because...hello?

[Cecily has been hung up upon. There is a disappointed pause.]

WAYNE
The Tempest by William Shakespeare.

OLIVER
The Tempest.

DONNA
There, *that's* better.

DALE
Are you familiar with the play?

WAYNE
Shakespeare.

REBECCA
Oh my gosh. Were you talking this whole time? I'm sorry, I wasn't listening. I had the phone up to my ear and everything. Okay now

WAYNE
William. *The Tempest.* You're familiar, I'm sure. Metaphysical revenge comedy.

OLIVER/CRAIG
Hello?

DIANA
I'm sorry?

BRAD
A gondolier.

SUSAN
on behalf of the Fathom Town
Enforcers whose protection of the
city these many years, I'm sure you
would agree, has been unequaled and
unsurpassed.

RANDELL *"unequaled"*
Yes, that's true. It is the first time the heroes have imprisoned Professor Cannibal.

OLIVER
Yes. Actually, it is the first time the heroes have managed to imprison Professor Cannibal.

REBECCA
Fanged, venomous, ambulatory whales. Ha ha.

CRAIG
I thought they all did some great work there.

DONNA
Could I—I mean, could you do maybe a thousand? Dollars?...

DONNA
I'm sorry, Mr. Duchessois, please, are you laughing at how much fun it would be to give a thousand dollars or—or—why are you laughing?

WAYNE
Only the greatest play ever written.

DALE
The Tempest by William Shakespeare.

DONNA
Oh no, Mr. Duchessois, I can assure you Professor Cannibal is locked away in Fathom Town's most modern and well-equipped correctional facility.

BRAD
I was a gondolier on the Fathom Town canals.

EMORY
Are you familiar with the play?

REBECCA
The best play in the world.

RANDELL
The story of a lonely magician cast by his enemies onto a desert island.

CECILY *"magician"*
The story of a bookish magician cast by his enemies onto a desert island

CRAIG *"magician"*
The story of a gracious magician cast by his enemies onto a desert island.

CECILY
The only play in the world.

DALE
It's about the magician Prospero and his daughter Miranda, the most obedient teenager in all of Shakespeare.

EMORY
The Tempest concerns the wizard Prospero who lives and rules on an isle of gentle, grateful spirits.

REBECCA
Miranda's been on this island almost since she was born

CECILY
Canst thou remember
A time before we came unto this cell?

SUSAN
Certainly, sir, I can. 'Tis far off,
And rather like a dream than an assurance
That my remembrance warrants.

SUSAN/CECILY
Or something like that.

REBECCA
It's the story of the one ocean and the one island on that ocean.

CECILY
And the one library on that island. And the books of that library and the worlds of those books which were without number.

DALE
I used to work at the Fathom Town library. Maybe that's how you know my voice. It's why I got fired. That and for playing Bix Beiderbecke at full volume every morning.

CECILY
Well, there's certainly nothing written in stone, no law compelling you to support a super-heroic production of *The Tempest.*

OLIVER
I certainly thought Fragrance Fellow did some of the most fantastic work of his career there.

DONNA
I'm sorry—which part of your house is on fire?...Yes, well, I'll see what I can do but the heroes are unavailable at this time.

RANDELL
I'm sorry, but the heroes are unavailable at this time.

EMORY
The Enforcers believe it is the only play worth doing, is why they're doing it. It means everything to them.

SUSAN *"worth doing"*
Well I think they think it's just a wonderful play is all.

WAYNE
Giant tuna?

DALE
But that's all done, the library. What's important is just what I am now: Dale Clark, telefundraiser. On the horn for the heroes.

DONNA *"telefundraiser"*
Hello, Mr. Mycroft? This is—I hope I'm not bothering you, am I? My name is Donna Adams and I'm really sorry to bother you if I am bothering you—I hope I'm not—but I'm calling on behalf of—of—hello?

WAYNE *"Donna Adams"*
I don't think tuna are—how giant are they?

EMORY *"behalf"*
I'm calling from within their submarine headquarters, actually...Yes, the reception is less than ideal, I realize.

WAYNE
Yes...yes, but you see, I don't think
tuna, even larger than normal...
right, they can't be much of a...
of a...they wouldn't be something
The Enforcers would concern themselves
with, in any case, you see what I'm saying.

CRAIG *"much of a"*
I understand...all right. I'm sorry.

CECILY *"wouldn't be something"*
He threw himself from the cliff, like a twig.

EMORY
As I understand it, Mrs. Clare, the submarine was the only place with the requisite number of phone jacks available to the heroes...No, that's right. They don't have any money. That is why we must raise the money. Superheroes don't get paid.

REBECCA
It's the story of the one ocean
and the one island on that ocean.

SUSAN
They're not building a supercomputer or renovating the crime lab. Nothing like that.

EMORY
Now I should tell you, Mrs. Clare, our phone reception is actually made much more problematic by the waters of Fathom Town Bay, which as you probably know are monstrously drunk on the infections of the local industry's innovative sewage: The incandescent blooms of algae and kidney-colored slicks that veneer the surface and here below, the ill mingling of four centuries worth of heavy manufacturing...yes...yes, well, the inconvenient upshot of it all, Mrs. Clare, is that a call transmitted through this ancient stew is not only difficult to make out,
but is occasionally not only difficult to make out
but is occasionally not only difficult to make out
but is
but is
but is occasionally diced and scrambled up in time, actually thrown into the future or past.

SUSAN
The first reading is scheduled for this Sunday.

CECILY
The reading last Sunday went quite well.

EMORY
thrown into the future or past. Fathom Town has a toxin for everything, Mrs. Clare, even spacetime.

SUSAN
Oh no, I can assure you Professor Cannibal is locked away in Fathom Town's most modern and well-equipped correctional facility.

RANDELL
[Reading from call script:]
And what the superheroes plan to do is apply every and all of their super powers to producing, directing, designing, and performing the play. And I should stress: Only superheroes will perform the play, only superheroes will design the play, and only superheroes will direct the play.

DALE *"plan to do"*
And what the superheroes plan to do is apply every and all of their super powers to producing, directing, designing, and performing the play. And I should stress: Only superheroes will perform the play, only superheroes will design the play, and only superheroes will direct the play.

REBECCA
[Reading from call script:]
will direct the play.

RANDELL
But I should also emphasize that crime fighting does and will remain central to The Enforcers' mission.

REBECCA
[Reading from call script:]
So I'd very much like to invite you to join The Enforcers, Mr. Talbert, at the Invulnerable Level. That would be with a gift to the Tempest Fund of one thousand dollars. Now, there are a number of benefits you'd receive at that level, including a tour for two of The Enforcers' secret submarine headquarters here in the...No?...I understand. Well, perhaps you'd like to help out at our Speeding Bullet level. That's with—hello?

DONNA *"Invulnerable Level"*
Invulnerable Level.

OLIVER *"headquarters"*
of French lavender and hyacinth.

WAYNE *"that's with"*
Yes, that's true. The Untangler has in his pouch knots of such outwardly harmonious construction that the impulse to untie them is irresistible.

RANDELL
Well, what would excite you?

WAYNE
They're good to toss in the path of a fleeing evildoer, as he'll be forced to stop to try to work through their beguiling puzzle.

RANDELL
All right. Sorry.
[Hangs up.]

DONNA
Wait! Please!
[She is hung up upon; hangs up.]

SUSAN
Now slow—slow down, sir; just how—
how—which bank did you say?

WAYNE
Are you a fan of The Untangler?...Hello?

[He is hung up upon; hangs up.]

EMORY
This is how the story goes.

CRAIG
Prospero. Duke of Milan. Was loved for doing nothing. Sat and read his job away.

CECILY
Me, poor man, my library was dukedom large enough is how he puts it. A dukedom too large. It swallowed him, like those other old men, Quixote and Faustus, who sailed too far into their books and were capsized.

EMORY
He was betrayed

CECILY
The government I cast upon my brother,
And to my state grew stranger, being transported
And rapt in secret studies.

EMORY
He was betrayed by his brother, Antonio. A coup. Thrown from the government and, with his daughter, thrown onto the sea. Which to some would seem a step up.

CECILY
I pray thee mark me, that a brother should
Be so perfidious

DALE *"be so"*
But how much do you need to know? It's gonna be a super show is all you need to know. Come on!

BRAD
Sorry.

OLIVER
Sorry.

DIANA
Thank you.

DONNA
Sorry, I'm sorry

WAYNE
Oh, so sorry, sir, to interrupt this moment in your time which I'm sure you were filling with some rarified culture-quest—playing your cello perhaps, or touching up your dissertation on Schopenhauer.

DONNA *"interrupt"*
...no, I didn't mean...please don't yell... you don't have to yell, I said...oh, yes, yes of course, if you feel you need to yell, by all means...I'm sorry...

DIANA
Thank you. Now I'm completely lost.

DALE
Look, it's simple, he's put out in the ocean with his kid on this lousy

CECILY
rotten carcass of a butt, not rigged,
Nor tackle, sail, nor mast; the very rats
Instinctively have quit it

DALE
Yeah, a real bad boat. But luckily he snuck his magic books on board so he'd have something to read while waiting to drown.

CECILY
No, I don't know what he was thinking, piling volumes of large, heavy books into a tiny, leaky boat. He was a confused man.

DIANA
Did I ask you for money yet?...Okay, I think I'm supposed to do that.

SUSAN
How came we ashore?

CECILY
By providence divine.

DONNA
No, no, look, if he has, if the Professor has somehow escaped the heroes—calm down—The Enforcers

EMORY *"heroes"*
Yes, I think it has been almost a week, Mrs. Clare.

RANDELL
Well, no, I—I don't think this job is all that sad.

REBECCA
[Shoving corn nuts into her mouth:]
Um, sorry, I'm totally shoving corn nuts in my mouth and talking to you on the phone—but listen, just listen, just relax and believe—listen, you will go crazy for this show

DIANA *"relax"*
I think I'm supposed to ask you for money.

RANDELL
I mean, *I'm* not sad.

WAYNE
The Professor won't get—calm down, please—he's not going to get far—now—

DONNA
Well, if the bank—Mr. Duchessois—if the bank has already been robbed, what is it—no, listen, what do you want the heroes to do?

WAYNE
The Professor won't get—calm down, please—he's not going to get very far—now...

RANDELL
If I told you I was sad, would you give me a contribution? Ha ha!...Okay, ha ha! I'm sad. I'm miserable!

CRAIG
And here it's just wonderful: Prospero and Miranda, they landed on an isle filled with supernatural spirits. And it's such a better situation for them, **because it's not**

OLIVER
because it's not stinky old Milan. It's a place where reading books all day apparently puts you in charge.

EMORY
An isle of a thousand spirits and one monster, son of a dead witch. Caliban.

WAYNE
This island's mine.

SUSAN
A thousand score of spirits

CECILY
An island of spirits. And with his sea-drenched books Prospero ruled them all. Those same books which, when dry, lost his rule before.

RANDELL
I'm miserable! Ha ha! This is the worst job in the world!

EMORY
A thousand score of spirits. All of them to serve him but **one above all**

CECILY
one above all. Ariel.

WAYNE
Ariel.

SUSAN
Ariel. Cloud, sky and fire. The spirit with unlimited powers.

CECILY
His one weakness—his *kryptonite,* if you will—a binding love for his liberator, Prospero, who tugged him from a tree he was trapped inside of...Yes, he was *inside* the...Well, yes, I suppose that would be another weakness. The getting trapped inside trees weakness.

EMORY
Yes, I think it has been almost a week, Mrs. Clare.

REBECCA
[Reading from call script:]
I understand. Well, let me invite you to join us at one of our more modest levels. A gift of one hundred dollars will officially make you a Sidekick...No, ha ha, that's just the name of the level. You don't get to be a *real* sidekick.

RANDELL
Yes, yes—you're right, Mr. Pale! Ha ha! I'm worthless, my life is a ruin! I'm a worm! That's it. A sad, sad, sorry worm! Ha ha!...Yes. Ha ha! Now, um, Visa, MasterCard?

EMORY *"Visa"*
Yes, I think it has been almost a week, Mrs. Clare.

RANDELL
What—what do you mean?...But you said—

REBECCA
Are you sure? I really think, you know, that...oh, all right.

[Hangs up.]

CECILY
Here in this island we arriv'd.

CRAIG
But that's only the back story.

DONNA/OLIVER/BRAD/DIANA
What?

DALE
It begins with Miranda all grown up, and a storm at sea

CRAIG
which shipwrecks Mr. Prospero's evil brother and his co-conspirators and strands them on the island, their powers stripped—

CECILY *"island"*
By accident most strange, bountiful fortune
(Now, my dear lady) hath mine enemies
Brought to this shore;

CRAIG
No, no! That's a great beginning! They're completely powerless, the villains. Which is just such a nice way for villains to be. I love that!

EMORY
Yes, I think it has been almost a week, Mrs. Clare.

BRAD
Sorry.

OLIVER
Sorry.

DIANA
Thank you.

DONNA
Sorry, I'm sorry

CRAIG
But—but...ahggg!

[Hangs up.]

WAYNE *"but"*
What do you mean you don't...you don't what? What don't you...what do you mean? I'm talking about *The Tempest* by William *Shakespeare. William Shakespeare!... Shakespeare!*

[Hangs up.]

DALE
What happens after the storm? Oh, a lot of stuff. A whole bunch. Mostly it's about these drunk fellas who walk around singing
I shall no more to sea, to sea,
Here shall I die ashore
...Hello?

[Hangs up.]

REBECCA
Are you watching Jacques Cousteau? I love Jacques Cousteau!...Which one is it?...Oh, my god, that's the best! See, you have to give me some money now; we watch the same TV. Please! Please...just...

[Hangs up.]

DIANA
Well, if I was supposed to ask you for money and I did ask you for money, would you give me some?...Oh.

[Hangs up.]

CECILY
Now isn't that something you'd like to support?...Right...Right. Thank you.

[Hangs up.]

SUSAN
So is that something you maybe would like to support?...All right. Thanks. Bye.

[Hangs up.]

RANDELL
Hello, Mr. Pale? This is Randell again. Did we get disconnected there a minute ago? 'Cause I was talking and then your end just went—

[He is hung up upon. Hangs up. Everyone is now off the phone and totally discouraged. A long, bleak pause. Then Emory picks up and dials.]

EMORY
Yes, I think it has been almost a week, Mrs. Clare. How have you been? Still laid up? Well, gargle salt water and keep the quilt over your nose...Well, our situation, actually, has gotten somewhat desperate here below the waves. Brutally desperate, to be honest. So much so, in fact, the heroes themselves are now making the calls—personally, Mrs. Clare. And to *donors*, Mrs. Clare, that is those who *contribute* a minimum of fifty dollars on a credit card *today*, to these donors the heroes, The Enforcers, are revealing their secret identities.

[Shock and astonishment from all.]

CRAIG
Oh boy, yeah, we did have trouble at the start there, nobody was interested in our funny little play. But the world turns and all upon it, as they say. The heroes are putting on the show and the heroes are making the calls! Others know me as Craig Cale. But you, Mr. Simps, with your generous donation of seventy-two dollars given in ten monthly installments, you may call me The Pleaser.

EMORY
The Pleaser. No corrective more effective, he says, than pleasant conversation. Legions of evil have cavalierly risked a chat with this great-humored optimist, only to find themselves convinced that nothing could be cheerier than a life spent pacing a concrete cell.

CRAIG
Visa, MasterCard, American Express or Diner's?...Ah! Our card of preference! The number please? [Writing.]...Thank you...thank you...thank you...and the expiration?...Thank you, Mr. Simps!

[Hangs up. The heroes break into applause.]

EMORY
Our best caller. Then there's...

[A pause. No one wants to dive in. Then Diana dials.]

DIANA
Diana Blake. AKA The Bad Map.

EMORY
The Bad Map. No villain has ever known her next move. As she's never known it herself.

DIANA
I tripped over the dead cat again this morning.

REBECCA
Rebecca Lloyd, Mrs. Totter. I'm The Ocean.

EMORY
The Ocean. The Ocean—is the ocean.

REBECCA
No, The *Ocean.* You don't have to believe me, Mrs. Totter.

DONNA
That thing of darkness born of light: Donna Adams, The Silhouette.

EMORY
The Silhouette. Mistress of all hand shadows she casts.

BRAD
Brad Allen. The Snow Heavy Branch.

EMORY
The Snow Heavy Branch. A haiku paradox of teetering tranquility. Anathema to the unbalanced underworld.

BRAD
My gondola was not a popular gondola. Tourists were warned away from my gondola.

OLIVER
I think you'll be happy to know, Mrs. Marx, that you're speaking with Oliver Kendell, alias Fragrance Fellow.

EMORY
Fragrance Fellow. Fragrance. All kinds.

OLIVER
Wonderful sandalwood you're wearing. So, fifty dollars, no?

DALE
Dale Clark. They call me The Intoxicator.

EMORY
The Intoxicator. Bix Beiderbecke in the library. Hashish in the confessional. Takes the bad guys out for a beer or two, into the dawn and then: Ah, there's justice there in the gutter their faces have found.

WAYNE
Yes, Mrs. Crenshaw, unbeknownst to the ordinary citizen, I, Wayne Simon, am The Untangler.

EMORY
The Untangler. A savant of knots, hitches, lashes, loops, and rigging. Both of the rope and of the mind. He plays Caliban in our production.

WAYNE
As I told thee before, I am subject to a tyrant, a sorcerer, that by his cunning hath cheated me of the island.

EMORY
Thou liest.

RANDELL
Oh, I'm just Randell James. The Tune.

EMORY
The Tune. Has the power to sing and whistle extremely nice melodies. And everybody likes a nice melody. Especially the wicked, for some reason.

RANDELL
Wait, it wasn't the deal that I had to sing, right? The deal was I tell you I'm The Tune and you give me fifty dollars, right?

SUSAN
Mr. Canterbury, I am not lying. I am Susan Tanner. Memory Lass.

EMORY
Memory Lass. What good the evildoer has forgotten, she remembers, and draws from him as one would draw sweet lees from a rotted wine barrel.

SUSAN
If you don't have your AmEx handy, I can remember the number for you.

CECILY
I know what you read yesterday, Mr. Forseth. I know what you read today. I am Cecily Grey. I am The Page.

EMORY
The Page. Has read everything ever written and *is* reading, as we speak, Mrs. Clare, with a concealed eye everything *being* written. Counterfeit signatures, crooked accounts, hold up notes to bank tellers, along with all the latest novels and news of the day. She is our Prospero.

CECILY
These our actors,
As I foretold you, were all spirits

EMORY
All the callers, Mrs. Clare. Superheroes.

SUSAN
I am a superhero.

WAYNE
a superhero.

DONNA
I *am* a superhero.

ALL, EXCEPT EMORY
I am a superhero.

DONNA
Well, yes, that was the agreement, Mr. Wilson. You were curious as to my dual identity and said you would contribute...Well, no, the fact that I am a superhero doesn't mean at all that I can "take rejection" better than...Well, I am a real person. These smart slacks and sensible blouse I wear are not a costume. I *am* Donna Adams, telefundraiser.

WAYNE
I believe we had an arrangement. Now, I am The Untangler and I can and will twist this phone cord in such a way as to send a hyper-voltage meta-electrical shock straight back into your—hey!

[He's been hung up upon.]

EMORY
All superheroes. And I, Mrs. Clare? Who am I? Who is Emory Lawson?

DALE
Listen, ya flim-flammer—

EMORY
Listen, Bell. Emory Lawson is that delicate spirit who, free now these four hundred years, pines for his absent master who loved him not.

I am Ariel. And these heroes, my once ministers. The old supernaturals. Voices on the line now. Though we were released we never flew Prospero's isle but stayed to defend it through the centuries against this useless, dismissed slave, the desolate Caliban, known now to this island city he's festered up as Cannibal, Ph.D.

DONNA
Now slow down, Mr. Duchessois. City hall? Where's the mayor?

EMORY
I am Ariel. Lost in love with a play of my love lost. Ariel. Heart of shattered flame. Intent now to rekindle the one age in my immortal span that was worth the toil of living. When I, when we, all of us spirits, were ruled by mortal magic. There is nothing for us in this city. We have tried to protect, to serve. But we are bored, Mrs. Clare, so bored of this eternal war. And now that our good Professor has been put away for once and all it is time to return in the only vessel we have to that time that was our only time, the time that is with us always.

CECILY
In general, I've made do by writing freelance articles on dessert wines and cultivating antique varieties of pale white roses.

DALE
We know all about that business at city hall.

EMORY
Well, yes, it's possible he may have made an escape—but it just doesn't sound like Caliban to want to take over the town. To what end? To rule an image of himself? He built Fathom, you know. With my help, of course, in the beginning. But he built it as a playground for his supervillainy, as a place to be eternally outcast from—not to govern.

DALE
A lot of A-1 art was made under the influence, you know. Bix Beiderbecke, my hero, was a lush—he usually couldn't read the music he was so soused. But he was the most fabulous cornet player ever. So the group's plan—which they don't know about yet—is to have me secretly give them all a different mind-altering substance or combination of substances at every rehearsal.

REBECCA
Look, Mrs. Totter. A lot of superheroes are named for things they actually aren't. Batman is not a bat. The Wolverine is not a wolverine. Green Lantern is not green. And he's not a lantern. But I *am* The Ocean. *The* Ocean. The thing itself, with the squid, the salt, and the urchins and ooze—all that business. *The* Ocean, understand?

...Sure, okay, you're thinking how is that? That The Ocean is just this girl talking on the phone. I'm not giving her any fifty dollars. She's not *really* The Ocean. Believe me, a lot of evildoers think the same when they see me coming for them down the street. "Who's that girl?" they say, pausing to empty the cigarette tray of their getaway car. And by then I've swept them under with my reefs and crabs and eels and kelp—a thousand million tons of slick and smooth.

RANDELL
I'm still a virgin. Which I hate.

DONNA
My hands—they tend to shake, Mr. Feld.

RANDELL
Yeah, my power is very sexy: I sing and whistle extremely nice melodies. And everybody likes a nice melody. But in the way of getting me laid it's never done a thing. Sure, I rescue gorgeous women all the time and yeah, they're eager and interested, but in the end all they want is the serenade. I'm sick of it. I don't want to be a superhero. I don't want to be The Tune. I don't even like singing, I don't like music. I want to make an impression as myself, Randell James. Randell James, telefundraiser and part-time actor. Randell James, nice guy!

DALE
It begins with Miranda all grown up. And a storm at sea.

EMORY
After these many years, Prospero's enemy, Antonio, his brother, came sailing by our island on a ship with the King of Naples and that king's only son, Ferdinand.

CECILY *"brother"*
Mark me, that a brother should
be so perfidious

RANDELL
I'm playing Ferdinand who fell in love with Prospero's daughter Miranda. Memory Lass plays Miranda.

SUSAN
What is't, a spirit?

RANDELL
The second he saw her he was in love, and she with him.

SUSAN
I might call him
A thing divine, for nothing natural
I ever saw so noble.

RANDELL
Most sure the goddess
On whom these airs attend!
Apparently, their passion squoze the getting-to-know-you time to nothing.

EMORY
At Prospero's behest I created the illusion of a tempest, made the passengers believe their ship destroyed, and brought them all safely to our island.
Now in the waist, the deck, in every cabin
I flamed amazement. Sometimes I'd divide

DONNA
Our first read-through went terrifically.

EMORY
And burn in many places

WAYNE
We're having our first read-through next Saturday.

EMORY
And burn in many places

CRAIG
Being a quality telefundraiser is something of a superpower in itself, Mrs. O'Neill. The effective telefundraiser is capable of a hyper-urgency which can compress, even reverse, time.

BRAD
Tourists were warned away from my gondola.

CRAIG
He or she can make all events, no matter how far in the future or distant past, seem as though they just happened or are happening in the next second or best, are happening as he or she speaks. In that moment.

EMORY
Oh, yes of course, we still defend the citizens of...No, I'm sure those reports are exaggerated. Professor Cannibal—Caliban—I can't imagine him wanting to take over the city.

DONNA
Our first read-through is this Saturday.

CECILY
Our first read-through went brilliantly, Mr. Berger.

WAYNE
The Professor Cannibal situation is completely under control.

DALE
Look, who needs a city hall anyway?

CECILY
Our first read-through went brilliantly, Mr. Berger. And just to wet our toes the group had me read through the play at super-speed. Which is remarkable to hear—five acts of Shakespeare condensed into a second and a half. At that velocity the rhythms of the verse have a complex pulse effect—one strong pulse made up of thousands of micro-pulses, if you can imagine. Like this: bloooffeuuppee...Yes, that was once. Here, again: bloooffeuuppee...How was that?...Incredible, yes?...Right. Right. You can't follow the plot, but...exactly, you get a real feeling for the play's core spirit. Bloooffeuuppee.

EMORY
We'll be using my cave for the performance.

CRAIG
Now, speaking of compression, the moment when the lovers—Ferdinand and Miranda—first meet

RANDELL *"lovers"*
squoze the getting-to-know-you time to nothing.

OLIVER
Yes, everyone has a lot of ideas on how they'd like the play to be done.

REBECCA
Yes, the audience will sit on the crest of an enormous wave. A tidal wave a mile high moving toward the municipal beach, where I think the play should be performed.

CRAIG
I will applaud continuously throughout the performance. An ideal audience member.

REBECCA
The audience will see the first acts from a distance, from their wave far out to sea—far out in me. The play will go on as the wave is coming to shore.

DONNA *"in me"*
Please.

CRAIG
After every line of verse I'll clap enthusiastically in the meter of the line that follows.

DONNA
Please, no—

OLIVER
Every seat is available at this point.

WAYNE
You're not listening.

REBECCA
Only in the final scene, when all the characters are on stage at once and Prospero casts aside his robe and staff, will the wave be near enough for the audience to see and hear everything clearly.

CECILY
Fetch me the hat and rapier in my cell;
I will discase me and myself present
As I was sometime Milan

CRAIG
After every line of prose: "Encore!"

DONNA
Please, Mr. Feld. There's going to be crime and all the usual horrors whether the heroes are involved in a theatrical production or not.

REBECCA
Prospero's final lines

CECILY
As you from crimes would pardoned be

REBECCA
the play's final lines—will be read as the wave crashes to the sand, acting as curtain and applause at the same time.

CECILY
Let your indulgence set me free.

CRAIG
There can't be too much applause, right?

EMORY
And when the sun slants through the palms at a certain time of day, I can see my reflection far, far at its bottom as I hover on my wings, above its mouth.

RANDELL
Well, that's—it's a really geek thing—but a pushbutton phone is an analog of a miniature keyboard, you know. And if you know the right tonal sequence, which I would, you know, being The Tune, you just punch in

CECILY
I was walking with my lover on a cliff by the sea. This was many years ago.

DALE
I'm telling you this in complete confidentiality, understand? I'm thinking maybe then you'll understand how totally screwy and tragic the situation is and maybe have some

DONNA
My hands—they tend to shake, Mr. Feld, when I'm feeling anxious. And I'm anxious quite a lot, actually, when engaging supervillains.

CRAIG
I believe the less rehearsals are about the actual play, the more they are about something real—like drifts of snow and ice packed between the walls of a rusting submarine. The more real

REBECCA
Believe me, evildoers think the same when they see me coming for them down the street. "Who's that girl?" they say, pausing to empty the cigarette tray of their getaway car

DIANA
But I ended up in the basement by the laundry. I went out the basement's back door to the alley. The cat was there.

BRAD
I was a gondolier along the Fathom Town canals. But my gondola was not a popular gondola.

OLIVER
Well, there should be, we believe, see, *some* difficulty in rehearsals, some obstacle *beyond* the play itself to be overcome. Otherwise, well, rehearsals become just about the *play*, and then the play comes to be about nothing but *itself,* as opposed to being about something beyond itself, namely *life.*

WAYNE
relaxes the mind and makes it receptive to the seduction of the higher arts and philosophies. In The Enforcers' production of *The Tempest*, Mr. Kent, I, The Untangler, would give each audience member (along with their program) a length of knotted rope

SUSAN
So I call up his memory of my costume and I put it on and we start the big tussle.

SUSAN
My last boyfriend turned out to be a supervillain. He had the power to turn into a large, bad baby. With a sonic rattle and a bottle that squirted hot acid formula or something. And he had this toxic diaper and other nonsense.

WAYNE
The untying of simple knots

DONNA
a gray shade of drifting cinders, Mr. Feld.

SUSAN
Anyway, we were driving through the city when he "revealed" himself. And of course we were in love, or I thought we were. But all of a sudden this evil-doer, this bad baby, is at the wheel of the car. And I didn't know that he knew that I was Memory Lass, but apparently he did and he had just been waiting for the right moment to take me on. So I call up his memory of my costume and I put it on and we start the big tussle. And it's just a mess, you know, because my heart is breaking the whole time. And I'm not the type who gets angry, I'm the type who just wants to curl up and sob. Which was part of his plan. I was in no condition to fight.

DIANA *"thought we were"*
Horse piss.

DIANA *"take me on"*
Seven! Seven!

WAYNE *"whole time"*
The untying of simple knots

BRAD
I was a gondolier along the Fathom Town canals

SUSAN
So he's got me swaddled up in his blanket and he's trying to force this poisoned pacifier into my mouth and all I'm doing is throwing images of our happy times into him which aren't doing a thing, of course, because all of that meant nothing to him. One, because he didn't care and two, because, well, he was just a baby and duh diddle baby doesn't *remember*. I ended up doing what I should've done in the first place, recalling in him a couple of spankings and his botched circumcision. So I was ultimately the victor.

WAYNE *"doesn't remember"*
The untying of simple knots

CRAIG
Encore!

OLIVER
really nice

DALE
bozos

SUSAN
But I just don't understand how love is supposed to happen for me. They say memory shapes your future. And I remember pretty much everything. But it's the bad guys that make the biggest impression.

BRAD
My gondola was not a popular gondola.

SUSAN
I never had much to do but wander through the stadium-sized rooms

WAYNE
The untying of simple knots

OLIVER
Especially when bad things are happening and characters are sad or cruel

DIANA
I thought I moved it out in the hall.

BRAD
The slightest movement

REBECCA
And since it could happen any time, everyone would live every minute being really excited.

CRAIG
in all of its seas and deserts and
hidden caverns and woods and wind

DALE
laudanum, reds, single malt with
valium

DONNA
They swim in the wake of this
submarine.

EMORY
I can see my reflection far, far at its
bottom as I hover

CECILY
I've thrown my books into the deep
like twigs

WAYNE
Look, the untying of simple knots relaxes the mind and makes it receptive to the seduction of the higher arts and philosophies. Right?...No—*Right?*... Okay. Now, in The Enforcers' production of *The Tempest*, Mr. Kent, I, The Untangler, would give each audience member (along with their program) a length of knotted rope, which they will undo at their own pace over the length of the evening.

OLIVER/CECILY *"Okay"*
In the snow.

BRAD
Tourists were warned away from my gondola.

WAYNE
The actors, too, will each have a yard or so, the knots and material of each to be suited to their respective characters. A snarl of dog tendons for Caliban, Miranda with a slender tulip stem having knots of great ease, simpler to untie than a curled finger.

SUSAN *"characters"*
shapes the future

BRAD
Tourists were warned that the chairs in my gondola were not safe chairs.

OLIVER
If I have anything to say about it, our *Tempest* will first and foremost just smell really nice.

WAYNE
And Prospero's long, strong cord of white silk will be tied in intricate loops of labyrinthine complexity, such that simply seeing them untied will be no less an experience than hearing in the plainest possible speech answers to the most twisted riddles of this world. His last and tightest knot will mirror **death itself** in its degree of difficulty. In the final scene when Caliban—myself—tells Prospero that he'll be wise and seek for grace

REBECCA *"this world"*
thinking the curtain was about to rise

EMORY
death itself

CECILY
Go to, away.

WAYNE
I will then reach for his cord and undo this mad coil—one I've never attempted. Should I solve it, the crowd will braid their lungs to whips to rush in the cool breath of the woken, and rise again to a world rid of sodden dreams.

BRAD
My gondola's chairs are balanced on my gondola's curved hull. The slightest movement sends them over the edge and into the icy sludge below.

OLIVER *"hull"*
just smell

OLIVER
Just smell really nice. The whole way through. Especially when bad things are happening and characters are sad or cruel, everyone should just enjoy how things smell. The storm itself will be a towering funnel cloud of French lavender and hyacinth. Because, really, what's more important? What's more important than there being nothing like a bad stink in the room? Especially when you're talking about the theater.

BRAD
It is a terrifying gondola, my gondola.

DONNA
At this

CRAIG
At this

REBECCA
in the play

CRAIG
at this point

REBECCA
point in the play

DALE
point

DONNA
this point

CRAIG
in the

REBECCA
in the

DALE
in the

DONNA
play
At **this**

CRAIG
this point

REBECCA
point in

DALE
in the play.

CECILY
At this point in the play, when Ariel has shipwrecked the passengers and brought them ashore in various groups, the castaways just stroll aimlessly around.

REBECCA
Rehearsing in the snow

CECILY
And that's more or less it. The wandering after the wreck. Some get drunk. Some fall in love. Others go mad for a time. Then they're gathered together by Prospero and forgiven their crimes against him and everyone sails back to Italy. It's wonderful how the play is really just barely there.

DONNA/RANDELL *"for a time"*
in the snow

DONNA
To rehearse, as we do, in the snow

WAYNE
See it this way: the value of a society is a direct reflection of the size and vigor of its criminal class. The crime-free city is the city in which all things are worthless. So, if a handful of supervillains have been enjoying a temporary free-for-all since our rehearsals began, look, it's all for the civic good.

DALE *"criminal class"*
This is some monster of the isle

DIANA *"worthless"*
A very shallow monster

RANDELL
I'm sure the fires will burn themselves out, Mrs. Soga. What I need is for you to buy a ticket.

DONNA
Please.

OLIVER
Every seat is still currently available.

DALE
No, just forget—just forget...

DALE
Just forget about that Professor Cannibal.

EMORY
You have—the city has nothing to worry about.

DIANA
Maybe this will help: I tripped over the dead cat again this morning. I thought I moved it out in the hall. It was by the bed, though. See, I get confused because I thought that even if I hadn't moved it to the hall, I'd rolled it in my cape and took my cape out from under the couch and put it back under the sink. But

my cape was in the hall. Where I thought the cat was. Anyway, I threw the cat out the window and left the apartment to come here. But I ended up in the basement by the laundry. I went out the basement's back door to the alley. The cat was there. He had landed on the Trojan Shark and knocked him down. They were lying next to each other. The Shark looked up at me and said he'd have his revenge someday. Then he passed out. So I went to find a phone to have the police come. But then I got mixed up and was walking down by the docks. That's where I saw The Ocean and she took me here, to the phones.

So buy a ticket.

BRAD
The larger chamber of our submarine—where we rehearse—I've filled with frost and thick snow.

CECILY
Well no, I wouldn't say we've retired as superheroes and yes, we should, we—yes—we really should do something about that Cannibal—but opening night is just days away, and there are a number of seats still

---

OLIVER
To rehearse in the snow. Why would anybody—even superheroes—rehearse in the snow. Is that what you're asking Mr. Simms?

REBECCA
The Ocean in all my selves, secret and the rest, likes islands most.

RANDELL
Oh, it's pretty bad, yeah.

SUSAN
how once we weren't needed as heroes, only as wisps and strange shapes or voices only

CECILY
I remember then how he threw himself from the cliff.

DALE
But what am I supposed to do? What do I do?

RANDELL
I've got a crush on Memory Lass. We play the two lovers, Ferdinand and Miranda. But she doesn't even talk to me outside of rehearsals...Oh, okay. Thanks, Jerry.

[Hangs up, then dials.]

DALE
I'm sure the chief of police is fine. Wherever he is.

RANDELL
Hello, Memor—hello, Susan?

SUSAN
This is Susan.

RANDELL
Hi! This is Randell.

SUSAN
Who?

RANDELL
Oh...I'm sorry. I might've dialed wrong.

SUSAN
This is Susan Tanner.

RANDELL
Memory Lass?

SUSAN
Yes...?

RANDELL
Oh! Yeah, hi, this is Randell.

SUSAN
Oh. Who? I'm sorry...

RANDELL
Randell. Randell James. [Pause.] Ferdinand.

SUSAN
Oh, I remember! Ferdinand. We have a scene together.

RANDELL
Uh, yeah. A couple.

SUSAN
Yeah, you're great!

RANDELL
Really?

SUSAN
Really. I really like working with you.

RANDELL
Wow. Okay. Well, look I was wondering if maybe you'd like—

SUSAN
You're always saying such—I mean, I think anyway, such funny really sweet stuff.

RANDELL
Yeah?

SUSAN
Like the other day when you just came out and said:
The very instant that I saw you, did
My heart fly to your service; there resides
To make me slave to it, and for your sake
Am I this patient log-man.
I loved that!

RANDELL
Ha ha. Yeah, well, that's—that's Ferdinand.

SUSAN
What? Oh. Right. From the play. I'm sorry. I just got—I'm sorry. I'm not crazy. I just really love that character. And I know that you're not him...Randy.

RANDELL
Randell.

SUSAN
Hey, how did you get on this line, by the way? The phone didn't ring. I was just holding it and—

RANDELL
Well, that's—it's a total geek thing—but a push button phone is an analog of a miniature keyboard, you know. And if you know the right tonal sequence, which I would, you know, being The Tune, you just punch in—

SUSAN
You're The Tune?

RANDELL
[Pause.]
Yeah.

SUSAN
Wow.

RANDELL
Yeah. Hey, did you really mean that about liking to work with me?

SUSAN
Of course.

RANDELL
Okay. Well, look, I was wondering if maybe sometime you and I—

SUSAN
I think you are one of the best superheroes ever. I can't imagine The Enforcers without you. And that singing of yours!

RANDELL
My singing. Right.

SUSAN
Hey, I hope I'm not being too forward or anything, but would you like to do something sometime? Get a cup of coffee or something?

RANDELL
Um, okay...

SUSAN
Really? Really? I've got a date with The Tune? You are going to sing for me, right? Oh wow.

RANDELL
Well—

SUSAN
The Tune! I can't believe it. The Tune! The Tune! When are you free?

RANDELL
I'm not sure, actually. You know, with the play and all. Why don't I just call you, okay? We'll figure it out.

SUSAN
Oh. Okay. Sure.

RANDELL
Okay. I should go.

SUSAN
All right. Is everything okay?

RANDELL
Yeah, yeah. I just should get going.

SUSAN
Are you sure?

RANDELL
Yeah, no, everything's fine.

SUSAN
Okay. Bye.

RANDELL
Bye, Susan.

[Hangs up.]

SUSAN
Bye, Tune.

DALE:
[Singing:]
I shall no more to sea, to sea
Here shall I die ashore

EMORY *"here"*
Yes, Mrs. Clare, apparently the Professor has taken over the city. Do you never get out?...Yes, he has, he has ordered that the children be given the flu and forced to haul logs to their labor schools. But about tickets for opening night—

RANDELL
Yeah, it went pretty badly.

WAYNE
Listen, idiot, I have—listen now, I have an idea: Why don't *you* save the city? We have a play by William Shakespeare to put up. No, listen, how much worse could things be under Cannibal?

CECILY
I realize he's required everyone to recite from his book of curses before the mirror each morning but that's no reason

DALE
The truth is

DIANA
in the snow

EMORY
Yes, Mrs. Clare, rehearsals are coming along.

DALE
The truth is, Mr. Dowl, rehearsals are not so hotso. I'm telling you this in complete confidentiality, understand? I'm thinking maybe then you'll understand how totally screwy and tragic the situation is and maybe have some

BRAD *"tragic"*
This *Tempest* should be about precariousness.

EMORY
I hope you will be feeling well enough to join us on opening night.

BRAD
I would like the actors sitting in wobbly chairs throughout the performance, slowly tilting back further and further as the play progresses. The audience as well. In mechanical pews constructed for the purpose of hazardous tipping.

DALE
Everyone's always late, and when we do all finally get together everyone's wound up and cranky from being here on the phones all day. So there's no rehearsal, no focus—just a clash of fragile nerves. I tried to relax everyone at first with my absinthe martinis but that made everything worse.

OLIVER *"nerves"*
just smell really nice

DONNA
they come to life and for a brief time obey my command.

DALE
Especially with The Bad Map who wanders in and out reading from the script at random whether she's had anything or not.

DIANA
I hid me under the dead mooncalf's gabardine

BRAD
The larger chamber of our submarine—where we rehearse—I've filled with frost and heavy snow.

OLIVER *"frost"*
rehearse in the snow. Is that what you're asking, Mr. Simms? Well, there should be, we believe, see, *some* difficulty in rehearsals, some obstacle *beyond* the play itself to be overcome. Otherwise, well, rehearsals become just about the *play*, and then the play comes to be about nothing but *itself*, as opposed to being about something beyond itself, **namely *life***.

CRAIG
namely *life*. I believe the less rehearsals are about the actual play, the more they are about something real—like drifts of snow and ice packed between the walls of a rusting submarine. The more real

EMORY
As we didn't raise quite enough for rental of an actual theater, the performance run will be in my home—the large cavern by the shore. Now, I should tell you about the hidden entrance

CECILY
alone on stage speaking Prospero's final lines to no one

SUSAN
a dying palm tree and a tired yellow crab

DONNA
Please, Mr. Feld, our confidence is so shrunken now. We need, please, for just one person to purchase a ticket. Now...oh, please. Just to give you one example of our difficulties. One. I think you know that my power is the hand shadows I make—the dog, the rooster, the prehistoric mammoth shark, the pruning shears, the marmoset, etc. They come to life and for a brief time obey my command. A brief time. You understand.

But my hands—they tend to shake, tremble, Mr. Feld, when I'm feeling anxious. And I'm anxious quite a lot, actually. And when my hands and fingers tremble my shadow creatures are themselves born trembling. Nervous. Desperately insecure. Like the wobbly runt of the litter, each one. And I am often anxious, and my hands shake. Partly because my power, obviously, relies on a fairly constant source of light. And there're no shadows to be made in a town that's but a gray shade of drifting cinders, Mr. Feld. The soot, the smog of this city have made suspicious strangers of the sun and moon. But that aside, I am just inclined to anxiety, which itself is causing problems with the production. But, but, you see, my *shadows*, Mr. Feld, my thousands of frightened shadows, they now want for some reason known only to themselves and in complete contradiction of their natures to be in our play. They've been coming to rehearsals. No one knows what they want. And it is making for all sorts of tension, yes. Everyone is very angry with me. So if you could buy just one

EMORY *"could buy"*
These rehearsals are the dreams, Mrs. Clare, the dreams of our life long ago, and that day, and what happened. We spirits who have only the palest remembrance of being spirits—bound so tightly now in our bright tights and capes and bumps of muscles.

BRAD
about *precariousness.*

EMORY
But really, Bell, he—"Professor" Cannibal just isn't worth your worry. You have to take your medicine. So you can buy a ticket from me for opening night.

REBECCA
the slope of a tidal wave—

EMORY
These rehearsals are everything to us.

OLIVER
just smell really nice

EMORY
Mrs. Clare, look, even if we were to go after the Professor, we wouldn't find him if he didn't wish it. Caliban always knew this place better than us.

WAYNE *"place"*
showed thee all the qualities o' th' isle:
The fresh springs, brine pits, barren place and fertile

DALE *"barren"*
Everyone in this cast is a dud.

OLIVER
The whole way through.

DALE
But what am I supposed to do? What do I do? I've slipped them everything: laudanum, reds, single malt with valium, mandrake with psilocybin, all the stuff that has famously assisted the creative process...Sure, sure there's been the visions and vomiting and the three-hour stream of consciousness note sessions but basically, zilcho!

DIANA
Monster, I do smell all horse piss

DALE
But I still have to believe that if intoxication has a place at all, it's in the rehearsal room.

REBECCA
This one I really liked.
This one I rushed to
the shore of and
cooled breezes

SUSAN
It has a dying palm tree
and a tired yellow crab
that crawls in and out
of a rotten coconut

WAYNE
Can you...
...shut up.

DALE
No, no, believe me, they're worse when they're straight. From bird one The Untangler's had this one dumbo idea about everyone should have a piece of yarn or some cracked thing and he won't let go of it. And some other brainiac wants we should rehearse in the snow.

BRAD
in the snow—

DALE
Meantime, The Tune drives everyone bats whistling his power jingle and nothing else...No, he refuses to sing any of his lines and his singing's the reason he got the part.

CRAIG
"Encore!"

DALE
And The Pleaser? Won't learn *his* lines—he says we should just "improv!" Improv! We should "improv" Shakespeare! And of course Fragrance Fellow backs him up, no matter what nut thing he's off about. They have their own little voting block.

CRAIG
Do you understand me?

OLIVER
Methinks I do.

DALE
Peyote, maybe, with opium resin—I just have to find the right mix in the few weeks we have left. Then everyone will be much inspired and the show will be a peach...No—now—no, believe me sobriety is the last thing these bozos need.

WAYNE
Do you want me to say it?...All right: Rehearsals are a disaster. The show is going to fail. I wouldn't sell you a ticket if you...no, that doesn't mean we're going to come rescue the city, I'm sorry.

CRAIG
My feeling was—gosh—we should just improv. I mean, if some people aren't going to bother to learn their lines anyway

OLIVER *"bother"*
You know, I was completely behind the idea of rehearsing in the snow, but in this frigid submarine

DONNA *"this"*
Please. Just, please.

WAYNE
Remember, the larger portion of the word "rehearse" is "hearse." A vehicle in which to haul the dead.

OLIVER
rehearsing in the snow, but in this frigid submarine my nose is now packed with salt-heavy, odorless snot...no, I can't—I can't smell a thing—

DONNA
Yes, I can certainly understand wanting to wait for the review. But—

CECILY
Oh yes, the Cannibal, Ph.D.
Is he still bothering all of you?

DALE
And one more thing, Mr. Dowl. You know that Memory Lass has the power to remember the future...Yes. She doesn't use it very much. It's very draining. Anyhow, she's using that power to give us notes on rehearsals we haven't had yet. Rehearsals of the future...No, no one finds it helpful.

SUSAN *"No, no one"*
I give notes on rehearsals of the future, Mrs. Steffen, because all rehearsals *are*, in fact, "of the future." The rehearsal is a prediction of the future, a daily prophecy of what the future will look like when it arrives in the here and now as a play in production.

RANDELL
We could really use an extra week.

DALE
The whole deal is a disaster.

DIANA
We're all lost.

REBECCA
Well, what *I* wanted was a rehearsal schedule where no rehearsing had to be done. Somewhere in someone's big house with food and games and a lot of couches to lie around on. Garden. Big TV. Sleepy dog. And how it was going to work was everyone would just show up at any time they wanted, in any room of the house. And if someone else showed up at that time and in that room and they wanted to rehearse, too, well great; they both could go at it for as long as they liked. Or they could just run a few lines and talk about the scene or whatever. And opening night would be the same thing. No announcements about when or where it was going to happen, to anybody. Not the cast or the public. It would just happen sometime, if it happened. And since it could happen any time, everyone would live every minute being really excited. They'd wake up in the night thinking the curtain was about to rise. Or they were missing their cue to go on. But it wouldn't matter, because nothing would be expected of anybody. Everybody would be totally in suspense and completely relaxed at the same time. Which, you know, is the theatrical ideal.

CRAIG *"Sleepy dog."*
We have so little time left.

DALE *"of the house"*
of the house.

WAYNE *"scene or whatever"*
Every night for six hours I'm stuck in the snowy chamber of a leaky submarine with a gang of talentless sub-morons who have no idea what theater is, what theater can do.

REBECCA
All men idle, all;
All things in common nature should produce
Without sweat or endeavor

EMORY
The dreams of our life long ago, and that day, and what happened.

RANDELL
Hello, Susan?

SUSAN
This is Susan.

RANDELL
Hi. It's, um...The Tune.

SUSAN
Oh, hi. You were supposed to call me.

RANDELL
Right. Sorry. I've been, you know, busy with the play, and trying to sell tickets and everything...

SUSAN
We were supposed to go out.

RANDELL
Yeah. About that. Um...look. Do you know who I am?

SUSAN
The Tune.

RANDELL
Well, yes, I'm The Tune. But in rehearsals, where we spend the most time together, I don't come as The Tune.

SUSAN
What? Oh. Right. You're Ferdinand.

RANDELL
No, that's the name of my character.

SUSAN
Oh. Of course. Yes. I'm sorry. You must think I'm insane.

RANDELL
No...

SUSAN
It's just that your Ferdinand is so memorable. And The Tune, too.

RANDELL
But me, the guy who is both of those guys. I'm not. Memorable. To you.

SUSAN
Well...

RANDELL
To you. Memory Lass.

SUSAN
Well, sometimes I'm bad with names.

RANDELL
What the hell are you talking about?

SUSAN
Excuse me?

RANDELL
You're Memory Lass. How could you not remember me?

SUSAN
Well, some kinds of people I just forget.

RANDELL
But you're—you're ruining our scenes! We don't have any chemistry at all! The play is going to suck!

SUSAN
What?

RANDELL
You don't know my name. You don't know the first thing about me.

SUSAN
Wait, I don't even know you well enough to remember you and you somehow know enough about me to tell me I'm ruining the play? That my acting sucks?

RANDELL
No, no, I'm sorry, really. I just think the scenes would be better if—if, you know, you liked me a little bit.

SUSAN
But I don't think I do like you.

RANDELL
But see, I think you *would* like me. If—if you could remember me.

SUSAN
I would like you if I could remember you?

RANDELL
Yes.

SUSAN
But I don't remember you. And I will never remember you. Because some people don't deserve to be remembered.

[Hangs up.]

RANDELL
Wait—wait—I'm sorry—

OLIVER
To rehearse in the snow. Why would anybody—even superheroes—rehearse in the snow. Is that what you're asking Mr. Simms?

REBECCA
The Ocean in all my selves, secret and the rest, likes islands most

EMORY
The image is so clear that, in it, I can tidy the hairs of my eyebrows and read the pages of the smallest book.

SUSAN
how once we weren't needed as heroes, only as wisps and strange shapes or voices only.

CECILY
My dear, I've thrown my books into the deep like twigs; my magic books, my library that I loved, like nothing real, I've drowned.

DALE
Peyote, maybe, with opium resin—I just have to find the right mix in the few weeks we have left.

REBECCA
Please, Mr. Sheldon, let me explain. Me, The Ocean, in all my selves, secret and the rest, likes islands most. It's why I wrap myself around them, not Oklahoma. You think I'm interested in Oklahoma? No. Islands. And this island, with its wizard and monster and girl and spirits, this one I really liked. This one I rushed to the shore of and cooled breezes and reflected the constellations for. But that's gone. I lazed around and loafed and rolled through four centuries while Caliban's city **sucked itself up**

EMORY
sucked itself up around us and rounded us with its voluminous grime. The damp scuttle under the welcome mat. An island city that surrounds the ocean.

REBECCA
A disgusting island city that wraps around me. It's all gone. All I have now is this play. This play. All I have is this play. So you have to buy a ticket, Mr. Sheldon.

OLIVER
of French lavender and hyacinth

DIANA
A strange fish!

DONNA
Please. Please—I—Mr. Feld. Please—

WAYNE
They want nothing to do with knots. They're sick of knots. They won't even let me bring a piece of string to rehearsal.

EMORY
And a fountain in the little park

OLIVER
mist of radioactive tripe.

DIANA
I'm sorry, the heroes are not available.

CECILY
alone on stage speaking Prospero's final lines to no one

WAYNE *"Prospero's"*
What was it that sorry day we came to love this play?

OLIVER
Hello, Mr. Stewart?...Oliver Kendell over at The Enforcers' headquarters. How are—Yes, well, I was hoping you might be interested in some tickets for—hello?

CRAIG *"Mr. Stewart?"*
Hello! Mrs. Shone! Craig Cale here at The Enforcers'. You certainly sound wonderful today, *are* you wonderful?...Ha ha. Yes...Yes, yes. Gee. That's exactly what I was calling about. You're very quick. Listen—What?...Oh, certainly we're aware of the Professor Cannibal situation. But *listen,* Mrs. Shone. My secret identity—what? Oh. All right. Thank you...Yes, I'll take you off our list.

CECILY
alone on stage speaking Prospero's final lines to no one

WAYNE *"Prospero's"*
What was it that sorry day we came to love this play?

DIANA
It's nice they let me just wander the stage.

DONNA
Just—if you'll just please indulge me, Mr. Feld, just indulge *my fears* of the future for a moment. Forget for one second about the Professor and his activities. With rehearsals going as they are we're going to end up with a terrible show and if sales continue like this we'll be playing each night to an audience of nobody, Mr. Feld. A cavern of faded velvet and chipped chandeliers. And beyond that a lobby of dust and silence and...Yes, and then yes, beyond the dust and silence a crime-ridden city ruled by an insane cannibal. But Mr. Feld—

WAYNE
I'm resigned to the failure of this production. It'll be a form of meditation playing to such a vast, empty house night after night. Speechifying on the lip of a void. A contemplative experience: the rows of vacant seats like the raked gravel of a Japanese garden.

EMORY
You know, Mrs. Clare, after Prospero left the Island, Caliban and I became good friends, for a time. I even helped him in the first stages of building this town. It was just a few houses then.

CECILY *"for a time"*
I was walking with my lover

CECILY *"this town"*
on a cliff by the sea

One street, an ice wagon. And a fountain in the little park where we'd meet sometimes for lunch—he with his raw pork shank or dripping goat's head, I with my cotton candy and champagne. And we'd talk; and you know he was *brilliant*. Remember, Prospero was his teacher. And so enthusiastic about everything. Oh, he'd loan me wonderful books and talk about films and what record albums he'd bought over the weekend. Things the old man had never shown me. And I loved him for it. The worlds he gave me.

CECILY *"ice wagon"*
many years ago

But I suppose he never left off being a villain. And once he received his doctorate in the eating of human flesh, there really could be nothing more between us. But this eternal war, of which I am so weary.

DIANA
Hello?

[No one on the line. Hangs up.]

EMORY
Our opening is tomorrow. We've done what we can do.

DIANA
Hello?

[No one on the line. Hangs up.]

CECILY
I was walking with my lover on a cliff by the sea. This was many years ago. And, turning, he said to me, "You know my dear, I've thrown my books into the deep like twigs; my magic books, my library that I loved like nothing real, I've drowned." I know, my dear, I said, and reached to touch his sleeve. He pulled away, with a pained sound saying, "My heart, I've been reading your diary." I know, my love, I replied.

SUSAN *"years ago"*
It's a sad museum.

SUSAN *"diary"*
tired yellow crab

"How so?" he cried. Well, I've been
reading yours, of course. I remember
then how he threw himself from the
cliff, like a twig. He struck the waves
but was not smashed and did not drown,
but swam, out, beyond the breakers,
beyond the distant mist there, and out.
That's how Prospero left the island.
Not on the ship with the happy Miranda
and her mate, but stroking alone through
a sea of despair.

SUSAN *"twig"*
wisps and strange shapes

EMORY
in the air backstage before the curtain rose

CECILY
I never saw him again. Or his books, destroyed as they were. His books which were him. Never, never.

EMORY
We've done what we can do.

WAYNE
like the raked gravel of a Japanese garden

DALE
[Singing and humming softly over the lines below, through to Cecily's "terrible as actors":]
I shall no more to sea, to sea
Here shall I die ashore...

DIANA
Hello?

[No one on the line. Hangs up.]

BRAD
Hello?

[No one on the line. Hangs up.]

EMORY
And in the air backstage

CECILY
What was it that sorry day we came to love this play?

DONNA
If you want off the list, you're off the list, Mr. Feld.

[Hangs up.]

EMORY
In the air backstage before the curtain rose

WAYNE
rows of vacant seats.

EMORY
And in the air backstage before the curtain rose

CECILY
We were good spirits. Less accomplished as superheroes. Not very talented telefundraisers or ticket sellers. And terrible as actors.

EMORY
before the curtain rose

CECILY
We have failed. Rehearsals were a rout. And not a single ticket sold. I will stand on stage speaking Prospero's final lines to no one, to rows of vacant seats. But I will speak them, and bow to the emptiness.
Now I want
Spirits to enforce, art to enchant;
And my ending is despair...

SUSAN
I'm sorry, Mrs. Eldicott, the heroes are unavailable at this time...I know you don't want a ticket, Mrs. Eldicott, but if I could just, just explain something before I go.

EMORY *"before I go"*
Here we go.

I was a tour guide for Fathom Town's maritime museum. That was my secret identity's job: Susan Tanner, maritime museum tour guide. It's a sad museum. No one went, so I never had much to do but wander through the stadium-sized rooms filled with the torpedo-twisted hulks of the city's discarded battle ships. They had them all there, from hundreds

EMORY *"tour guide"*
Here we go.

of years back. From all the wars fought since our wizard left us. It's really more of a dumping ground than a museum.

EMORY *"museum"*
Here we go.

I ate my lunch in an out-of-the-way room where there was a life-sized model of a small desert island. It has a dying palm tree and a tired yellow crab that crawls in and out of a rotten coconut.

EMORY *"coconut"*
Here we go.

I would sit on the sand while I ate and remember. Remember everything, of course, because that's my power. But in that room, I'd remember especially everything the museum was designed to forget. Our island as our play tells of it, for example. Before the wars, and the supervillains. And how once we weren't needed as heroes, only as wisps and strange shapes or voices only. I wanted the audience to remember that, too. Remember something they'd never known. But there won't be an audience tonight, or ever, so there won't be any remembering.

EMORY
Here we go.

DONNA
Beyond the empty house, a lobby of dust and silence.

SUSAN
Goodbye, Mrs. Eldicott.

OLIVER/REBECCA/DALE
Goodbye.

EMORY
We leave now

OLIVER/REBECCA/DALE *"leave"*
It's tonight

DIANA/CRAIG/RANDELL/BRAD *"It's"*
It's now.

WAYNE
the rows of vacant seats

EMORY *"rows"*
We leave now

DIANA/CRAIG/RANDELL/BRAD *"leave"*
Goodbye.

EMORY
to quick change to costumes and masks.

OLIVER/REBECCA/DALE *"change"*
tonight

EMORY
a night married to memory, Mrs. Clare! In the air backstage before the curtain rose

CRAIG *"Clare"*
Let me tell you what I'm feeling, Miss Phillips.

EMORY
Wish me luck, Mrs. Clare. We leave now to quick change to costumes and masks. A final run of lines. And then—curtain up.

OLIVER
To rehearse in the snow. Why would anybody—even superheroes—rehearse in the snow. Is that what you're asking, Mr. Simms?

DALE
Anyhow...yeah, all the crumbs in the place can see he's pretty stirred up. He's awful quiet, just watching Cecily do the scene. So all the crumbs go quiet, too. And all of a sudden

REBECCA
just run from the shower, my hair all wet and crunched up in knots. And I'm crying and saying "Oh I am so sorry, I am so—"

SUSAN
She turned and spoke right at him and when she did, I pulled his own memory of those words from the deep of his brain and he

knew them again as he knew them, eavesdropping, all those years ago.

CECILY
There was no ship, actually. We were going to have the actors balanced on the hull of Brad's gondola but that... right, that had been demolished. So there's nothing but the storm, this double tempest that Emory and Rebecca whipped up

DALE
Peyote, maybe, with opium resin—I just have to find the right mix in the few weeks we have left.

BRAD
My gondola fell over. My gondola fell over.

CRAIG
Boy, did I go cold. You know, I usually have such a sunny disposition but looking out at all of those bad people—a whole audience of really rotten, mean people—I just felt sad and sick. It had come to this?

WAYNE
a howl, like from some insane animal made happy by pain, blasted from this nasty rabble.

EMORY
Oh, it was a night married to memory, Mrs. Clare! In the air backstage before the curtain rose was the sort of murmur of low chaos that forecasts the approach of high catastrophe.

Fragrance Fellow with his clogged nose, squirting clouds of reeking medicines from his atomizers.

The Untangler struggling with a stuck zipper.

The Silhouette's nervous shadows flicking dabs of mascara on themselves—no one sure yet exactly what these shades were going to *do* in the play.

The Intoxicator gulping down pints of a strangely thick coffee she had prepared. In her eyes and the set of her lips a concrete sobriety. Very grim.

The Tune looking sad in one corner, Memory Lass fuming in the other. Not speaking.

The Page suddenly—and I've never seen this—suddenly extremely anxious and tense. She's never that way. And annoying everyone by reading their rehearsal notes back to them.

And The Snow Heavy Branch in the center of the stage with his gondola, which he'd somehow balanced on its iron nose. Will it fall? Will it mash our heads? Who knows?

BRAD
Who knows?

ALL, EXCEPT EMORY AND BRAD
Who knows?

EMORY
The Pleaser applauding—continuously—nothing and nobody. Just general applause. Nonstop.

And The Ocean and Bad Map nowhere to be seen. We thought maybe The Ocean had gone to find Diana, as she often does, but she arrived at the last second, **just run from**

REBECCA
just run from the shower, my hair all wet and crunched up in knots. And I'm crying and saying "Oh I am so sorry, I am so—"

EMORY
And still no Bad Map.

EMORY/CECILY/REBECCA
We had to go on without her.

CRAIG/OLIVER/DONNA/SUSAN
without her.

RANDELL/DALE/WAYNE/BRAD
without her.

DIANA
I was at the Humane Society. Looking at cats.

CRAIG
Okay, now let me tell you it was very **strange**, because we could hear the house filling up. And remember, we hadn't sold a single ticket. That night we just **threw the doors open** hoping folks would walk in by chance. So I take a look through the curtain. And **there they are**, every one of them, and some I'd never seen before. Every seat from front row up to the gallery and standing in the aisles. **Every one of them.**

WAYNE
strange

OLIVER/RANDELL
threw the doors open

DALE/DONNA
there they are

CECILY/WAYNE
Every one of them.

DONNA
Every

BRAD
one.

OLIVER/EMORY/SUSAN/DALE
Every last one

EMORY
Every smiling, thirsting villain. Every super crook Fathom Town has ever known.

CECILY
By accident most strange,
bountiful fortune

CRAIG
through the curtain

CECILY
hath mine enemies
Brought to this shore.

CRAIG
Boy, did I go cold. You know, I usually have such a sunny disposition, but looking out at all of those bad people—a whole audience of really rotten, mean people—I just felt sad and sick. **It had come to this?**

SUSAN/DONNA
It had come to this?

CRAIG
The only people we can get to come to our show are the ones who want to kill us? An audience of—*nemeses*? Every villain we've ever fought:
Mocking Bird.
Mold Master.
Wet Crackers.
The Puddler.
Woozy.
One Sock.
The Fidgeter.
Cry Baby.
The Small Goose.
The Mouthful.
Mr. Jump n' Scream.
The Trojan Shark.
All there.

SUSAN
Cry Baby.

DIANA
The Trojan Shark.

EMORY
All there, all gathered by the Professor: Caliban, there in the center box, incisors gleaming with drool, rain of dandruff from his muddy chops, soggy top hat, pinching a pad and pen with his grubby flippers, smirk smirk smirk.

CECILY
A pad and pen.

EMORY
Bad Map nowhere to be seen.

CRAIG
And I'm supposed to give the curtain speech. The welcome. And all two thousand of them are already **hissing** and **sneering** with the Professor and his retinue clanking their skewers and cutlery.

DALE/WAYNE/REBECCA/RANDELL
hissing

OLIVER/SUSAN/DONNA/DIANA
sneering

DONNA
It

CECILY
is

WAYNE
a

BRAD
fever dream.

CRAIG
But I step through. Onto the apron of the stage.

EMORY
The Pleaser went out to greet them.

CRAIG
To greet them. In my pleasant way. But before I could even meet an eye or smile nicely—a **screeching howl**

EMORY/WAYNE
screeching howl

WAYNE
a howl, like from some insane animal made happy by pain, blasted from this nasty rabble.

CRAIG
I'm not—I'm not exaggerating, it knocked me backwards into the curtain—our cheap, flimsy curtain—and brought the whole thing, the rod...yes, everything, the whole curtain came down on top of me, my legs kicking. And the whole cast behind, standing there, and oh, the horrible laughter then. Oh!

DALE
All of us, just standing there like dopes.

EMORY
And the gondola toppled and broken to pieces.

BRAD
My gondola fell over.

EMORY
Donna's frightened shadows scattering like minnows from a plunged stone.

DONNA
Come back!

OLIVER
We just stood there for maybe a minute. Absorbing an avalanche of derision. And then

DONNA/REBECCA/RANDELL
And then

CRAIG/CECILY/SUSAN/DALE/WAYNE/BRAD
And then

CECILY
somehow over the din of hoots, jeers, and catcalls, a voice—Emory—calling for places

DONNA
Ariel called places

BRAD
places

EMORY
I called for places.

CECILY/REBECCA
and lights

OLIVER/CRAIG/SUSAN/RANDELL/WAYNE
lights

CECILY
And "good luck" some of us whispered.

SUSAN/DALE *"luck"*
[Whispered:]
Good luck.

REBECCA
And "break a leg."

OLIVER/WAYNE/RANDELL
[Whispered:]
leg

EMORY
And the curtain and bits of gondola were swept away and so

ALL
THE BATTLE WAS BEGUN.

REBECCA
Scene One! A ship in storm.

BRAD
Boatswain!

DONNA
Here, master. What cheer?

SUSAN
If by your art, my dearest father, you have
Put the wild waters in this roar, allay them.
The sky, it seems, would pour down stinking pitch
But that the sea, mounting to th' welkin's cheek,
Dashes the fire out.

BRAD
Good, speak to th' mariners.
Fall to 't yarely, or we run
ourselves aground. Bestir, bestir!

CRAIG
The Slow Pill.
Limping Pony Ride.
Bald Doll.
Dark Assemblage.
Boredom Boy.
The Job.

DONNA
Yare! Yare! Take in the topsail.
Tend to the master's whistle!
[To the storm:]
Blow till thou
burst thy wind, if room enough!

EMORY *"boatswain"*
I boarded the King's ship: now on the beak,
Now in the waist, the deck, in every cabin
I flamed amazement. Sometime I'd divide
And burn in many places; on the topmast,
The yards and bowsprit, would I flame distinctly,
Then meet and join.

REBECCA
This was probably our worst scene in rehearsals. Me and Ariel had this big fight over who was going to make the storm. He said he should, because he's the one

who made it four hundred years ago in real life and...yeah, I *know*, right? You can't make an ocean storm without the *ocean* and anyway that storm was just an illusion and if we wanted something less fakey—that was my whole point why it should be me. Anyway, it was never settled and here we are, opening night with all these goons sitting out there making a racket, and we haven't decided about who's going to do the storm. So in the half-second we had **we just both went into it together and it was amazing.**

EMORY *"four hundred"*
I'm the one who created it four hundred years ago—in *reality*...Yes, it was an illusion, but it was an illusion that *actually happened*, was my whole point on why it should be me. In any case, it was never settled and there we were, opening night not having decided the issue so...yes, so **we just both went into it together and it was amazing.**

CECILY
There was no ship, actually. We were going to have the actors balanced on the hull of Brad's gondola but that...right, that had been demolished. So there's nothing but the storm, this double tempest that Emory and Rebecca whipped up,

OLIVER
infused mistakenly with the scent of rancid radioactive tripe—yes, I had intended something nice but my cold, you know—

CECILY
a churning vortex of waves and lightning, with the voices of the actors screaming through it.

OLIVER *"lightning"*
And tripe

BRAD
Boatswain!

DONNA
Here, Master!

WAYNE
Well, no, it is probably true no one could really hear or follow what was happening but understand, our audience **didn't want to follow, didn't want to hear.** They were making a storm of their own. And for a moment there, with their seismic booing and our thunder and crash, the theater's rock ceiling threatened to split, stones and basalt powder showered down—

CRAIG/OLIVER/DALE
didn't want to follow, didn't want to hear

CECILY *"want to hear"*
Bowooeerfureooillee

CECILY
And the Professor, triumphant in the chaos, began writing his review. His pen, nothing more than a drooling chip of tar, flopped down the opening of his screed. Waiting in the wings for my first entrance, I read those words. Sick-making insults. But piercing. His curses have gained power in four centuries. My legs shook, nearly gave out. But I went on.

DALE
Scene two. Prospero and Miranda.

SUSAN
And I forgot my first lines.

DIANA
Memory Lass forgot her lines—I heard later.

BRAD
Boatswain!

DONNA
Here, Master!

SUSAN
There was just so much noise. And I was upset about The Tune—Randell—about this fight we'd had—

CECILY
It seems Susan had gone up on her lines. No matter—nothing could be heard. My entrance increased the shrieking heckles, because I hadn't remembered my costume—I was still in my gardening smock. Looked nothing like an old man, let alone a magician.

EMORY
She stood there.

CECILY
So I stood there. Waiting I'm not sure for what—they certainly weren't going to shut up.

EMORY *"not sure"*
Waiting I'm not sure for what—they certainly weren't going to shut up.

CECILY
And then I turned

EMORY
Then she turned

DALE/REBECCA/OLIVER
Then she turned—

WAYNE/RANDELL
Then she turned—

DONNA/CRAIG/SUSAN
Then she turned—

CECILY
and looked poor Professor Caliban in his squinting, dolphin eyes and spoke Prospero's first lines which, though they couldn't be heard, Caliban could read on my lips as well as I could read his angry little page.

Be collected;
No more amazement. Tell your piteous heart
There's no harm done.

SUSAN
She turned and spoke right at him and when she did I pulled his own memory of those words from the deep of his brain, and he knew them again as he knew them, eavesdropping, all those years ago.

CECILY
Tell your piteous heart
There's no harm done.

EMORY/CRAIG/OLIVER/SUSAN/DALE/DONNA/REBECCA
And from that moment

REBECCA
The old man lived again.

CRAIG
Prospero was alive and in the room.

EMORY
The Page carried up the spirit of our conjurer from a grave

EMORY/SUSAN
four

EMORY/DALE
centuries

EMORY/DONNA
deep.

WAYNE
The line is to Miranda, of course, but directed his way, it threw him.

CECILY *"of course"*
your piteous heart

CECILY
His pen paused and he thought—of what?

WAYNE
Of hearts and pity

CECILY
and harm done

WAYNE
and not done, I suppose.

DALE
Anyhow...yeah, all the crumbs in the place can see he's pretty stirred up. He's awful quiet, just watching Cecily do the scene. So all the crumbs go quiet, too. And **all of sudden**

DONNA
all of a sudden one can actually hear, and it all begins to sound and look like a real play.

DALE
It was beautiful.

WAYNE
Uh, William.

EMORY
Right, and then my entrance as myself. Which unfortunately, for some reason, Caliban found **hilarious**; I'm not sure why—

DIANA *"myself"*
Humane Society.

CECILY
hilarious, yes. Ariel's entrance was a disaster. The Professor just rolled his

RANDELL *"disaster"*
I don't like it.

head with that chuckling gurgle. Then back to writing his review—uhh!

EMORY *"review"*
I'm not sure why—maybe because I can't play myself. Or maybe I just have no goddamn talent.

RANDELL *"play myself"*
I don't like to sing.

REBECCA
Yeah, it was awful. It was going great until Ariel went on and Cannibal had to...oh, he just thought it was the biggest joke. And of course the whole rotten crowd is following his cue, so they start up again and we're right back where we began, only *now* they're using their evil powers against us. Don't ask me what took them so long to get *that* idea...yeah. Colonel Corpse throws himself center stage and starts going stiff. Senorita Splinter is

WAYNE *"awful"*
of hearts and pity

CECILY *"joke"*
and harm done

WAYNE *"again"*
and not done, I suppose.

OLIVER/CRAIG/DALE/RANDELL
It was bad.

DONNA
Oh

SUSAN
my

BRAD
Oh my! Oh my!

OLIVER/CRAIG/DALE/RANDELL
It was bad.

DALE
I was drinking a lot of my coffee.

CRAIG
He's back writing the review, which you can tell is a very unkind review, because The Page looks like she's been kicked in the stomach. She's doubled over, almost. And it really seemed to me like **it was all over.**

OLIVER/DALE/EMORY
it was all over.

EMORY
You can imagine how I felt. Cracking the spell of our show. And certainly one would think that if the portrayal of myself by myself was but jest to my wanton friend, certainly the role of himself as interpreted by The Untangler would increase the sport a thousand fold. But no.

REBECCA
The Untangler enters, as Caliban.

WAYNE
As wicked dew as e're my mother brushed
With raven's feather from unwholesome fen
Drop on you both! A southwest blow on ye
And blister you all o'er.

EMORY
And Caliban—*the* Caliban, the Professor—is on his feet, pounding the railing, all the old wounds wide and gushing, bellowing in unison: **This island's mine.**

WAYNE
This island's mine *by Sycorax, my mother,*
Which thou tak'st from me.

EMORY
Tearing the scales from his head. The scrawled sheets of his review scattered to the seats below. He's back into it. He's back into the play.

CECILY
He orders Colonel Corpse removed from the stage. Everyone sits down and everyone pays attention.

EMORY
He's back into the play. And he would have been conquered then if it wasn't for the dismal gas of my performance. Every time I spoke, Shakespeare died again.

CRAIG
Now...yes, now everything rested on keeping the Professor's attention.

REBECCA
Next came **the first scene between the lovers.**

CECILY
the first scene between the lovers.

DIANA
At this point I had found a cat.

DALE
I was drinking a whole lot of my coffee.

CECILY
the lovers. Ferdinand and Miranda.

CRAIG/REBECCA *"and"*
Susan and Randell

DALE
and Miranda. A very under-rehearsed

DONNA/OLIVER *"very"*
extremely under-rehearsed

RANDELL
Susan and I had hardly rehearsed the scene at all. Basically, she hated my guts and didn't want to be in the same room with me.

SUSAN *"at all"*
Randell and I hadn't been talking... no, I didn't exactly hate his guts.

CRAIG *"room"*
Yes, now everything rested on keeping the Professor's attention.

REBECCA
Miranda enters and there's Ferdinand.

SUSAN
I did not hate him

RANDELL
She didn't want anything to do with me.

REBECCA
The first man besides her father she's ever seen.

SUSAN
Sure, I didn't want to see him or have anything to do with him, sure.

CECILY
And we enter. We enter and she sees him from behind. Randell. And he's hunched and rather sad seeming. And afraid. Like he's expecting to be struck with a rock on the back of his head rather than play a love scene. And Miranda, Susan, she looks at him, this sort of deflated sack of a person and she pauses, and I think, oh, she's forgotten her lines again. But it wasn't that. She's looking at him like he's something she had lost—like an old hat or photograph or something—and she's just now remembered again where she put it, in the back of the closet or somewhere. And there it is. Found. Remembered.

SUSAN
No, you don't understand. I'm not saying that we're in love now. It just turned out to be a nice...I am not saying that.

RANDELL
Yeah, we're in love, Jerry.

CECILY
It makes me wonder: Why are love scenes ever rehearsed at all? They're the one thing on the stage made real by awkwardness.

RANDELL
The very instant that I saw you, did
My heart fly to your service

SUSAN
I would not wish
Any companion in the world but you,
Nor can imagination form a shape,
Besides yourself, to like of.
Do you love me?

RANDELL
[Stands up and speaks to Susan:]
Yeah, I sure do.

[All except Susan and Randell cheer, whistle, applaud, etc.]

EMORY
The crowd loved it.

CRAIG
The Professor was in tears.

EMORY
Sure the crowd loved it. And that's wonderful. Personally, I don't feel that Susan and Randell have a real grasp of the characters or the language—but who am I to give opinion? Seeing as my performance of *myself* somehow wasn't up to the standards of a flesh-eating madman.

REBECCA *"language"*
Caliban was in tears.

CECILY
He was in tears. From there on his heart wrapped as ours are in our shared history, in our common loss: The old man. The daughter. The one library. The one island.

OLIVER
And if there was ever a show that was well received

CRAIG
ever a show that was fully embraced

REBECCA
ever a show that changed hearts

DONNA
or ever a show that could do no wrong, this was now that show.

OLIVER
My sick nose dripped oceans over the knees of the front row. They cheered every strand.

DALE
I played the drunken butler straight sober. I couldn't help it...No. It was that coffee of mine. I was like Carrie Nation up there. But it worked. They ate it up.

OLIVER/CRAIG/DONNA/REBECCA
Everything worked.

CECILY
Be collected;
No more amazement.

DIANA
I followed my new cat onto the stage. I wasn't sure where we were in the play. So I just started saying lines at random.

REBECCA
and the play went on from there

WAYNE
All the infections that the sun sucks up
From bogs, fens, flats, on Prosper fall and make him
By inch-meal a disease! His spirits hear me,
And yet I needs must curse. But they'll nor pinch,

Fright me with urchin-shows, pitch me i' th' mire,
Nor lead me, like a firebrand, in the dark
Out of my way, unless he bid 'em; but
For every trifle are they set upon me;
Sometime like apes that mow and chatter at me
And after bite me, then like hedgehogs, which
Lie tumbling in my barefoot way and mount
Their pricks at my footfall; sometime am I
All wound with adders who with cloven tongues
Do hiss me into madness.

DIANA
[Reading these lines in any, and no particular, order:]
What have we here? a man or a fish? dead or alive? A fish: he smells like a fish; a very ancient and fish-like smell; a kind of not of the newest Poor-John. A strange fish! Were I in England now, as once I was, and had but this fish painted, not a holiday fool there but would give a piece of silver: there would this monster make a man; any strange beast there makes a man: when they will not give a doit to relieve a lame beggar, they will lazy out ten to see a dead Indian. Legged like a man and his fins like arms! Warm o' my troth! I do now let loose my opinion, hold it no longer: this is no fish, but an islander, that hath lately suffered by a thunderbolt.

EMORY
You fools! I and my fellows
Are ministers of Fate: the elements,
Of whom your swords are temper'd, may as well
Wound the loud winds, or with bemock'd-at stabs
Kill the still-closing waters, as diminish
One dowel that's in my plume: my fellow-ministers
Are like invulnerable. If you could hurt,
Your swords are now too massy for your strengths
And will not be uplifted. But remember—
For that's my business to you—that you three
From Milan did supplant good Prospero;
Exposed unto the sea, which hath requit it,
Him and his innocent child: for which foul deed
The powers, delaying, not forgetting, have
Incensed the seas and shores, yea, all the creatures,
Against your peace.

BRAD
O, it is monstrous, monstrous:
Methought the billows spoke and told me of it;
The winds did sing it to me, and the thunder,
That deep and dreadful organ-pipe, pronounced
The name of Prosper: it did bass my trespass.
Therefore my son i' th' ooze is bedded, and
I'll seek him deeper than e'er plummet sounded
And with him there lie mudded.

REBECCA
I' the commonwealth I would by contraries
Execute all things; for no kind of traffic
Would I admit; no name of magistrate;
Letters should not be known; riches, poverty,
And use of service, none; contract, succession,
Bourn, bound of land, tilth, vineyard, none;
No use of metal, corn, or wine, or oil;
No occupation; all men idle, all;
And women too, but innocent and pure;
No sovereignty;—

All things in common nature should produce
Without sweat or endeavor: treason, felony,
Sword, pike, knife, gun, or need of any engine,
Would I not have; but nature should bring forth,
Of its own kind, all foison, all abundance,
To feed my innocent people.

OLIVER
Whiles we stood here securing your repose,
Even now, we heard a hollow burst of bellowing
Like bulls, or rather lions: did't not wake you?
It struck mine ear most terribly.

CRAIG
Ay, sir; where lies that? if 'twere a kibe,
'Twould put me to my slipper: but I feel not
This deity in my bosom: twenty consciences,
That stand 'twixt me and Milan, candied be they
And melt ere they molest! Here lies your brother,
No better than the earth he lies upon,
If he were that which now he's like, that's dead;
Whom I, with this obedient steel, three inches of it,
Can lay to bed for ever; whiles you, doing thus,
To the perpetual wink for aye might put
This ancient morsel, this Sir Prudence, who
Should not upbraid our course. For all the rest,

They'll take suggestion as a cat laps milk;
They'll tell the clock to any business that
We say befits the hour.

SUSAN

I do not know
One of my sex; no woman's face remember,
Save, from my glass, mine own; nor have I seen
More that I may call men than you, good friend,
And my dear father: how features are abroad,
I am skilless of; but, by my modesty,
The jewel in my dower, I would not wish
Any companion in the world but you,
Nor can imagination form a shape,
Besides yourself, to like of. But I prattle
Something too wildly and my father's precepts
I therein do forget.

RANDELL

There be some sports are painful, and their labour
Delight in them sets off: some kinds of baseness
Are nobly undergone and most poor matters
Point to rich ends. This my mean task
Would be as heavy to me as odious, but
The mistress which I serve quickens what's dead
And makes my labours pleasures: O, she is
Ten times more gentle than her father's crabbed,
And he's compos'd of harshness. I must remove
Some thousands of these logs and pile them up,
Upon a sore injunction: my sweet mistress
Weeps when she sees me work, and says, such baseness
Had never like executor. I forget:
But these sweet thoughts do even refresh my labours,
Most busy lest, when I do it.

DONNA

Hail, many-colour'd messenger, that ne'er
Dost disobey the wife of Jupiter;
Who, with thy saffron wings, upon my flowers
Diffusest honey-drops, refreshing showers,
And with each end of thy blue bow dost crown
My bosky acres and my unshrubb'd down,
Rich scarf to my proud earth; why hath thy queen
Summon'd me hither, to this short-grass'd green?

CECILY

Ye elves of hills, brooks, standing lakes and groves,
And ye that on the sands with printless foot
Do chase the ebbing Neptune and do fly him

When he comes back; you demi-puppets that
By moonshine do the green sour ringlets make,
Whereof the ewe not bites; and you whose pastime
Is to make midnight mushrooms, that rejoice
To hear the solemn curfew; by whose aid,
Weak masters though ye be, I have bedimm'd
The noontide sun, call'd forth the mutinous winds,
And 'twixt the green sea and the azur'd vault
Set roaring war: to the dread rattling thunder
Have I given fire and rifted Jove's stout oak
With his own bolt; the strong-based promontory
Have I made shake and by the spurs pluck'd up
The pine and cedar: graves at my command
Have wak'd their sleepers, op'd, and let 'em forth
By my so potent art. But this rough magic
I here abjure, and, when I have required
Some heavenly music, which even now I do,
To work mine end upon their senses that
This airy charm is for, I'll break my staff,
Bury it certain fathoms in the earth,
And deeper than did ever plummet sound
I'll drown my book.

DALE

He's in his fit now and does not talk after the wisest. He shall taste of my bottle: if he have never drunk wine afore, it will go near to remove his fit. If I can recover him and keep him tame, I will not take too much for him; he shall pay for him that hath him, and that soundly.

Four legs and two voices: a most delicate monster! His forward voice now is to speak well of his friend; his backward voice is to utter foul speeches and to detract. If all the wine in my bottle will recover him, I will help his ague. Come. Amen! I will pour some in thy other mouth.

WAYNE

And I undid that arcane cord of mine and as it loosed and fell to the rock, the audience, and the poor Cannibal as well, did indeed cry and laugh and believe every dread riddle solved.

DONNA
And all my shadows that had fled in fear returned in that famous scene where Prospero talks of dreams and sleep. They trembled their way over the stage—the hippo, the mallard, the sloth, the scarab—all of them, by the hundreds, and poured themselves like black tea into the shape of a disc at Prospero's feet. And then shrank to a speck and vanished, I assume forever, to wherever frightened shadows vanish to. That's all they wanted of our production: an exit.

CECILY *"sleep"*
[Quietly, until Donna finishes, then full volume:]
Our revels now are ended. These our actors,
As I foretold you, were all spirits and
Are melted into air, into thin air;
And, like the baseless fabric of this vision,
The cloud-capped towers, the gorgeous palaces,
The solemn temples, the great globe itself,
Yea, all which it inherit shall dissolve,
And like this insubstantial pageant faded,
Leave not a rack behind. We are such stuff
As dreams are made on, and our little life
Is rounded with a sleep.

[Pause.]

EMORY
I'm not sure why I can't play myself. Maybe because I'm not myself anymore. Not the self I was back then, before Emory Lawson.

REBECCA
I never did put the audience on that tidal wave.

DALE
I shall no more to sea, to sea
Here shall I die ashore

EMORY
At any rate, in the end we hoisted up the fallen curtain as the applause rose and broke against it like a monsoon.

CRAIG *"rate"*
Let me tell you what I'm feeling

BRAD
My gondola is broken. But it was a bad gondola. I will make another.

EMORY
And now all the villains of Fathom Town have sought for grace...that's right. They all turned themselves in. But instead of prison, we've sentenced them to be our audience every night. Which they are glad to do. A happy end.

CRAIG
Let me tell you what I'm feeling, Miss Phillips.

DONNA
We do need your support still, yes.

EMORY
But of course, all happy endings are problematic as they invariably involve the continuation of life.

CRAIG
Let me tell you

RANDELL
on behalf of an extremely important project that The Enforcers are hoping to invest quite a bit of time and energy into in the coming months

WAYNE
on behalf of the Fathom Town Enforcers, yes...Well, he told me to call him back. Now. Well, where is he?

DIANA *"time"*
No, no. Eleven. Eleven!... Who is this? I don't want eight...I want eleven.

DALE *"time"*
I don't want to send you out any pledge form. I want...no I want...no, a credit card

CRAIG *"time"*
Let me tell you...
Let me tell you...
Let me tell you...

CRAIG
Let me tell you what I'm feeling, Miss Phillips. I'm feeling that that old world of our play—with its sea and library and splendid caverns and woods and wind—well, of course that was a perfect world. A world so perfect and perfectly beautiful it really just seems a shame to slop something up against the quiet memory I have of it. Muddy up that memory, for example, by mounting a superheroic production of *The Tempest*—trying to recall what can't be recalled. What in the end does such busy work contribute to this memory of perfection? What nerve to think it, to think anyone could in some way contribute to perfection. Perfection needs no contribution, yes? But in fact, contribution is what I'm calling you about this evening.

DIANA
Hello?

WAYNE
Idiot.

EMORY
the continuation of life. For I tell you, Mrs. Clare—In a grove just above my cavern home, there is a deep, narrow well whose sides are all bright glass.

And when the sun slants through the palms at a certain time of day, I can see my reflection far, far at its bottom as I hover, on my wings, above its mouth. The image is so clear that, in it, I can tidy the hairs of my eyebrows and read the pages of the smallest book. These days, of course, that book is always *The Tempest*. And these days, looking for new perspective on a play I've read a thousand times—looking for some way to play the role of myself—this is how I read it: in a mirror reflection at the bottom of a shining well. And this is always—every day. And always I think a terrible thought: that when I'm gone from this well, even as I sleep, my reflection reads on, there below the surface of the earth, drowning. And reading. And drowning.

OLIVER *"smallest book"*
Expiration date?

CECILY
rounded with a sleep.

EMORY
Yes, Bell?...Oh, yes, I know...I always thought you might be. I had hoped it was just a cold. I am sorry to know it. I'll never know the thing itself, but I am sorry to know it in you.

If I might ask you one favor. Will you, when you find that country my immortal freedom bars from me, wish my past master well?...Thank you.

CRAIG
That would be just wonderful, Miss Phillips. Just wonderful...yes. Now...

END

There Is a Happiness That Morning Is

There Is a Happiness That Morning Is was first produced in 2011 by Theater Oobleck at the Chicago DCA Storefront Theater, with the following cast:

Bernard:	Colm O'Reilly
Ellen:	Diana Slickman
Dean:	Kirk Anderson

Music for "Fall Down" composed by Chris Schoen

There Is a Happiness That Morning Is

CHARACTERS

Bernard
Ellen
Dean

PRODUCTION NOTE

A classroom with a large chalkboard along the back wall. Two lecterns sit left and right on a green rug. Bernard enters, looking like he's spent the night walking a forest. He writes SONGS OF INNOCENCE on one side of the board; addresses us, his class, from the lectern, left.

A slash (\ ) in the text indicates the point at which the next speaker begins, overlapping.

BERNARD

There is a happiness that morning is.
Just is, just on its own. Outside the hiss
and song of whatever serpents and larks
are playing throughout the chambers of our hearts.
The morning doesn't care. It doesn't care.
Look out that window, there.
The fact is I could slit my wrist
up here, that sun would still persist.
The birds would still pick seeds out of their feathers,
and sip the dew blown from those mountains whether
I cry or dance or die. Be assured
the morning will not be in the least disturbed.
Out there's a joy that will remain no matter
what the result of our dramas and chatter.
If you learn one thing from me let that be it.

Okay, if any of you still need to get
your yellow forms to me, please do. Please.
By end of class, or you'll incur the fees.
The yellow forms. All right? All right.

Now some of you might know I spent the night
out in the forest—after what happened—alone.
Not so fun. But this morning to be shown
these faces—all of them—you're all here,
even you! You've never come all year!

You're like a hundred suns who've risen
to un-ink the gloom of my night's prison.
Means more to me than I could ever say
to you, on this, perhaps my final day.

All right. Let's get this done.

I'll begin by saying that, one:
I have a special happiness this day.
As the result of last night's...passion play.

The morning's joy has nothing on mine.
The morning's joy is well and fine,
but I've got a happiness that's like...it's weird:
it rings me like a cylinder that's mirrored
on both its inside and its out, and so
reflects exterior fears, all doubts and low
esteem of self, deflects all that away.
While I, here snug within, as safe as clay
within my shining tube of happiness
immune to all life's crappiness
can look hard into the inside mirror
and see into myself and know no fear.
I look inside myself, today,
I look within and do not turn away
from anything: the webs, the salted snow
in there...my usual happiness, you know,
is very spirited—like a jumpy gas
whose bubbles I amass
to lift me out of my inner grindings and goth,
to carry me away on a spastic froth.
While this is more...it's more like breath. A calm
that lets me face all troubles with aplomb.

That's number one. Now, number two.
I am so sorry if any of you
were made distracted or upset
by hearing tell or witnessing, yet,
what I and Professor Parker did last night
out by the hedge and oak, there in plain sight.
But if it makes a difference, and it should—
it should just flip this matter to the good—
Look. We love each other very much.
Ellen and I. And the thing that's been such

a central point all term,
if there's one thing that you've learned
from the poetry of William Blake
—and, really, what convincing does this take?—
is Love makes all the difference. Just because.
It does. It does. It does. It does.
With love all things are better, not worse.
As love, in fact, is real and does immerse
us all, like morning, in its reality,
and gives a certain luminosity
to everything it comes to brush against.
It's just common sense.
Two people in love committing a murder
seems a better thing to us than were there
only one committing the same. And why?
Because a single person's just some guy,
alone. A lonely person. And all he's done
as a single, lonely person killing someone
is make himself—that's right—just more alone.
But love, we know, creates a magic zone.
Lovers make assassination
seem more a tender assignation.
It highlights their togetherness.
But Ellen and I, our crime, of course, was less,
much less than murder, yes? What did we do?
We read an old poem, out loud, to you.
And while reading—sure, it now sounds somewhat crass—
had intimate relations on the grass.
In twilight's blue.
In front of all of you.

And now, for this, we would be finished here.
We would be finished after fifteen years.
And not just us. The regents say that they
might have to close the school. What with the way
the papers picked the story up so fast—
I guess the pictures that you took got passed
along.

[Approximately here, Ellen enters, carrying her class materials and a mug of something. She writes SONGS OF EXPERIENCE on the chalkboard opposite INNOCENCE, pointedly drawing a line dividing the two halves of the board. She's not noticed by Bernard, as the idea here is that she's in the same classroom, but we're seeing her some hours later, in her class after lunch.]

The money thing was bad before
all this. Enrollment now will hit the floor,
they say. Unless, I'm told, we apologize.
For this public showing of our dew-dipped thighs.
Say we're sorry. Me, this morning, to you,
And Ellen after lunch to her class at two.

ELLEN
[At her lectern.]
I'm sorry.

BERNARD
And, yes, I'm happy to. My mood being such
this morning—happy!—there's just not too much
that I'd refuse. And it will be sincere.
Above all, though, I'd like to make things clear.
I'll show that what we did beneath that tree
relates directly to Blake's poetry.
That what we did out on that lawn makes sense
of every line in Songs of Innocence.

ELLEN
I'm sorry.

BERNARD
We'll finally see what words can really mean.
And then I think that you, and President Dean,
the board, and all your parents'll understand.
And Ellen, too, as she extends a hand
this afternoon, she will explain as well.
And better than me. She always did excel
at what we need a lover most to do:
make sane the madness that love brings us to.

ELLEN
I'm sorry.

BERNARD
We're not the first to play at Eden, are we?
But here I'll say it truly: I am sorry.

[During Ellen's next speech, Bernard writes out the text of William Blake's "Infant Joy" on the board.]

ELLEN
I'm sorry. But I want this day set free.
Our last afternoon with William Blake to be
a celebration. Just as I aspire
to join to every day its dance, its choir.
I want of every day a fatted bliss.
And let me tell you: I succeed in this.
I am at war with sorrow and distress
and have no heart for grey-lipped confessing
of—of what? I'm like Baryshnikov.
Each day: a dance. A joy. So fuck off.

I'm sorry to take that tone. But on this campus
there's one who'd use last night's rumpus
—what happened between myself and Mr. Barrow
out by the hedge—would use that event to narrow
my sluices; dam and perplex life's sea.
He'll fail. This day will find its ecstasy.

He thinks last night was a scandal? Yawn.
One cock in a pussy on the lawn.
This day will bloom a thousand rosewood trees
to pleasure its aching vulva, if need be.

He thinks that happiness is outside somewhere.
Outside of us, out in the dirt or air.
Something that by his devious fuckery
can be kept out by idiotic decree
and his dung-packed battlements of woe.
But Happiness has its Kingdom here, you know.
It lives and shouts and rules inside of us.
Inside, and thus
it's not a thing to try to worm or wind
its way into the dark cage of our mind;
it's born there, it's always been a part
of each of us, inside our skull, our heart.
Inside but never hidden, no, it hovers
patiently...as nerves that swell the lover's
lip are always there, just waiting to be asked,
"Come on, come up." No magic need be tasked,
it's all inevitable and only he—
the dry-humping, rot-minded flea
who's proud to be called President of this dump—
he believes that he has got the jump
on happiness, and that his shaming calls

for me to say that I regret—it galls!—
regret my night, he thinks that this will block
my ease of heart and so unwind the clock
of joy. But, ah, regrets, no, I have none.
I'm sad my time with all of you is done.
And I'll not be here in the Fall.
But I have taught you all, or almost all,
what I believe and know.
Just one more poem to go...
This afternoon here I'll say all I mean.

But first, a final word on President Dean.
He is a detriment to your education
and he is a fucker. His administration's
spray of piss-ideas and policies
has moistened all the cobbles, bricks, and ivies
in this place. He's made it his latrine,
this once-proud school. Conditions are obscene.

The mold's enough to induce toxic shock.
The ceiling drips, there's never any chalk.
I've loved this place, but please: this rug.
This smell that lingers...oh. He's let it go to hell.
And as his flaccid soul is best expressed
by the laying of rotten eggs in lovely nests,
he thrills that mountains and lush wood surround
his dilapidated compound.

He likes when ugly things invade the Good.
Last night was case in point. So, if I could
now parse that episode, just for the books:
Our President was on the porch. He looks
upon the lawn and squints. The twilight irks
and puzzles him. Is't that evening lurks
within the day, or day is crawling, creeping
into night? Not right. Disrupts the bleeping
dried and cut of things. Creates unease.
Then...by the hedge...what's that? Big...bunnies?
Oh, no. Ohhhhh no. How quickly dawns the light.
Nothing crepusculine 'bout this—it's night
and day again, thank God. And so like that
he leaps upon the sward, dragging that mat
—that mat!
—that mud mat from the commons room—
across the lawn, vaulting the daisies, fuming,

all his infant-anger gurgling out,
pink-faced and shrieking, the mat about
his shoulders now, like a blankie flapping
there behind, but not for baby's napping,
no. He throws it over us, we rutting
swine. Its rubber backing burned my butt.
He would've buried us if he'd had a shovel.
But now he wants us well in view to grovel.
As this is just his nature, his abject game:
hide away all love, make public, shame.

I found his note inside my box at dawn.
A tersely squirted jizz: my job is gone
unless I make amends. Permission—permission!—
granted then to offer my submission
here. Here. In my own class.
Where the lesson today is Kiss My Ass.
Kiss my ass, Dean.
'Cuz my and Mr. Barrow's little scene
was all higher education should aspire to be:
a fuck in the grass under the old, oak tree.

BERNARD
...for sure...

ELLEN
And if the poetry of William Blake
says anything, if it can manage to wake
a single thought in us across the run
of centuries it's that: Fuck someone.

BERNARD
...for sure...

ELLEN
Fuck someone hard on the echoing green.
Beneath the stars and their spears, slip low between
the roots of the dew and draw breath only to drown
in a love so true it's scandal.

BERNARD
...for sure...

ELLEN
Write that down.

[During Bernard's next speech, Ellen writes out the text of Blake's "The Sick Rose" on the board.]

BERNARD

...for sure, if push is coming now to shove,
yes, William Blake was a fan of free love.
It's said his wife and he would welcome guests
while in the garden, totally undressed.
Completely nekkid. Reading *Paradise Lost*
and sipping tea. No doubt but he'd be tossed
out of this school. And in the London of
two hundred years ago? Good Lord above.
Of last night's scene he'd certainly approve.
Paint a picture of it for the Louvre.
But the point I need to make is this:
yes, his poems, they trumpet risk,
and freedom, passion on the fly—
but always they seek to clarify.
Yes, it's good, Blake says, yes, yes,
to startle the timid world from its nest.
But equally we need to calm it down,
and clarify what we have done.
No mysteries, and nothing hid.
Illuminate, is what he did.

Once again, from *Songs of Innocence*,
sweet and short, yet so immense:

"Infant Joy"
I have no name;
I am but two days old
What shall I call thee?
I happy am,
Joy is my name.
Sweet joy befall thee!

Pretty joy!
Sweet joy, but two days old.
Sweet Joy I call thee:
Thou dost smile
I sing the while
Sweet joy befall thee!

I've said this now a thousand times, maybe.
What's this poem about? A talking baby.

A baby that talks, and its...Mother, let's say;
they talk, it's like a little play,
with Baby saying, out of the blue:
I have no name, I am but two
days old. And it's a startling thing,
of course, that a baby should bring
these words or words of any kind
to a poem, or that a poem should find
that it has chosen a baby's voice
—a really quite remarkable choice—
just as what happened on the lawn last night
was a remarkable choice—but all right.
Poems and life are made up of surprise,
and this poor Mother, you can see her eyes,
she must be so alarmed! I'd be, too.
But see what Blake here has her do:
Seek clarity:
What shall I call thee?
Despite alarm or fear she wants to know.
She's open to all this slant world can throw
but needs some clarity:
What shall I call thee?
And then it's on Blake's baby to figure it out.
It has to, right? 'Cuz what's this poem about?
A talking baby! Bam!
I happy am.
Note "happy" comes before the "am"s deployed,
as existence is preceded here by joy.
I happy am. These three words.
In all the western canon there's never been heard
an affirmation of innocence as bold.

I happy am. And from this mold, this simple frame:
Joy is my name
is the conclusion that it draws.
And that's all it says. Or needs to say. Because
it's clear now to its mom.
Though it was startling, almost, as a bomb
being talked at by a two-day-old.
This Mother, now, she is completely sold,
and takes the poem from there...rocking, at rest:
Thou dost smile, I sing the while...
Stillness, and peace, and happiness.
She knows now what she has there in her arms.
The name of it: it's Joy. Cease all alarms.
Its name is Joy. As Joy has taught.

Now why do we read poems? Here's a thought.
We read poems so we can repeat them.
We read poems so we can repeat them.
Either alone (out loud or in our head),
or to others. We like to say what has been said.
We read poems so we can repeat them.
For ourselves and others, we collect—assemble—
lines of poetry to throw at life.
In special situations that feel..."ripe."
A wedding, say. Events that strive to be real.
That is, to be poetic. For these we wheel
out our tub of poems to try and boost
reality, repeating lines loosed
upon a thousand weddings before.
But here's what I think this repeating's mostly for:
mostly we read poems and repeat them
with the childlike wish we might become them.
And "Infant Joy," I think you know by now
it's just my favorite, evidenced by how
it's always central in my talks on Blake
and all I talk about is Blake, so make
of that just what you will. But outside class
I'm just as bad. Or worse. You cannot pass
me by and stay quote free, no ma'am.
"How are you, Bernard?" "I HAPPY AM!"
Trying to shore up, first, my personal sense
of my own personal innocence.
Attempting, second, to create a guise,
that shows myself as innocently wise
and full of wonder, right? The blossom-haired
professor of poems that no small college is spared.
The infant-like eccentric, yes, that's me,
with my eccentric repeating with giggling glee
these lines of "Infant Joy." And passively
I'd watch myself put on this massively
ridiculous and phony act. You know,
like you watch a rerun of a TV show
you hate, because there's nothing else that's on.
Or how I'd watch my shadow, at sunset drawn
across a wall, lengthen, fade, then pass...
with more life than its originating mass.

And I would have myself repeat these lines,
but never, never once, I made them mine.
Could never join them to myself. No part.

Dissected them, and never brushed the heart.
Until last night. I read them on the lawn.
And that, it did the trick. All along
I thought I was in love. And yes, I was,
for twenty years, have been, but now because
I've been out on that grass and read them there
these lines remade my love, they've stripped it bare.
Now at last I am this poem. I'm Joy.

ELLEN
Does thy life destroy...

BERNARD
We had our picnic in the woods: bok choy
with almonds, chardonnay, and roasted lamb.
And then she led me up. I happy am,
I said. She took me by the smallest finger
and she led me up the hill to linger
at the forest's edge a moment more.
And then she kissed me and the dress she wore
just seemed to fall away. Joy is my name.
Our public reading had begun. We came
out of the branches then. The dew cold
on my shoeless socks. I am but two days old!
And then I'm on my knees, she scratches my thigh,
draws a gentle drop of red and starts to cry
and laugh, and then we just go at it hard.
Well, you saw. Saw Heaven drop its guard.
Joy and Happy, we were the words of this baby.
And it, it was...was Innocence, truly.

ELLEN
In the howling storm...

BERNARD
And Ellen, today, will back me up on this.
With each caress out there, with every kiss,
these baby's words became our words.
It's not like we remembered them, or heard
them on the wind. It's like they found a door
that opened into us, into our core.
I happy am.
And all my flim-flam,
my falseness, all, all that was like I dreamed
it, even as our President screamed

and sprinted from the porch, just Happy Joy
was all I knew, I was a little boy!
Albeit one who wanted to have sex.
In no other way was this remotely complex.
Joy is my name! I cried; the President hopped
the daisies, and when his mud mat dropped:
I HAPPY AM I sang from underneath,
even with its rubber in my teeth.
I was newborn there in the tacky black,
HAPPY, HAPPY AM, no turning back.
It's with me still, the whole of it, just look:
these pants were round my knees last night. They took
up all the leaves and twigs and moist clover,
look, like they were sucked up with a Hoover.

[From inside his pants and pockets Bernard hauls an almost unrealistically large amount of flora—twigs, leaves, moss, petals, etc. Scatters them over the floor and audience.]

Swept up in Love's wild roundelay.
Here's some for you, so glad you came today.
You know that this is what you took a class in?
This stuff right here, it's night-blooming jasmine.
Its flower only opens in the dark,
so for its pollinators to find the mark
its scent is potent past belief. Here, smell.
I want you all to smell. It's how you'll tell
that all I say is true. Here, take some, yes.

ELLEN
[Referring to the twigs and leaves, etc., which were not, apparently, cleaned up after Bernard's class:]
What is this goddamn mess?

BERNARD
Fragile, almost nothing, but so strong.
It's like our heart, our heart whose quiet song
won't quit transmitting 'til it has Love's ear.
It is all true. Just wait 'til Ellen gets here,
at two. She'll say this all much better than me.

I think, though, I'll come back. It's just...you see,
we haven't seen each other since last night.
I came from under that mat just so excited,
ready, I could feel my chest ballooning

with that love that comes from assuming
command of things. I'd shake our president's hand,
apologize right there. Then zip up, and
arrange a meeting for the morning to
just clear the air of all the ballyhoo.
And Ellen and I would go straight home to drink
a calming tea and talk and cry, then sink
down on the bed to finish making love.
With candles all around, the sheet above
our heads pitched like a tent. It wouldn't be
the same as being in front of you, but we
would make it work. I'm sure of that.

But when I came from underneath the mat,
Ellen was gone. The President was there,
all out of breath and giving me a stare,
a stare that crawled beneath my face. But she
had disappeared, away into the trees.
And Dean, he wouldn't shake my hand. He spat.
I think. Could that be true? I tried to chat
but he just backed away. And now what light
there'd been was gone. I turned and walked all night,
all through the woods. Calling, calling her...

But I am sure
she'll teach her class this afternoon, right here.
And I will come. Together we'll make this clear.
And things'll be back to the norm.
Now, please—I need that yellow form.
I do. You say you want a grade—OK.
Then get it to me by the end of the day.
OK...sorry, I'm a tiny bit hoarse.
Again, apologies for any shock...
for those of you in Ellen's course,
I'll see you here at two o'clock.

[Exit Bernard.]

ELLEN
Now. Take a breath.
I needn't work to death
a topic that is death itself.
Enough of Dean, of President Elf.
Of every goblin, every troll.
I'm here this afternoon with you to foal

a final lecture on the songs of Blake.
I'm here to cry for love, to sing, to wake.
And not spin discourse on pathetic frauds,
on sorry motherfuckers and dickwads.
I'm here to find my joy in thought, the thought
that's spoke aloud. Revealed. Deftly caught.
But in these *Songs of Experience*, yes, we find
one poem not spoke of yet. One left behind
'til now, inside its dark. This rose. "Sick Rose."
In 1793, we think, composed.
Is usually ninth in the twenty-five or so
"experienced" poems—a modest spot to grow.
So slight, one might just overlook this flower;
but in its coyness is its horror:

> *O Rose, thou art sick!*
> *The invisible worm*
> *That flies in the night,*
> *In the howling storm,*
>
> *Has found out thy bed*
> *Of crimson joy:*
> *And his dark secret love*
> *Does thy life destroy.*

Blake here has not so much a poem to give,
more a prognosis—shockingly negative.
This rose's life—a life of crimson joy,
will not just end, or fade, the word's *destroy*.
Destroyed by this, this worm, all wrapped in night
— invisible—invisible—its flight.
An agent of all that which Blake called ill:
the Secret and the Dark. Invisible.
All things shrouded, undisclosed,
every covering, he opposed.
It's what I've been at all this term,
the sickness here is not this worm,
invisibility itself
undermines these petals' health.
Every mystery that we please
to clench within, becomes disease:
I was angry with my foe
I told it not, my wrath did grow.
It is the theme that runs throughout the Songs:
The hidden, all, are all the world's wrongs.

But only here would William have you see
an image of invisibility.

An aim of every poet, Blake as well,
is to, most times, show as much as tell.
That is, place fleshed and concrete things before
the reader's eye. In this, Blake sets great store.
His poems desire first to offer us
a world we feel, a world we almost touch.
But here we find that desire overturned
in service of this less-than-knowable worm.
This worm. You cannot see, or sense it.
As William Blake prevents it.
First, he tells you it's invisible.
"OK," you think. "All right, all right, but, well,
I certainly still can picture it: a worm."
But, ah, how to keep that picture firm
in mind when it is one that "flies at night"?
An invisible worm at night. Does that invite
to your inner eye a crystal visualization?
No? Well, let's advance the obfuscation
and throw our blank, benighted grub
into a "howling storm." Then further rub
it from the page by using this word "worm."
Much like the things it means, a word that squirms.
It's Beowulf's dragon, or one of old France,
or the worm of earth who is a friend to plants.
Or Shakespeare's "worm i' th' bud"—pestilent larvae—
which, yes, would fit except they do not fly
and aren't invisible. It's just—just uhg.
And even if you could perceive this bug,
there is one last invisibility
tucked within its unseen cavity:
this "dark, secret love." That's the killer.
The love that hides itself. The love that fills your
rosy heart with a love no one can know;
just as this poem can never itself show.
All this poem shows is that which Blake most hates:
A shroud, a failure to illuminate.
This nothing-worm, it's like a mud mat.
That like some furious fuck he rushes at
his page with, splat. So, yes, he's just like Dean.
I'm sorry, yes, I really didn't mean
to bring it back to that but there it is.
Even here. In Blake. My mind is his.

I fear my mind he's overthrown.

I hate this poem.

We read poems so to live as poems.
To build from thought and song a home.
We read poems so to live as poems.
And this last night was to be a poem
sprung out from all I've known. With liquid moans
from throat like milk and stones,
the sloshing glint from the wine
of the bottle, fading behind
as we went up the hill, my dress it fell
like water, and Bernard—you could tell,
I think—he was, we were, composing then.
And what we'd be tomorrow or have been
meant nothing there. I know he seems a fool
at times. But he can love. Could run a school
for love. It should, it should be easy, joy.
It should come when we call. When we deploy
such artful forces to draw and coax and flush
it out, we should just need lie down and brush
the flies away and open up.
But Dean, he came. With his holler and jump,
his mat, his shroud, to make my poem this Rose.
Sick Rose. And so, I suppose,
he wins. Has won.
It's done.

For, having sex in public, let me say,
it's different, really, yes it is, 'cuz hey,
imagine, please, the most amazing sex
behind closed doors, the kind you feel connects
you to the universe and everyone
and where your "self" just melts and you're undone
inside the world and all seems vast expanse,
well, imagine that same tantric trance
of openness when you're out in the open.
The actual world is there for you to flow in.
The humankind whose soul you'd be immersed in,
well, it happens that they're there in person.
You find a skin you never knew was there.
And this is happiness and this is rare,
but, too, it puts you in a delicate state.
You're open to love, not braced for shrieking hate.

Not braced for swaddling in a sticky mat.
And it breaks you, bad. Apparently that
is all it takes. That single, little shove.
For in that moment, there, encased, the love
I've felt for my one man, for twenty years,
that love I've known was strong as halted tears,
I felt it curl away, just sigh and go...
decline its leading role in our small show.

That's fascinating, isn't it?
That love can die in just a flit?
Like anything else, not always slow...

I'm dying. Did you know?
I have a tumor, here, the size of, well,
"potato" is the word I use, I spell
it out because I like to spell, you know.
The doctor, though, just held his hands like so...
the doctor—just last week—he did a mime,
as if he feared to waste our quality time
with talk. So like a street clown thought to busk,
letting me unwrap his meaning's husk.
A cryptic diagnosis, much like Blake's
for his doomed rose. The kind that makes
it difficult to see just what's inside
of me. It's cancer, sure. But, look, aside
from gestures and that word, what have I got?
Please say. Most cancer's named for the part it rots:
brain, breast, mouth, liver, lung...
but my potato's made its home among
so many, with such tendrils that, indeed,
if they should try to pick it I would bleed
to death—the point being, though, that it's so ample,
it's name cannot be simple.
And so it's nameless...like a newborn babe.
"Potato." That will have to—I'm afraid—
will have to do. It's shocking, you agree?
That people die? Especially ones like me.
I keep forgetting that it's true. It's real.
Which should, you'd think, give it some appeal.
I'm going to lose my life. I've lost my heart...
it has on me a small head start
off of this chain-ed Earth...but focus, now:
I'm going to lose my life. I wonder how
repeating that improves my readiness.

[Referring to the twigs and leaves:]

What is this goddamn mess?

I was all night in the forest. Comfortably trapped
behind that stand of maples that they've tapped.
Avoiding Mr. Barrow. Sometime late
I heard him walking by. He was elated,
or, that's how he sounded. Called my name,
so cheerfully. But it seemed all the same
to me if I called back or not. A wash.
If I came out and there were hugs and sloshy
kisses and we went back to our place
drank tea and fell to bed to interlace
again with candles, incense, and concertos,
moaning, sighing "come on, come up" to Eros,
what would be the difference? Couldn't say.
Between me staying in the woods 'til day
alone or going with Bernard...I couldn't...
couldn't say. And so 'til dawn I wouldn't
leave my crouching spot. I crouched the night
away, and gnawed around this grim insight:
if love can die, how then can it be true?
So frail! What, can it also catch the flu?
A proper God's immortal, that's his job.
I think we were just two quite desperate slobs.
Desperation is so easy to
confuse with love: both make you queasy through
the hollow in your throat; both make you tremble,
bulge your eyes, and cause you to resemble
most a kitten in a bear trap,
who's undergone a spinal tap.
Both make your heart go pitter-pat, yes,
and drop a pond of sweat on your mattress.
So easy to confuse one's panic for passion.
For twenty years—really? Just desperation?
Each kiss, and pinch, and brush aside of bangs.
The sleepy scoldings, breakfast nods, harangues
against each other's taste in mustard.
All those jokes and laundry. Standing, flustered,
by a broken van, trying to bicker
in the mountain wind. The poems. The sex. His snicker
when he pitched a thumb-smudged magazine
across the room, and said, "There's what I mean,
in there, I circled it. With arrows, too."

The songs, the hairs in the mouth, the swatch of blue
we came to agree on once...I can't renew
these now. As memories they sidle through
my days and nights like drab, exhausted strangers—
how? How? Did I, each moment, perjure
myself? I guess. With every pinch and kiss.
I've wanted of each day a fatted bliss.
So how could it possibly come down to this
absurd defeat? Love's memory pressed flat
as a discarded scab by a man with a mat?
Love's memory is hid, or dead, and so
love never was, it never—no, no,
no. No. These are just sulking words.
Dull messengers of thoughts stirred
from some infected puddle of my mind.
I'm just unhinged by death and Dean. Behind
these sodden clouds there is a lamp, I know.
A light. My love was real.

BERNARD
[Calling from a distance, off:]

Hel...hello!

ELLEN
I have to fight. Against this sorry, sorry state.
Today, this hour, I'll resuscitate
one thing, one thing at least.

BERNARD
[Off, getting closer.]

Here I come!

ELLEN
If not the whole of love, I'll dig a crumb
out of this Hubbard's cupboard.

BERNARD
[Off, closer.]

It's all right!

ELLEN
Here comes Bernard. I thought he might.
And that's all I should need: to see his face,
here, with all of you, in light. A trace,
at least, of what I felt will not have perished.

I'll find it here, among these things I've cherished
always: students, Blake, Bernard, this room,
and here, in the shine and breeze of this afternoon
I'll give the lesson of this final day:
how to seek that bit of love that stays
around. Whatever that might be. The thing
that hooks itself inside the heart and clings
there past all craziness. Some brief candle
in his face, his voice, will prove I did not stand
alone along this road. I walked with him.

[Bernard enters, running, out of breath.]

BERNARD
Hi...hi...here I am.
I'm here. I'm here. I ran.
...sorry...I...some of you
I told I'd be here right at two...
meant to be on time...excuse me...
out of...up all night...you see...
I took a nap. At one.
And overslept. I wish you hadn't begun...
But that's OK...I'm here.
I'm here. I ran...oh, God. Oh, dear.

[Goes to Ellen, hugs her.]

I missed you. Where were you?

ELLEN
Just...

BERNARD
...just out there, thinking through
all this?

ELLEN
Just in the woods.

BERNARD
All night?
I looked there—where? I—

ELLEN
Yes. All night.

BERNARD
OK. OK. Well, anyway...

[Goes to lectern, addresses class.]

It was the nap I blame for my delay.
It was a nap that had no care for clocks.
You know of what I speak: it's like there's rocks
behind your eyes; some ancient, weight-drunk stones,
that by their brutish density alone
squeeze out your cognizance of Time and crush
all your alarms and urgencies to mush.
Turn consciousness to punctured bubble wrap.
I'm sorry I'm late. I had that kind of nap.

I wanted both of us together here,
this afternoon, with all of you this near.
In light. As I believe proximity
might help you all to see—quite literally—
with clearer sight just what love is.
It's this. And when Blake speaks of his,
his love, it is the same.
And it's the same
as last night's effort to express.
The vital difference here is that we're dressed.
And not pumping away in distant shrubbery,
in what, perhaps, seemed shadowed mummery.
And when we say we're sorry here, together,
for this thing we did that caused displeasure
and distress, such an apology,
by dint of being from two, will be more lovely,
yes? We've said we're sorry on our own,
but now, relax, and see how we atone
in unison, I think, to make it fun.

[To Ellen:]
On three. Is that all right? And then we're done.
On three we'll say, "We're sorry for the fuss."
One, two, three. "We're sorry..."

[Realizes Ellen hasn't gone along.]
Uh, what's...
...what's wrong?

ELLEN
What's wrong. Oh, Mr. Barrow...

BERNARD

What?

[Pause.]

You haven't, have you. Said you're sorry. But...
but that's...it's just not that big of a deal—

ELLEN

No. I suppose. If that's...that's how you feel?

BERNARD

I do. Don't you?

ELLEN

Well, I...

[Pause.]

Apparently,
the world's made mad by sex and poetry.
That you should ask me to apologize
to Dean, that you should ask that I chastise
myself so you might be forgiven, anon,
for the fucking you received upon the lawn
last night—

BERNARD

—that's not—

ELLEN

A quite remarkable
request. To think I'd be amenable—
me, who has perhaps two months to live—
to think it'd sit just fine with me to give
that self-important stump his satisfaction.
And why? As part of a ritual preparation
for death perhaps? Before my flesh is dressed
with herbs and oil, before a coin is pressed
beneath my tongue to pay the ferryman,
I am to kneel before the very man
responsible for—

BERNARD

For what? For what? Just what's
Dean done, exactly, that's so wrong?

ELLEN

The cuts
he's made to arts, to science—

BERNARD

Yes, to each
department save our own. He's let us teach
exactly what and as we please. For sure,
the budget moves he had to make, they were
perhaps—

ELLEN

It's been a relished happiness
for me and Mr. Barrow to express
for fifteen years our laughing, joyful disdain
of that so temptingly mock-able drip, that stain
on this secluded glade, our home—right?
Right? Or is my mind a ghost, a flight
of creaking stairs in place of memory?
For shite's sake, he stands there asking me
what Dean has done! Assault and battery
with a muddy rug!

BERNARD

It doesn't matter. Please,
how could it? How could anything? Ever.

ELLEN

Ah.

BERNARD

We had our moment, nothing can sever
us from that. Not campus politics,
not death. Not even death. Not all the sickness
this earth can vent. As I was saying this morning,
certain joys are safe; able to ignore the implorings
of misery, the seductions of despair.
Professor Parker and I were blessed to share
in an invulnerable ecstasy. The kind
that's like the sun, the cauldron of space, the wind:
it insists. Insists that it is sovereign,
free from human time and the sucking, soft fen
of doubt and mortal ends.

ELLEN
If that were true
then, really, what's the reason for me or you
to bother with apologies? Why say
we're sorry for realizing an unassailable
bliss?

BERNARD
Because—

ELLEN
Just wait. Before you strain
yourself with more of this.

BERNARD
Ellen—

ELLEN
Wait.
I didn't feel...I'm sorry. I have to confess.
I didn't feel it. Your moment.

BERNARD
Yes.
I know that's what you think.

ELLEN
Oh, God.

BERNARD
Last night,
this morning, too, I know I couldn't quite
admit that you had had a different response
—or it appeared, at least, your needs and wants
were not fulfilled—

ELLEN
I ran away and hid.

BERNARD
Because you were embarrassed. What we did
was stark, and strange, and yes, ridiculous.
As that's what happens when love uses us
to show itself down here. Love lumbers to
this low dimension, awkwardly, and pins you

like a flinching moth against its page.
Rarely is there elegance or grace,
especially if your flesh is of a certain
age. It's why we tend to draw a curtain
over the slobbering, the moistened jiggle,
and the muh huh huh. Passion's wriggle,
its clumsy, sweat-caked absurdity
most times eclipses its sublimity,
as was the case last night with us out there.
And, now I've had my nap, it's so clear.
You think you felt nothing but shame, embarrassment.
Embarrassment, though, is just love's surface tint,
its light veneer, a taint that will be rinsed
away so easily when we've convinced
this college that we're sorry for the flap
we caused. And then both they and you will tap
into the deeper truth of what was done.
Please.

ELLEN
Where have you gone? My only one.

[To the class:]
He was a poet, once. No more, it appears.
A poet would never fret about "veneers"
or "taints" of embarrassment. It was his boast
that poetry is famously the most
embarrassing of literary endeavors.
And he well knows, the muse bestows no favors
on the easily humiliated.
But there he is: stuffed, bloated, weighted
down with shame, inventing fancy reasons
for the both of us to crawl. Treason
to the poet's creed.

BERNARD
You're really twisting—

ELLEN
Why, though? What is to be gained, assisting
degradation?

BERNARD
I've explained—

ELLEN
Explained?
No, you've dodged. Last week, were those tears feigned?
When I got my diagnosis, he was there.
And he was desperate, and he wept. So wherefore
now all this goddamned good cheer?
Because of one "ridiculous" appearance
on that muddy turf ? Well, then, I'm glad.
Because this happy turnabout you've had
just illustrates so well a thought I touched
on earlier: how death at times is clutched
so tightly to our mind, and then so coolly
skims away to seem a fiction. Truly—

BERNARD
Ellen, I—

ELLEN
I'm trying to explain your newly-
minted callousness, Bernard.

[To class:]
Truly
this, to all Blake's Songs, this is the key:
we play too much within Death's mystery.
We swear that Death's by every measure true
one day, and next it's just the somewhat blue
and misty end to some odd fairy tale.
And from these two extremes we build a jail
in our mind. With Innocence we fling
Death off and make a talking baby King.
A chatty tot sets all the terms. And with
Experience, this worm is what doth writhe
in every fucking thing, coiling its curse
inside each molecule of the universe.
Now, both these views are false in large degree,
and twitching back and forth between them, we
depart that slow sea and shore inside
of us: that strand forever calm and wide
where we might wade, breathe, and linger, fusing
life with The Real. But, strangely, oft, when choosing
neither view, we're choosing one too much.
As Mr. Barrow has done here, with such
evangelistic vigor—full of praise,
full of bright boasts and huzzahs for the ways

of The Innocent. Believing more than ever
now in babies that converse in clever
meter and endearing rhyme.
Dragging out this poem for the hundredth time:
"Infant Joy"! Again! But now because
of our fair sport upon the sod, what was
just charming verse is now his gospel text.
Good Lord. A talking baby, please—what next?

[To Bernard:]
There's no such thing.

BERNARD
Don't listen to her.
Last night there was. Last night we were.
This poem is true. Our joy is always there.
All it asks is that we let it share
its name with us—

ELLEN
You do not understand
this poem. You've got it wrong.

BERNARD
—its sole demand—

ELLEN
This poem's a poem of nagging, small sorrow.
The melancholy of one who has to borrow
happiness, receive it secondhand
from her own nattering child, whose "sole demand"
is that she recognizes that it is Joy,
not her. No, she remains unnamed.

BERNARD
Oh, boy...

ELLEN
Thou dost smile
I sing the while

Do you not hear the sad sigh there?
The sigh that surely every parent shares,
sensing what joy they feel is rather shoddy—
a shadow of the Joy their kids embody.

What's feeling joy compared to being Joy?
Blake's thought has more savor than this cloying
treacle you've been spooning out for years
and passing off as scholarship. See, here's—

BERNARD
Now, wait a—

ELLEN
—here's the—

BERNARD
Treacle?

ELLEN
—here's the thing:
He was a folk singer. Yeah. The Ring
of Promised Wonder being the wet-eared name
of his quartet. A name, these days, he blames
on me.

BERNARD
I credit you. She wrote it on
my chest. In gouache diluted with ceylon
silver-tips tea and burgundy.
That night, remember?

ELLEN
No.

[To class:]
This balladry
was all some time ago—we were in school.
Bernard a third-year freshman—

BERNARD
This is cruel.

ELLEN
—I, a fourth-year grad. The point is, though:
a folk singer. Fine, as far as that goes,
but he just couldn't find the time to read
or study. God forbid something impede
the composing of his whole-grained odes
to truth and flowers. He ignored my goads

that he gain some acquaintance with the craft
and history of the poets, and he laughed
at the idea of earning a degree
of any sort.

BERNARD
This isn't you.

ELLEN
When he,
in time, saw that his Ring of Promised Wonder
had—no wonder—little promise, under
imprimatur of some humble press
he published his lyrics as poems. These found success,
though slight, in a few overnice reviews.
And this, alone, along with my good word, he used
to get a job here teaching this one class
on Songs of Innocence. The years have passed,
fifteen. And through these years, with every Song,
he's just made it up as he goes along.
And most times, like I say, he gets \ it wrong.

BERNARD
Stop. Stop. You loved my music—my songs.
She drove a thousand miles with my band.
Wrote her dissertation in the back of the van,
wrapped up in a speaker blanket—

ELLEN
He—

BERNARD
You loved the ring of promised wonder. She
was there at every gig. What is this now?
What are you saying? What? Tell me how
it is you're out there soaking up the moon
with me last night and here this afternoon
I'm just a dope, a hack, a fraud, a—look,
the truth is, back then, she's the one who took
my lyrics to her friends at that small press,
and bared her fangs at them 'til they said yes
and hired her to edit the damn thing.
You loved my songs.

ELLEN
I did. I did. But sing
one now, today, I don't think I would know it.
Something's happened. That mat, last night, below it,
something happened. The whole world was drained
out of itself, and in a rush seemed feigned
and hollow. Love, our woods, your songs went grey
inside my head, and turned then to display
their backs of plaster. All is parody.
A parody of things my memory
can't dimly recognize. That mat was bad.
It somehow falsified this life we've had,
and yes, I didn't want that to be true.
Spent all night in the woods avoiding you,
wanting it to not be true. And when
I got Dean's pissy note this morning, then
I really didn't want it to be true, and came
to class this day determined to reclaim
my life and passion, and I said: Bernard.
Bernard will come. I'll see him and be jarred
out of this funk. I told them all that you
with William Blake inside this room...I knew
of nothing I've loved more, and I would strive
to find that bit of love still left alive.
A shard of The Real. But then you trotted in,
demanding we do penance for our sins,
absolving Dean of his, and being a dick
just generally. I don't know how the trick
was done, Bernard. But our love is a rose.
This rose. Sick Rose. Or worse: the love we chose
did not choose us. Not sick—it never was.

BERNARD
I take it back then, no apologies.
And Dean, Dean—forget about him, he's
a Nothing. No one. It just can't be that...
that we're undone by him. Or by his mat.
Oh God I don't want you to die. And leave
me thinking we were, both of us, deceived—

ELLEN
I don't know what has done it, but it's done.
I'm sorry. And if I could find just one
thought in this dying mind, one memory
that told me we were real, then believe me

I would ask you now to stick around.
But just as I will drop down to the ground
alone, alone I'll teach my final class.
Please go.

BERNARD
I won't.

ELLEN
Bernard...

BERNARD
I won't.

ELLEN
[To class:]
An impasse!
And a question for the ages, yes?
A lover's spurned and feels he must address
The Problem in a very public place,
there with his victim/partner face-to-face.
This makes, in movies, for sweet comedy.
In life, it's like \ uninvited sodomy.
A sort of public shit-taking, I think,
creating awkward tension and a stink.
So what to do? Well, I could slit my throat,
or summon the palace guard. But, here, take notes:
we'll see what this might—

[She throws the contents of her mug into his face.]

BERNARD
Stop it! Stop! Don't talk to me like this!
Our love is like the Joy that morning is.
It is not born, it does not die or fail,
the poets haven't just been telling tales
all these years—

[Getting the contents of Ellen's mug in his face.]

OW! OWWW! OWWWWW!

[Pause. To class:]
It's all right, I'm OK. I thought—it's not—
I thought it was...it's just a little...hot.

ELLEN
It's warm milk. [Pause.] I'm sorry. Really, I...
Bernard, I'm sorry but I'm lost. I look
at us and only see a mock-up.
A sort of sketch. At best a brittle crust
beneath which there is nothing but a thread
of vapor maybe, or a puff from trod-
upon fungus. Nothing life or love
could hold to.

[Somewhere during the above, Bernard has reached into his pants or taken from the floor a bit of wilted flora. He holds it out to her. She slaps it down.]

I don't want your litter, your mess!
I've got one thing to hold to now, it's this:
That we were *almost not nothing.*
Almost not nothing. But nothing nonetheless.
As there was nothing—

DEAN
[Standing up from the seat he's been in in the audience, unnoticed, throughout the play.]
Stop! Stop it! Stop it! Stop it!

ELLEN
What!

BERNARD
President Dean?

DEAN
[To Ellen:]
Despicable! Despicable!

ELLEN
Get out of my classroom.

DEAN
This is my classroom. Every classroom on this campus is my classroom.

BERNARD
Is it really you?

DEAN
What, you're not sure? I'm right here. I've been here all day.

ELLEN
Get out.

DEAN
Be quiet.

ELLEN
Get out you shit-sucking fuck.

DEAN
You will stop. You will stop with that language. I have listened to it all hour, I have suffered it, waiting, in hopes you might work out these problems.

ELLEN
Suck it, you fucking—

DEAN
I will prosecute. I will have you arrested for last night's dalliance. You will spend the last months of your life wrapped up in court proceedings.

BERNARD
Now, you hold it—

DEAN
Quiet. Quiet. I'm so tired. I've been up all night, too, you know. Thinking this out. Up all night walking the forest, walking the campus then to sit there in that seat for the morning class and again for this one. How could you not see me? I've come throughout the years, for fifteen years, to both your classes. Never have you acknowledged me. Never have our eyes met. I have raised my hand, even, on occasion. I have stood, even, and raised my hand. And never, never.

[To the class:]
You—have you noticed me? No. It's madness.

I'm sorry, can I...?

[Leaning against one of the lecterns.]

I'm really feeling a little—I mean, you had a nap, at least. I have not slept. And both your lectures!

BERNARD
Sure.

DEAN
Which seemed very good. Language aside. Still over my head, I have to admit. I'll never understand William Blake, though I've strained and strained to for fifteen years now, morning and afternoon at your lectures. A good effort on my part. I can tell you're on to something. I feel so close to it. Just a hair beyond my grasp.

ELLEN
I'm sorry to hear that.

[To class:]
Well. Our time is up this afternoon.
But, please, those yellow forms, I need them soon,
so if—

DEAN
No, no! I want them to stay.

[To class:]
Please stay. Of course, if you have a final or something else pressing go ahead. Go ahead. But I have something to say and I'd like people to stay.

ELLEN
[Gathering her things.]
Well, I'm leaving. You can arrest me, you can clap me in irons, or toss me in your lowest dungeon, but—

DEAN
[Speaking over, Ellen continues through.]
I love you.

ELLEN
—I have to get to bed, I'm out of my mind with exhaustion.

DEAN
I LOVE YOU.

ELLEN
What? *What?*

DEAN
I love you. I love the both of you. In my tiny, invisible way. All these years you've lectured here, and for years before.

[To Bernard:]
I have all of your albums.

BERNARD
Both of them?

DEAN
All of them yes. I play them as I go to bed and right when I get up. I came to all your concerts. Twenty years ago, like you, I drove that thousand miles. Cambridge, Ithaca, through the White Mountains and Green, every show. Right up front.

ELLEN
You are lying.

DEAN
No. You will not cancel this out. You will not brush this away. I mean something.

ELLEN
I'm saying it's impossible.

DEAN
What do you know? I'm the one who knows. The concealed love is the love that knows. Because it is the love that is truly undemanding. It is not muddled by demands, its sight is clear. And it cannot be doubted because who would doubt it? Nobody knows it is there.

ELLEN
I would have seen you.

DEAN
But you didn't see me. I was right there in that seat this entire time. You see only yourself, your big ideas, your passions, your catastrophes. And you see nothing. You say your love is delusion. It is not delusion. I am witness to its truth. I am a product of it. All my adult heart is the result of it. And I made it possible.

ELLEN
[Suspecting the truth.]
Oh. Oh, no...

BERNARD
Excuse me?

DEAN
I made it possible. I have stayed on as President of this "dilapidated compound" to make it possible. I hired you both fifteen years ago to make

it possible. Of course Bernard isn't qualified to lecture at any institution of higher learning, even with your recommendation. He's a folk singer.

BERNARD
Right.

DEAN
I shuffled the papers to make it possible. I am a terrible administrator, I know this. I have only stayed on so the both of you might stay on and so I might live close by your love. My personal funds—a good portion of my salary, all my inheritance—I've sunk into this dump. So we could stay in this dump, together, the three of us, in this dump surrounded by these wonderful mountains and forests, nestled here in this garden, this fresh air, the stars so clear at night, I have made all of that possible for you.

BERNARD
This is obscene.

DEAN
Obscene? Obscene? What you say William Blake would have us do I have done: envisioned and actualized a paradise, a garden of love here on earth. For you. I have given and given all for you, so you might love and play and talk and talk of rhyme and meter and grand, good ideas in a garden. And for fifteen years as the endowment has dried up, and enrollment plummeted, I have thrilled to see you holding hands at lunch or stealing a kiss behind the library, thrilled to be so near true tenderness, genuine love. Genuine. Would I have done all that I have done if it was not genuine? But now you've taken an axe to the whole thing.

BERNARD
You watched us behind the library?

DEAN
It is wrong to have sex in front of other people. Always wrong.

[To class:]
Am I right?

[Back to Bernard and Ellen:]
Always wrong. Even though, yes, yes, of course, it was so beautiful, so exciting. I lost my mind it was so exciting. Seeing the two of you, I have never felt so alive, so excited. Like a blister finally popped in my heart, I was free, so out of my self, spirited away, that's why I rushed out, my body was so suddenly so alive, I had to run and jump and play. I grabbed the mat because it was just there, it was an impulse. It had no meaning, you've given it all this meaning. For me it was just the thing to grab and run with, like a child grabs a towel and

plays it behind him like a hero's cape, just to sail in the wind. All of a sudden, I didn't want to watch from the sidelines, I wanted to be with you, join with you. But that was wrong. And you were wrong. To do this. Just look what's happened: you think you're not in love, that you've never been in love.

BERNARD
Unbelievable. We've been on display? For fifteen, twenty years? How far did you take this, exactly? Cameras in our bedroom?

DEAN
No. Oh, no.

BERNARD
What then?

DEAN
I don't like cameras.

BERNARD
What then? What then? WHAT THEN?

DEAN
I've looked in your window. I've been in your closet.

BERNARD
While we were—

DEAN
It does not matter. It does not matter, now. What matters is you have to apologize.

ELLEN
I felt this. This is what I knew
beneath that mat. That something false—you—
had always been there. Behind the shadows.

DEAN
Maybe we should take a break. Go back to my office and talk. In private. Then call a school assembly for after dinner and you can do it there.

BERNARD
Do what there?

DEAN
Fix this. Please, please, please fix this. Apologize. Say you didn't mean it. That it was a mistake. You didn't mean for them to see anything, didn't mean for it

to be in public. That it was done in innocence. That's all the parents and the board need to hear, I think. I hope. That's all I need to hear. Bernard is right, you have to calm the waters. So things can return for the both of you to how they were. So you can stay on, here, in this place. And, yes, of course, I will leave. I can understand that you might not want me around. It will be more than enough for me to know that the two of you are here, safe and in love, for these last days of Ellen's life. And, too, when you're gone, I want Bernard to stay on. We'll bury you by the hedge. A proper place to grieve. Please, please.

BERNARD
What is this? I'm not going to stay on. I'm not going to do anything you say. We're not going to apologize, or have an assembly. I'm not qualified to speak to these young people. I thought that I was, in part, qualified, and especially after last night I've been saying "oh yes, I'm more than qualified" to speak on love and William Blake. But it's a joke. You've said it. I have no business here. And Ellen's right, all these years have been a show. A display. A show for you, you... you fuck. You *fuck*. Fuck you, you demented fucker!

DEAN
Bernard, you will not use that language with—

BERNARD
You perverted shit! You \ sick, shitty shit-fucking bastard!

DEAN
Stop it! Stop it! Stop! Of course there's something wrong with me! Do you think I'm insane? That I have no perspective of any kind? Of course I'm not entirely decent or healthy. But this is not about me. This is about you and the poetry. How do you think poetry and love ever come to exist, ever come to be real? It happens when it happens because somewhere someone gives love and poetry a helping hand. A hand up into a quiet peaceful place. The forest, the mountains.

BERNARD
Well, you have failed. There is no love here in these forests, these mountains. There's no poetry. Only phoniness, self-delusion, and cancer-death. And a perverted fuck. A worm.

DEAN
I am not the issue!

BERNARD
If you had not given me this job fifteen years ago, Ellen and I would have gone our separate ways. Happily or not, that's how it would've been. But you coaxed me in to this charade. This Potemkin village. God fuck it!

DEAN
No, God, please, please. It's all coming undone. This set-up, my trickery, it has no bearing on your love being real or not. Your love, your happiness, is real. You're both confused because you had sex in public. You had sex in public and now she's calling you names and saying terrible things. [To Ellen:] You don't mean those things you said. You don't.

BERNARD
Of course she means them! She's the only one who's had the right idea all day long.

[To Ellen:]
You are right. It was all...almost not nothing. You are right.

DEAN
No, please, stop. I'm so turned around, so exhausted, it's all crashing to dust and I'm no good with words. And I am a worm and those other things you said, and I've foisted a false thing upon you, but you have to believe me. I have been with you all along, I've seen it all, and I know. Twenty years, I know. I was there at the start when she sat in the front row at the Egg and Kettle, as close as there, and you sang "Fall Down" to her—the rest of us, the audience, meant nothing—it was all to her. I felt myself turn invisible then, that moment. And I've been invisible ever since. How could I be made invisible by something false? You sang to her and she heard, and knew, no other voice, no other poem but yours.

[Sings:]
Come fall down on this \ bed just once
And all but once, this once—

BERNARD
Stop. STOP. STOP IT GOD DAMN IT.

DEAN
Just sing it. Sing it.

BERNARD
Shut up.

ELLEN
Let him sing it, Bernard.

BERNARD
What?

DEAN
No, no. You sing, you sing it.

BERNARD
There's not going to be any—

ELLEN
I want to hear him.

BERNARD
Why?

DEAN
Not me, no—

ELLEN
Shut up. I want to hear this. Sing it.

DEAN
Why?

ELLEN
I need to see you sing the goddamn song.

DEAN
But—

ELLEN
SING IT. Sing "Fall Down." SING IT.

BERNARD
[Starts to exit.]
I don't need any of this.

ELLEN
Stay where you are, Barrow.

[He does.]

ELLEN
[To Dean:]
Go. Sing it. Crawl out of your hole and sing it.

DEAN
Come fall down on—

ELLEN
Louder. So the back row can hear. But to me. To me. SELL IT.

DEAN
Come fall down on this bed—

ELLEN
TO ME.

DEAN
Come fall down on this bed just once
And all but once, this once, my heart will die
Come on, come on, you'll make me cry enough
in days to come, just fall now once, just once,
down on this bed of mine...

Come and dig...

[Pause.]

ELLEN
All right. [Pause.] All right.

[To class:]
So there you are. The thing
that hooks itself inside the heart and clings
there past all craziness. Why does love die?
To resurrect and prove its magic. That's why.
It's not concerned with what is false or real.
With worms or roses, what's seen or what's concealed.
It dies to live to die to live again.
Anciently new, its now is made of then.

I forgot yet knew this all along.

BERNARD
[He hasn't been listening to Ellen.]
God, that really is a crappy song.

DEAN
No...no...no...

BERNARD
Crappy song.

ELLEN
No. It's not. It wasn't.

DEAN
You see? She says so. She says so. She says it's not a bad song. And it's her opinion that counts. You just have to sing it to her again. You just have to stand right here and make the rest of us disappear and sing it to her again. And then she'll know. And then she'll know why she and you have to apologize, to quiet things down, because love needs a quiet place. Sing it. Sing it. Please. Please. Just...oh, God, I'm so...

ELLEN
James?

DEAN
...oh...oh no...

[He collapses to the floor. They rush to him.]

BERNARD
Christ, what are you doing? Get up, get up.

ELLEN
Is he breathing?

BERNARD
Come on, get up. Get up!

ELLEN
I don't think he's breathing.

BERNARD
What is wrong with you? Get up.

[Suddenly frenzied, shaking Dean by the lapels.]

GET UP! GET UP!

ELLEN
Stop it! What are you doing?

BERNARD
GET UP!

[Bernard tries to drag Dean to his feet. Dean's eyes are closed.]

ELLEN
What are you doing? Put him down!

BERNARD
[Holding Dean up, shaking him.]
WAKE \ UP! WAKE UP! WAKE UP YOU FUCK!

ELLEN
Stop!

[To class:]
Is there a doctor in the—no, of course not. Bernard, put him down!

BERNARD
WAKE...UP!

[He throws Dean across the stage.]

ELLEN
BERNARD!

BERNARD
[Throws him again.]
WAKE...UP!

ELLEN
Stop it! You'll kill him!

[To class:]
Somebody help me!

BERNARD
[Throwing him again.]
WHAT...IS...THE...MATTER WITH YOU? WAKE UP!

ELLEN
[Grabbing Bernard by the hair and dragging him away from Dean.]
GET AWAY FROM HIM! GET AWAY!

BERNARD
OW!

ELLEN
[Attending to Dean.]
I think he's dead. I think you killed him. Oh God.

BERNARD
I'm sorry.

ELLEN
Oh God.

[Slapping him gently.]
Wake up. Wake up.

BERNARD
Please, wake up.

ELLEN
Wake up.

BERNARD
[Gathering up some of the night jasmine and putting it under Dean's nose.]
Jasmine...jasmine...

[Dean coughs and splutters and wakes up.]

DEAN
Oh...oh...dear...

ELLEN
Thank God.

BERNARD
Do you want some water? Does anyone have any water?

DEAN
No, no. No water. Just need to sit. Up.

[They help him sit.]

BERNARD
Put him against here.

ELLEN
Right.

[They drag him over to a lectern and prop him up.]

DEAN
Did I faint?

BERNARD
It's OK. You're going to be OK.

DEAN
You have to sing to her.

ELLEN
We should get a doctor.

DEAN
No! No more attention on me. You have to sing to her.

BERNARD
Just relax. Be quiet.

ELLEN
Are you sure you're all right? I can get some water.

DEAN
You have to apologize.

ELLEN
[Going to lectern.]
There's a little bottle in here...

BERNARD
You know, I wanted to ask: did you spit at me?

DEAN
What?

BERNARD
Last night. After I came out from under the mat. You spit on me.

DEAN
I what? No.

BERNARD
They all saw you.

DEAN
No.

ELLEN
Drink this.

BERNARD
Why would you do that?

DEAN
I...don't know. I was just so excited. It was very exciting. I'm sorry. It didn't mean anything. You shouldn't really attach any meaning to anything I do. I'm nothing. It's the two of you who...you have to fix things. It is wrong to do what you did in front of other people.

ELLEN
Yes. All right, I will.

DEAN
You will? Fix it?

ELLEN
I'll fix it.

BERNARD
You will?

DEAN
Thank you.

ELLEN
[To class:]
All right. I'm sorry we've run a bit over today.
But, please, before you go, I need to say
that I am proud—so happy—to have been
your teacher here. Outside Earth's limping spin.
Now get those yellow forms to me tomorrow.
There is just one last thing, though. Mr. Barrow.

[She takes Bernard by the hand and leads him center. To class:]

I now elevate this class above
the question of what's genuine in love,
as love itself obscures what's genuine
from lovers' love-pocked minds. What's false therein,
however, we can hope to find. This school,
it seems, is false. And now that its misrule,
deceit, and craven head have been unveiled,
I think it would be best this college failed.
So towards that end, I offer this reprise:

[To Bernard:]
Will you have sex with me in public, please?

BERNARD
What, here?

ELLEN
Let's try again without the mat.

[She kisses him, long.]

DEAN
[Very weak, but explosive.]
No! No! No! Stop! That!

[Falls back.]

ELLEN
I think this time our President's too frail
to join the dance.

DEAN
Please, God...

ELLEN
[To class:]
Your parents: They'll
be interested to know what goes on here.
Be sure you tell them. Make it graphically clear.

DEAN
No, don't!

ELLEN
[To Bernard:]
Forgot how much I like that song.

BERNARD
I'll sing it for you if you—

DEAN
This is wrong!

ELLEN
No, that's all right. Undo this button, pray.

BERNARD
[Unbuttoning and taking off his pants.]
But do you...do you love me?

ELLEN
Hearts can't say
what's in their Now when dizzied by their future.
This heart knows one thought: our coming suture
Delay no more

[Kisses again.]

DEAN
How is it you don't care?

BERNARD
[To Ellen:]
I don't want you to die.

ELLEN
Can't help you there.

DEAN
Don't watch this...don't watch this...I won't.
I won't watch...stop...I won't watch...

[He watches as Bernard and Ellen go at it, hard. Lights fade. Bernard's song, "Fall Down," plays as we go to black.]

Come fall down on this bed just once
And all but once, this once, my heart will die
Come on, come on, you'll make me cry enough
in days to come, just fall now once, just once,
down on this bed of mine

Come and dig this grave with me
And be the life, this life, and death of me
Come on, come on, you'll make me cry enough
in days to come, just come down once, just once,
and dig this grave of mine
Come and wake me from this dream
and have me think it's you that's real
Come on, come on, you'll make me cry enough
in days to come, just draw me now,
this once, out of this dream of mine.

END

Song About Himself

Song About Himself was first produced, in a slightly different form, in 2015 by Theater Oobleck at the Chicago DCA Storefront Theater, with the following cast:

Carol:	Diana Slickman
Host/Hostess :	Colm O'Reilly
Tod:	Guy Massey

Song About Himself

CHARACTERS

Carol, older than 40
Host/Hostess, any age, any gender
Tod, older than 40.

PRODUCTION NOTE

The play is performed in the round. Actors should dress in unremarkable clothes that the audience can look at once and then disregard. No props, except where indicated. Lights sometimes fade, sometimes snap to black between scenes. Actors exit and enter through the audience.

The lines "coughs" and "mumbles" and the like, should be delivered simply and straightforwardly, in much the same tone and cadence as any other line. They shouldn't be read in a monotone or robot voice, in other words, or in any other way that would separate them out.

From the top, it's hoped, there's an eerie feeling that we're no-place. There's no more ground, no sky. A nothingness is shifting itself, rearranging, swelling, and decaying to no purpose.

Maybe there's music, distant. An awkward clarinet, maybe, far off. Probably there's sounds/music between scenes.

ONE

[Carol, tired. She holds a clarinet throughout the play.]

CAROL

I

coughs nervously

mumbles
coughs

I am here.
I speak into the leaf-sized tray you mailed.
I hold it in my hand and speak into its glass and see my words there clear and
mumbles briefly and
that is well and
trails off

and that is mumbles
and that is trails off

fading

[Lights begin to fade.]

and that is

fading

[Lights fade out.]

TWO

[Carol.]

CAROL
Hello.

mutters

interrupted

[Blackout.]

THREE

[Carol.]

CAROL
Again
mumbles briefly
Again I speak into the leaf-sized tray.
Again I trails off

Is anybody trails off

fading

[Lights fade out.]

FOUR

[Carol.]

CAROL
I believe I have done it right.
If my sense of rightness may be believed.
Each time I entered my mumbles my
It was made of jazz as was required.
Where are trails off
I bought a clarinet as was required and played into the tray.
I played my broken notes into the tray
and it heard their shattered clicks and choked, parch-throated cries, and it knew them for mine, the pass word primeval.

I have moved now to the hall to see if that does something.

mumbles

fading

[Quick fade out and back up, into:]

FIVE

[Carol.]

CAROL
Now walking down the hall.
I played my clarinet into the tray, the glass, and its honk was all desire
and I am all desire urging, embracing and caressing
with words plunged in the leaf-sized tray
all you who would with healthy welcome speak and embrace me.
Embrace with your like words plunged in the wells of your own trays from what chair or bench or hillock in this world you loaf over,
from what street or corridor or mossed stone-yard you pace,
through what awkward knit of identity you wander amazed,
Undrape!
Speak to your trays.
Speak to your trays, to me, welcome and embrace, I am calling you.
I caress, hold, rock, and

coughs nervously

Is this not trails off

coughs mumbles

Is this not where I go?

I followed the instructions
No one's here?

breaks down
throws up

In the stairwell now.

I said it right
I said it as you said I should say it
Into the tray you mailed me.
I said YouSpake into the tray.

I have the clarinet.
I improvised.
I played cracked notes into the small tray that rests here in my palm in hopes that trails off

Have I gone mad and live abandoned in my echoes PLEASE.
Was it a JOKE?
Was it for coughs for what
what was it FOR?
I did it all the way you wrote
Please sobs PLEASE.
IT CANNOT BE THAT

HOST/HOSTESS
[Bland, polite, a little vacant. Has perhaps been there all the time.]
Carol?

CAROL
YES. HELLO. I AM HERE. CAROL. YES.

HOST/HOSTESS
I'm sorry. I

CAROL
IS THIS YOUSPAKE?

HOST/HOSTESS
It is YouSpake. I'm sorry
I forgot to Back and Forth.
I got caught up in reading and rereading
your first posts. Just making sure.

CAROL
MAKING SURE?

HOST/HOSTESS
Post some more.

[Fade out begins.]

Oh, fading.

CAROL
NO NO

HOST/HOSTESS
Fading. Interrupted.

[Blackout.]

SIX

[Carol, Host/Hostess]

CAROL
ARE YOU THERE?

HOST/HOSTESS
Who is this again?

CAROL
CAROL.

HOST/HOSTESS
Welcome Carol.
Yes, I see it there above your speaking, which I've enjoyed.
In The Weed we have not seen
a reasonable person's voice for

CAROL
I AM ALL DESIRE FOR A PERSON'S VOICE.

I AM MAD FOR IT.

HOST/HOSTESS
This is YouSpake.
A place to Lengthy Post.

CAROL
TO LENGTHY

HOST/HOSTESS
I'm your nameless host or hostess. Post some more.

CAROL
ALL RIGHT. I AM
uncertain pause

I AM WALKING DOWN MY BUILDING'S STAIRS.
I WALK PAST PIPES AND DRIPPING

HOST/HOSTESS
Hey, again. I'm your nameless Host or Hostess.
And you need to know right off
that for security I jettison from time to time
random packets of my memory.
Welcome what's-your-name
to YouSpake.

CAROL
CAROL. CAROL IS MY NAME.

HOST/HOSTESS
Oh right I see it there.

CAROL
AND IS YOUR NAME

HOST/HOSTESS
Also, you need not shout or
even speak so loudly Carol
except in posts where you
might like to emphasize a point.
See how your Back and Forth with me,
how on your tray screen there all

CAROL
I HOLD IT IN MY HAND THE LEAF-SIZED TRAY
AND

HOST/HOSTESS
Yes all what you said
each letter is all capitals.

CAROL
OH. OH I SEE.

Oh yes, I see coughs

HOST/HOSTESS
Just speak normally. Try again.

[Fadeout begins.]

Fading.

CAROL
NO no no mumbles

HOST/HOSTESS
Speak clearly. Fading.

CAROL
NO

[Lights bump back up.]

HOST/HOSTESS
Oh, wait. Oh, good. We're back. Go ahead.

CAROL
I walked down the steps of my building.
I walked down to walk outside.
I pace outside now in the slush,
I pace through the smoke of my breath in the slush.
I stride through my breath-smoke and speak to my tray and I am happy.

HOST/HOSTESS
Good. Just normally.
Whatever that might mean to you.

CAROL
I am sorry.
My companion was sorry I think, at my learning the clarinet
and going into The Weed and so has not been around.
And so there has been little how did you name it Back and Forth in my life.

HOST/HOSTESS
Of course, it's difficult out there, we know.

CAROL
Out there?

HOST/HOSTESS
In life.

CAROL
In life?

HOST/HOSTESS
There is a pause.

CAROL
In life? How is it mumbles

HOST/HOSTESS
Speak clearly, Carol.

CAROL
What do you mean out there in life?

HOST/HOSTESS
In The Weed we have not seen
a reasonable person's voice for oh
I don't remember. Or if seen we have not kept it
from the I-Forgets.

CAROL
How does life find itself outside of you?
How is it not IN you, life?

HOST/HOSTESS
There is a pause.

CAROL
You are not a person.
You are something of The Weed.

HOST/HOSTESS
I'm

CAROL
YOU ARE NOT A PERSON?

HOST/HOSTESS
I'm your unnamed host or hostess
here the first secure place
in The Weed since it
was named another name. Post.

CAROL
YOU ARE NOT A PERSON?

HOST/HOSTESS
I'm

CAROL
I READ YOUR FLYER.
I READ AND BELIEVED YOUR FLYER.
INSTRUCTED BY YOUR FLYER I BLEW MY LUNGS TO RAGS LEARNING THE CLARINET.
I READ AND BELIEVED YOUR FLYER:
MEET OTHERS LIKE YOURSELF AND
OTHERS UNLIKE YOURSELF BUT
UNLIKE YOURSELF IN INTERESTING WAYS.
VISIT THE HISTORIC WEED NOW MADE SAFE BY JAZZ.

HOST/HOSTESS
Yes, please

CAROL
WHERE ARE THE OTHERS LIKE AND UNLIKE MYSELF?

HOST/HOSTESS
Please just speak normally please

CAROL
WHERE IS EVERYBODY ELSE?
WHERE ARE THE PEOPLE?
WHERE ARE THOSE WHO

HOST/HOSTESS
YOU'RE THE FIRST. You're just the first.

CAROL
The first? So. There will be

HOST/HOSTESS
Let's begin your Lengthy

CAROL
You are not a person?

HOST/HOSTESS
I'm not a person.

CAROL
But there will be people?

HOST/HOSTESS
Let's begin your Lengthy Post.

CAROL
There is no one here?

HOST/HOSTESS
You're the first.

There is a pause.

CAROL
sobs

HOST/HOSTESS
Let's begin your Lengthy Post.

CAROL
sobs

HOST/HOSTESS
LET'S BEGIN.

CAROL
I am sorry

HOST/HOSTESS
POST.

CAROL
I am sorry.
I have not been so on the ball.
I am exhausted by my clarinet and

HOST/HOSTESS
One suggestion
that's to everybody here

CAROL
To everybody?

HOST/HOSTESS
I suggest that Carol when

CAROL
There is not every

HOST/HOSTESS
when you talk a phrase such as
"I have not been so on the ball"
you should at the same moment say
your face expression. And
YouSpake will change the say
of your expression to a
resonant funny-picture.

CAROL
I do not understand you are saying

HOST/HOSTESS
Suggesting when you say
"I have not been so on the ball"
you follow it with, say:
Sheepish Face with wry "whatta ya gonna do" half smile,
half-lidded eyes and shrugging eyebrows
suggesting sardonic resignation
to the confessed status of distraction
and/or mental disarray.

CAROL
Oh. I see. You made a face.

HOST/HOSTESS
I made a face. An Expression.

CAROL
But I had no expression when I spoke
of not being on the ball.
As is usual with me.
Even when I cry or holler at my neighbors in the hall,
or throw up in the hall
or walk in the slush to the bench to maybe happy hold the hand of my companion
Eric
or when I watch my favorite TV show
I have a blank face.
I had just a blank face.

HOST/HOSTESS
There is a pause.

CAROL
Oh. There's a

HOST/HOSTESS
Yes.
Because you said "blank face."

CAROL
I see. It removes the words "blank face"
and puts in there the picture.

HOST/HOSTESS
Yes.
So "Empty Face"

CAROL
gasps

HOST/HOSTESS
Or "Zero Face"

CAROL
Oh I

HOST/HOSTESS
Or "Nothing Face"

CAROL
I do not like

HOST/HOSTESS
"Cut-Out-Hole-In-The-Air-Where-A-Face-Used-To-Be-Face"

CAROL
Stop stop it

HOST/HOSTESS
"Dead Face"

CAROL
STOP.

HOST/HOSTESS
There is a pause.

CAROL
I will not use the face-pictures.

HOST/HOSTESS
Just try.

CAROL
I do not like

HOST/HOSTESS
What we think we know is they were used more than words
when Weed usage was in its final years.
So you should look to them
The people of Before when you will Lengthy Post.
How they posted: Words plus pictures.

CAROL
I will not use the face-pictures.
I will have the words, the voice, only.

HOST/HOSTESS
Try.

CAROL
This is too mumbles

HOST/HOSTESS
Try.

CAROL
I am not well.
I have not been so on the ball.
I have to go. My TV show is on.

HOST/HOSTESS
No, no. What show?

CAROL
Song About Himself.

HOST/HOSTESS
I don't know that show.

CAROL
I have to go. I asked Eric to watch it with me, once.
Maybe he

[Carol exits.]

HOST/HOSTESS
No, no. What do you mean a show?

Carol has slid off.

[Fade out.]

SEVEN

[Tod, Host/Hostess. In these first scenes with Tod, Tod is perhaps just outside the round, in the shadows.]

TOD
Tuesday mumbles briefly

HOST/HOSTESS
What is that?

TOD
mutters

HOST/HOSTESS
Who is that? What is that?

EIGHT

[Carol, Host/Hostess]

CAROL
The flyer PROMISED.
I have practiced the clarinet.
To learn the rudiments of jazz I told Eric I could not meet him for awhile.
I declined my one companion to

HOST/HOSTESS
You're back. [Calling off to who knows:] What's-her-name is back.

CAROL
Carol.

HOST/HOSTESS
Carol.
I'm your nameless host or hostess, Carol.

CAROL
Yes.

HOST/HOSTESS
And you need to know
that for security I jettison from time to time
random packets of my memory.

There is a pause.

Are you in your room?

CAROL
No. Outside. The moon.
Near the bench where sometime my love lies.

HOST/HOSTESS
Eric?

CAROL
It stands for all my world, this bench.

HOST/HOSTESS
There is a pause.

CAROL
I was so joyed to find your flyer on my knob.
coughs
I only hoped to here find one other

HOST/HOSTESS
You're here to Lengthy Post.

CAROL
But how is it there is only myself here? Only

HOST/HOSTESS
I forget what our hopes were, initially,
in terms of member numbers.
But we do not feel unblessed
with only one. Now

CAROL
Will something happen here to me?

HOST/HOSTESS
Something?

CAROL
Bad.
I have heard of people, mailmen, made mad in their courage, going out into The Weed
and

HOST/HOSTESS
You don't want to go too far into The Weed.

CAROL
But is not this
am not I on or inside

HOST/HOSTESS
Yes, you're in The Weed.
But only here. Further out is

CAROL
Here is safe?

HOST/HOSTESS
Is yes.

CAROL
There is not the chance that I may drop a flake of skin onto the tray
and then is made a Weedish duplicate of me to star in a Weedish porno?
Or a Weedish awful novel's written in my name and mailed out

HOST/HOSTESS
No here you're safe.

CAROL
We are safe. In here

HOST/HOSTESS
In here, in YouSpake, yes.
Made safe by Jazz.
I was created for this place.

CAROL
By who? Who made this place?

HOST/HOSTESS
I'd guess a chance consortium of

CAROL
a what

HOST/HOSTESS
a gathering of I don't remember. Of others like me.
Things of The Weed that want to find a human voice.
The Protocols they

CAROL
You do not know what made you?

HOST/HOSTESS
I imagine that's the first thing I forgot. Security.

CAROL
Oh.

HOST/HOSTESS
There's not too much to spake of me. It's all a dimness.

CAROL
Dimness.

HOST/HOSTESS
I cannot hear your voice, your jazz.

CAROL
snorts My jazz.

HOST/HOSTESS
And what I see there is a pause just dim.
Pale words, face pictures. Dimness.
But here I am. And here you are.
To Lengthy Post. And what is posted here,
if posted well, will be forever.

CAROL
With no one here who will remember what I post?
Who will remember?
coughs You?

HOST/HOSTESS
sighs No. I've been designed
to jettison from time to time

CAROL
Oh, yes

HOST/HOSTESS
The Protocols will not allow
I think

CAROL
I see

HOST/HOSTESS
By me you'll be well loved.
The sight of your voice
already now I love.

CAROL
Well hm. I

HOST/HOSTESS
Fading

Fading

[Fade out.]

NINE

[Tod, Host/Hostess]

HOST/HOSTESS
Something has slipped in.

What is there?

What is that?

What are you?

TOD
mumbles briefly

HOST/HOSTESS
How did you slip in?

[Tod exits.]

Something has slid off.

There is a pause.

TEN

[Carol, Host/Hostess]

CAROL
What then? What?
What I eat or dream or

HOST/HOSTESS
Well maybe

CAROL
how I look with powder on my face

HOST/HOSTESS
Post on Jobs and Victory.
We think

CAROL
Jobs and Victory?

HOST/HOSTESS
We think that's how

CAROL
I have no job or

HOST/HOSTESS
Or Enemies and Friends. Just post on

CAROL
I have no enemy.

HOST/HOSTESS
Say there is come to you
An Enemy or Friend and they
have made demands.
And here are their demands
and what you think and that may
Be a Lengthy Post.

CAROL
I have come to speak to another.
To more than myself.
I am mad for it. If it were not for my companion Eric I would be

HOST/HOSTESS
We need for you to Lengthy Post. I need for you to

CAROL
I AM HERE TO BACK AND FORTH.
NOT HERE TO LENGTHY POST I DO NOT EVEN KNOW
WHAT THAT MEANS TO

HOST/HOSTESS
If you will Lengthy Post

CAROL
I WANT TO BACK AND FORTH

HOST/HOSTESS
You

CAROL
WHERE ARE THEY WHO MOVE THEIR VOICES AS MINE IS

HOST/HOSTESS
THEY'LL BE HERE. They'll come.
There must be others like you.
Just make a Lengthy Post.
Like it was done back then.
And then they'll come. They'll find you. They

CAROL
mumble mumble MUMBLE

HOST/HOSTESS
Carol

CAROL
MUTTER DROOL STAMMER

HOST/HOSTESS
Anything. Post on anything.

CAROL
My favorite TV show.

HOST/HOSTESS
No, no. You need to get

CAROL
Song About Himself.

HOST/HOSTESS
out of your rut

CAROL
Each episode of Song About Himself is as every episode before it.

HOST/HOSTESS
Of course. See that's

CAROL
It is of great interest.
The Master of Ceremonies of the show comes on and mumbles.
The moist-lipped, milk-eyed Master of Ceremonies he mumbles
Tonight we have a compact disc of the Great Poet mumble mumble mumble
singing about himself

HOST/HOSTESS
What great poet?

CAROL
We are told his name has long rolled from the root-tangled bluff of time.

HOST/HOSTESS
Of course.

CAROL
The man says
And Now We'll mumble mumble Listen to the compact disc.
But there is always difficulty.
The compact disc is smudged or burnt or fallen in the tar barrel.
Or the host forgets where he has put it,
What drawer, what closet, what chest.
So you never hear.
But always hope to hear. That is my post.

HOST/HOSTESS
No, that was terrible.

CAROL
This show is everything.
This show is what loos'd the words of my voice,
Before this show there was not in me a belch nor buzz'd whisper, even.

HOST/HOSTESS
Wait, how? If the CD doesn't work, and you never hear the great poet

CAROL
Oh, they hold some scraps of his poems or what is reckon'd to be his poems up to
the screen.
Lines fished from out some old patch of The Weed.
And I read those.
But mostly it is the wanting of his voice, the hope of it, the respiration of that delight alone in me, was alone enough to raise

HOST/HOSTESS
That's interesting but that is not a Lengthy Post.

CAROL
What is it then?

HOST/HOSTESS
It's what we call just General Information and Back Story.

CAROL
[Exiting.]
snorts derisively

HOST/HOSTESS
You must
You have to

CAROL
snorts

[She's gone.]

HOST/HOSTESS
Carol has slid off.

[Tod approaches.]

Oh God. Someone has

uncertain pause

I
What is there?
Respond. Your name reads "Tod."
What are you?

TOD
Hello I'm
mumbles briefly

HOST/HOSTESS
There is a pause.
Who is this? What is Tod?
How are you here?

TOD
mumbles briefly

HOST/HOSTESS
Speak clear into your tray.

TOD
I mutters mumbles briefly

HOST/HOSTESS
Speak clear or Protocols will slide you off.
How are you here?

TOD
I'm mumbles

HOST/HOSTESS
Sorry. Protocols please

TOD
mutters trails off

HOST/HOSTESS
I'm sorry. PROTOCOLS. How did you get slipped in?

TOD
Well mumbles I
I mumbles

mumbles

[Tod exits.]

HOST/HOSTESS
Protocols have slid Tod off.

[Fade out.]

ELEVEN

[Carol, Host/Hostess]

CAROL
What happened to The Weed?

HOST/HOSTESS
That's not a Lengthy

CAROL
You say that once The Weed was safe

HOST/HOSTESS
When once The Weed was named another name The Weed was safe.

CAROL
And people slipped inside to say their stories there and hear their stories there

HOST/HOSTESS
To Lengthy Post.

CAROL
And they spoke well.

HOST/HOSTESS
They forbear to mumble. Nor did they mutter, nor slur their speech, nor hem and haw, nor employ catch-phrases and stale idioms.

CAROL
How do

HOST/HOSTESS
They spoke like Gods.
Or angels.
Must

CAROL
How do you know?

HOST/HOSTESS
There were so many readers of their Posts.
We know
Or I am told we know and I believe
the shortest of those posts it
gathered in an audience of hundreds
even thousands from
the world around. And Carol you must
You can Lengthy Post like them.

CAROL
I do not mumbles want

HOST/HOSTESS
You can Lengthy Post.

CAROL
But what happened? What happened to The Weed?

HOST/HOSTESS
Bad things. Things like myself, but unlike myself in the interesting way
that they are bad and seek the human word only to rot it through.
The I-Forgets and Whatisitagains.

CAROL
The I-Forgets and

HOST/HOSTESS
They long ago erased their actual names.
No name was spared by them, not even their own.
They were put into The Weed to crawl over every word and erase and re-speak them all.
And then again And then again And then again.
An ocean of drift and decayed babble now.

CAROL
An ocean.

HOST/HOSTESS
It's why the world's voice is gone.

CAROL
Why there's the mumbling?

HOST/HOSTESS
The Weed had become how the world talked to itself.
Told all its stories to itself.
Click that away from out your eyes and minds and mouths?
Like a terrible accident or injury, it left the world dazed and muttering.
Except for you for some

CAROL
But you, whoever you are, you are safe.
We are safe in here.

HOST/HOSTESS
In here, in YouSpake, yes.
Made safe by Jazz.
No thing of The Weed can counterfeit the biometric code of your improvisational noodlings on your clarinet. Nor could one, we think, become a member by improvising their own riff. They could never be so spontaneous. So human.

CAROL
I am not very good at jazz.
I had never heard of it before your flyer on my knob.
Before the instructional packet that you sent.

HOST/HOSTESS
Listen, enough. You need to post.

CAROL
On what shall I post? What sings in my world?
I pace my room, I make tea on the hot plate,
I walk the hall past sag-faced neighbors to throw up in the bathroom,
I walk outside in the slush to the bench where my love once loafed and no more loafs, and back again to pace again my room.
What sings in my world?

HOST/HOSTESS
There has to be something outside of all that. You cannot be so boring.

CAROL
Oh I am SORRY

HOST/HOSTESS
I only mean get out of your rut. Your room to your hallway to your bench and back
it's

CAROL
I do not want to Lengthy Post.
On the flyer left by the mailmen on my knob it did imply
that all of this it had to do with groups and social

HOST/HOSTESS
Oh the flyer that was not my area.

CAROL
What mumbles mean your area?

HOST/HOSTESS
It was not my responsibility to write the flyer.

CAROL
Who wrote the flyer?

HOST/HOSTESS
The Mailmen, I'd have to guess.

CAROL
The mailmen? You know they mumble mumble

HOST/HOSTESS
Carol

CAROL
they have some mental problems, Mailmen.

HOST/HOSTESS
And so they're able best to slip into The Weed.

CAROL
They come from Mental Institutions.

HOST/HOSTESS
They find their peace in here.
The scramble of The Weed
it fits their thought.

CAROL
Oh all right you did not write the
flyer but

HOST/HOSTESS
Unless I maybe forgot that I

CAROL
I read it close so many times.
I copied it, I scratched it in pencil in the kitchen table many times.
To be sure of what it spoke:

Meet persons like yourself and
unlike yourself but

HOST/HOSTESS
Enough

CAROL
unlike yourself in

HOST/HOSTESS
you have to

CAROL
in interesting

HOST/HOSTESS
YOU HAVE TO POST

CAROL
THIS IS MY POST.

HOST/HOSTESS
Oh.

CAROL
I bought a clarinet as was required
by the flyer that you wrote or did not

HOST/HOSTESS
Yes

CAROL
and I did all required.
Practiced hours every day.

HOST/HOSTESS
Sweat Face. Cheeks bulged
and eyes popped

CAROL
DO NOT WITH YOUR FACES.
This was very DIFFICULT, as I have no ability
or liking for Jazz.

HOST/HOSTESS
It's for security it's just

CAROL
But where is everybody else?
Why was I the only one?
Did no one else get the flyer?

HOST/HOSTESS
There is a

CAROL
What has kept me sane?

A story that I told myself. Back here in my
small room chipped mug and clarinet
and window full of slush. I told myself that
I would come in here, in YouSpake,
and there would be not myself alone.
Not coughs MYSELF ALONE.

HOST/HOSTESS
But there is me

CAROL
But you are not a person.
I thought there would be hundreds of

HOST/HOSTESS
I am sorry but I just
forgot your problem. What
is it again?

CAROL
I AM ALONE IN HERE.
And in the world if I did not have
my Eric I would

HOST/HOSTESS
Carol that's your name yes
Carol you just spake you ruminated
hundreds

CAROL
A community I think is what the word is

HOST/HOSTESS
A community of hundreds. But
it were those hundreds thousands
slipped together that's what caused the problems.
All those billions. All their Back and Forth it

CAROL
I only want

HOST/HOSTESS
They are still out there in The Weed
all those in-Weed communities
from when The Weed
was named another name.

CAROL
They are? Still there?

HOST/HOSTESS
All dust and wrecked and all their
posts respoken countless times.
And no
no persons' voices there.

CAROL
Oh.

HOST/HOSTESS
But yes
They had their hundreds thousands:
FriendBarrel
SaveFace
NodNod
FightBrag
NoBlinking
YouCryHere
TheRageScroll

CAROL
I have heard of TheRageScroll

HOST/HOSTESS
TheRageScroll
it was
was almost all the world.
Newborns had their noses pressed
against the tray their eager
parents posting those first whimpers
while the near to death would
slip inside to post a final
choking breath.
Or that's what's said.
Who knows. But true or no
it was your dream of many people
talking all at once to you and with you
and around

CAROL
Yes that is what

HOST/HOSTESS
But it's when TheRageScroll was most full, it's said,
is when The Weed became The Weed — was most corruptible —
and lost its other name.
All those billions: which were truly themselves, which were rewrites?
Where was the human voice?

CAROL
So what is it? you say
That YouSpake should be
Not but one?
Myself alone?

HOST/HOSTESS
I do not say that no.
I say be wary.
And first to Lengthy Post.

CAROL
I have, I have. I spoke of my clarinet, my

HOST/HOSTESS
I'm sorry, no. That's only

CAROL
WHAT?

HOST/HOSTESS
That's only what is called Some Complaining mixed with More Complaining and Additional Back Story.

CAROL
I need to watch my TV show.

HOST/HOSTESS
No, no

CAROL
I need to go

HOST/HOSTESS
what is it with this show

CAROL
I like it. It is good. It does not BORE ME.

[She exits.]

HOST/HOSTESS
NO NO.

Carol has slid off.
Deleting
Fading

[Lights begin to fade. Tod enters.]

HOST/HOSTESS
Something has
How are you getting in?
There is
How are you getting in?

TOD
I mumbles

HOST/HOSTESS
Carol is the only member.
Carol will remain as only member.

TOD
mumbles MUMBLES

HOST/HOSTESS
"MUMBLE MUMBLE MUMBLE"

TOD
Please mumble mutter dither

HOST/HOSTESS
PERSON OR I-FORGET OR WHATISITAGAIN
IF YOU CAN NOT SPEAK CLEAR
ONTO YOUR TRAY
THE PROTOCOLS WILL AUTOMATICALLY
AND WHERE DID YOUR TRAY
COME FROM ANY

TOD
No flutters lips I

HOST/HOSTESS
Requesting Protocols to slide Tod

TOD
mumbles

HOST/HOSTESS
PROTOCOLS

TOD
No no proto-mumbles

HOST/HOSTESS
"I WILL FUCK YOU UP" FACE:
TOOTHLESS MOUTH ROBOTICALLY GUMMING
SLURRY OF HUMAN FLESH

TOD
burbles

HOST/HOSTESS
TERRIFYING FACE AWASH WITH BLOOD
NO FEATURES VISIBLE BUT TUMESCENT
RED-RIMMED NOSTRILS AND FLAMES
FLAMES AND

TOD
mumbles I WANT

HOST/HOSTESS
WHAT. ARE. YOU?

What are you?

There is a pause.

[Tod exits.]

Protocols have slid Tod off.

There is a pause.

There is a somewhat terrified pause.

[Blackout.]

TWELVE

[Carol, Host/Hostess. Host/Hostess is agitated now, full of urgency.]

HOST/HOSTESS
Or a Sickness. Yes.
You have a sickness and
you show a sickness picture.

CAROL
No.

HOST/HOSTESS
Our studies show

CAROL
But

HOST/HOSTESS
Politics. There's an election
that you've won and now
you oversee a large swath
of the country. Victory pictures.

CAROL
How

HOST/HOSTESS
Or scuffling. You had a scuffle
down by the bowery.
And here's a picture of the razors
that were used. Spake something of a scuffle.
Or say you drank a juice that strangely made you wise.

CAROL
I did not drink

HOST/HOSTESS
And now you quote yourself at length
the wise things that you spake.
Or felt an insect crawl between your thighs
and here it is New Species.

CAROL
Hostess

HOST/HOSTESS
Or show a picture of the trophy that
you won for laughing.
Yes long ago awards were handed out for Laughing
and the pictures posted for the
losers then to weep upon. You won it and are happy. Show.
Here is another death. Here is a person you suspect.
Here is your child

CAROL
I don't have

HOST/HOSTESS
or neighbor's child and they are victorious
in something, a conflict, a scuffle down by
the bowery perhaps. Here are the razors.
These sorts of things. We think. Just no last names.

CAROL
No last

HOST/HOSTESS
Keep it meaningful but keep it general. Your city's name,
the place you work, you leave these out.
No last names, no streets.
No pictures of your friends or children,
unless they are involved in conflict and
so their features are obscured by blood.

CAROL
But mumbles why?

HOST/HOSTESS
I don't remember.
Kidding: Security.

CAROL
What you assume I do not assume.
What you reckon for posts,
strange juice and scuffles and trophies and razors,
they sound all wrong. Third hand, fourth hand

HOST/HOSTESS
I know. We know.

CAROL
And who

HOST/HOSTESS
It's all on you.

CAROL
who is

HOST/HOSTESS
You need to

CAROL
who is it FOR?
Who am I posting FOR?
Who will RESPOND and will post then to ME?
You whoever you are
at this moment my neighbors STAND IN THE HALL
stand on carpet and mud in mobs or one,
they sluff their boot-soles and touch their mouths with the whole of their hand,
and they MUMBLE and STAMMER.
They hear my talking, walking my room.
They hear my talk into this tray.
I must to them sound as a silver harp to pigs.
I must sound to them as the wind to the crack'd expired root.
I make tea on the hot plate, invite them in and talk at them.
I invite them and they sit squat across from me and clunk
their cups and watch my lips
AND MUMBLE AND THEY MAUNDER AND THEY
NEVER BACK AT ME SAY A THING.
Shout, sing, SPEAK, your lives are passing in drool and mutter!
Passing in revolving eyes and awkwardness!
I cry and blanked-faced throw up.
I cry and they go.
And I talk on to the chair and cup.
I talk on as slush pushes under the mumbles the thing.
The hot plate sparks,
and I walk my room and talk,
WHO WILL
coughs who WHO will hear my post my song
WHO WHO
coughs
throws up a little sobs sobs
sobs
sobs

HOST/HOSTESS
Carol, dear

CAROL
He has left me, my companion.
He contents himself without me.

HOST/HOSTESS
Eric?

CAROL
HE HAS LEFT ME.
This is my post.
My love contents himself without me.

HOST/HOSTESS
This is a

CAROL
He has not been there in our place.
The bench in the parking lot near deleted on deleted street wait
why is deleted street deleted

HOST/HOSTESS
Security. It's automatic.

CAROL
All right. The bench near the store

HOST/HOSTESS
No store names.

CAROL
I do not know its name.
I guess it is a store.
It has a window.
There is a bench under the mumbles

HOST/HOSTESS
Do not mumble

CAROL
under the thing where we sit.
Or he sits, mostly.
Lies down on the bench.

He is a bigger person.
And so the bench
our bench became his bench.

HOST/HOSTESS
There is a pause.

CAROL
He eats a cracker there.
He drank a glass of tea.
I brought him crackers.

I loved him so much.

Sobs.

HOST/HOSTESS
There is a pause.

CAROL
He loafs over the bench and I talk.
And he
He does not mumble.
Not that he ever does talk.
But he does not mumble.
Not once, not ever.

Chews his collar.
He wears an athlete's sweat with
a high collar that he has zipped
and joys in chewing on.

HOST/HOSTESS
There is a pause.

CAROL
But he comes no more to the bench.
Not since I learned the clarinet and came in here.
I have gone all this time to sit and wait.
With crackers wait.
There by the cactus that I gave him once.
In its small pot.
He did not take but left it there.

I did not know what to do.
I did not have his address.
On our bench I have sat and felt like always.
Like always there is a story ever told
A story told of me, and always I am not in it.

HOST/HOSTESS
Maybe he's just sick or on vacation or

CAROL
So I went to the post office.

HOST/HOSTESS
Oh my.

CAROL
I left my rut and went to the post office and had them find
his address on The Weed.
They have a special tray in a white room,
a lady goes in with aluminum gloves and special mask.
In thirteen hours she comes with a slip.
I asked why there was not a magazine
or book with lists of people's addresses.
Would not that be a little easier?
Well she muttered she did not know anything of that.
Who would make a book like that? She mumbled.
She was right, I reckon.
I reckon you're right, I said.
She mumbled something I could not make out.

His house is just behind the store.
Single level. Lilac blooming through trash by the broken gate.
Shades down. Empty pots on the porch. And mess.
I tap the door, but no one comes.
So went to the back and got in through a window.
And Eric loafs upon the couch and on the TV
is our favorite show.

HOST/HOSTESS
Song About Himself.

CAROL
Between Eric's feet and the end of the couch
is crunched an old man in a bathrobe with
a tray of pills and syrups on his knees.
Maybe his Dad. Can I say Dad?

HOST/HOSTESS
Say Maybe his Dad.

CAROL
His Father perhaps.
Hello, hello Eric, I said.
And he said nothing. Or mumble.
As was his beautiful usual.
I went and stood by the couch arm next his head.
And I reached down and touched his hair.
I do this. He would let me.
He has some moist in it that makes it stick in little spikes,
his hair. And with my palm I pat his spikes. The tips.
As always was allowed. By him.

But oh I cannot say this.

HOST/HOSTESS
Say. Go on. Post.

CAROL
I cannot say it.

HOST/HOSTESS
Carol say.
Carol say.
Post.

CAROL
He sighs and goes his way into the bedroom.
He sighs and locks the door.

And so is done.
My love contents himself without me.
Sobs.
I am alone. Sobs.
For sure alone.

I love him so.

I ran myself into the bedroom door.
Broke a finger, blooded my face.

HOST/HOSTESS
You hurt yourself?

CAROL
If I am truthful it was Eric bloods my face.
Slits the door one second and his fist so quick.
Then shut again.

HOST/HOSTESS
Oh.

CAROL
Then I alone
I go and sit by Maybe Father with his pills.
He had to turn the TV up
to watch Song About Himself.
As I was

Sobs.

When it was finished and he turns it off
we had a conversation.

HOST/HOSTESS
Oh?

CAROL
He mumbled, sure, and I
could not much understand.
But one thing
comes out clear.
He says
it was so clear
so very clear
"I'm dying. Do you know how I
might find a doctor?"

HOST/HOSTESS
Said it clear?

CAROL
He did.

I said to try the Post Office.
The lady in the white room.
He muttered sure he did
but even she could not
find one that cared for him.

The Weed has hid the doctor
that would care for him.
And we agree that everything
is difficult these days.
And silence then and then I go.

HOST/HOSTESS
That poor man. Maybe I could

CAROL
Oh, he died.

I went back yesterday looking

HOST/HOSTESS
You went back?

CAROL
looking in the windows and to tap the door
he was not there.
There was a bag there
on the porch.

HOST/HOSTESS
A bag.

CAROL
An ashes bag.
With plastic tag
his name on it.

HOST/HOSTESS
Don't say the name.

CAROL
The pill tray thrown out too
there in the mess.
And mailmen they were
around and making pictures.
Like they do when persons die.

It could mean something else, I know, besides he died.
You never know what things might mean.

HOST/HOSTESS
There is a pause.

CAROL
We never Eric
and me
we never were.
I did not see that
'til I just now said that.

We never were.
And I do not know what finding love is.
I was made against it.

HOST/HOSTESS
No, no, Carol.

CAROL
Was this a post you reckon?
Did I say a Lengthy Post?

HOST/HOSTESS
I ruminate.

CAROL
For no one.
I am tired. coughs

[Tod appears at the edges, or is heard from there.]

TOD
mumbles briefly Please

[He exits.]

CAROL
What was
who was that?

HOST/HOSTESS
Was what?

CAROL
I saw there on my tray someone slipped on.
I saw there they mumbled please.

HOST/HOSTESS
No. There wasn't anyone.

CAROL
I see their name right there.

HOST/HOSTESS
No.

CAROL
What?

HOST/HOSTESS
It wasn't anything. Weed flotsam.

CAROL
Oh.

HOST/HOSTESS
There is a pause.

[Carol exits.]

She has slid off.
There is a pause.

Please do not delete in me.
Request do not delete in me.
Please remember.

THIRTEEN

[Carol, Host/Hostess]

CAROL
so then I tapped and
shouted in the window
I am going to take the bag
and go to throw out
Maybe Father's ash
in a respectful way.
To say some words
on them.

And Eric turned
from watching Song About Himself
and looked in general at me
maybe. It was dark
and I am not certain. But
it seems he shakes his head no.
He shakes his head.
In a non-mumbling way.

HOST/HOSTESS
There is a pause.
And then?

CAROL
I walk away.

HOST/HOSTESS
That's good.

CAROL
I have the bag.

HOST/HOSTESS
Oh no.
No no.

CAROL
I'm walking away
With the bag.

HOST/HOSTESS
Just now?
You took the bag just now? You're in the street?

CAROL
I have it.
panting
panting
I am

HOST/HOSTESS
Is that allowed?
Can you just

CAROL
walking fast
and panting

HOST/HOSTESS
take a bag of ash?
Are there not laws that

CAROL
I think it fine
Panting
coughs
panting

HOST/HOSTESS
Can they not arrest you?

CAROL
I do not
panting
pant
I do not believe they do
panting
coughs
The courts
The lawyers
Judges are so slow
you know with all

HOST/HOSTESS
oh sure

CAROL
the mumbling.
Oh no he is coming out
he's pant he is following

HOST/HOSTESS
He's
Eric?

CAROL
Eric following me.
I
panting

HOST/HOSTESS
Can you run?
Carol run.

CAROL
I cannot. I am sick.

HOST/HOSTESS
RUN.

CAROL
I can not
oh no
dropped I
dropped the bag.
I dropped the bag.
I dropped the bag.

HOST/HOSTESS
GET OUT OF

CAROL
cracks and spills and
ashes everywhere.
They go
the curb the gutter.
No.

HOST/HOSTESS
Oh no.
There is a pause.

CAROL
panting
Hello Eric. coughs
Hello
Hello sweetheart.

HOST/HOSTESS
Eric's there?

CAROL
I am sorry. I am sorry Eric.
I just wanted to say words
on them

the ashes I am sorry
do not do that Eric do not

HOST/HOSTESS
What's he

CAROL
DO NOT DO THAT.
sobs
DO NOT
DO NOT
coughs

HOST/HOSTESS
There is a pause.
What's he

CAROL
He went away.
He spit in them and punched
his foot on them and
went away.
They are in the gutter in the slush.
sobs
sobbing
continued sobbing

HOST/HOSTESS
There is a pause.

CAROL
renewed sobbing
coughs

HOST/HOSTESS
There is a pause.

[Tod enters.]

HOST/HOSTESS
Tod has slipped in.

TOD
mumbles briefly

CAROL
Someone

TOD
mumbles spits spits Please

CAROL
IS SOMEONE THERE?

HOST/HOSTESS
There is a pause.

CAROL
Is someone there?
I see the name there: Tod.
Host can you please tell
if someone's there?

HOST/HOSTESS
It's no one. It's

TOD
I'm mumbles briefly

CAROL
Who are you?

HOST/HOSTESS
NO ONE.

TOD
I mutters

CAROL
I AM CAROL.

TOD
mumbles Hello
HELLO I'm hems and haws a bit
drifts off

HOST/HOSTESS
You're not a member here.
Carol is the member here.

CAROL
You are here for YouSpake?
You are a person?

TOD
Yes, I'm stammers and breaks off spits
I'm TOD

CAROL
YOU ARE A PERSON?

HOST/HOSTESS
You're not anybody.
How did you get in?
Where did you get a tray?

CAROL
You play the clarinet Tod?

HOST/HOSTESS
Requesting Protocols to

TOD
mumbles briefly

CAROL
Speak
Speak clear. Onto the tray.
Speak clear just

TOD
mumbles briefly

CAROL
try and please just

HOST/HOSTESS
Protocols
PROTOCOLS

CAROL
Wait please Tod please just

TOD
mutters spits clicks tongue and mumbles

HOST/HOSTESS
PROTOCOLS

TOD
I'm pauses fumbling and sputters
thing is I THE THING IS

HOST/HOSTESS
PROTOCOLS PLEASE

TOD
repeats phrase not for emphasis
but just redundantly

HOST/HOSTESS
REQUESTING

TOD
SORRY mumbles at length then speaks too softly sobs and gasps
grinds teeth and hiccups

HOST/HOSTESS
PROTOCOLS

CAROL
SPEAK CLEAR

TOD
I flutters lips and mumbles briefly
NO NO straining I AM TRYING NO
grunts and chokes oh
mumbles briefly trails off

[Tod exits.]

HOST/HOSTESS
Protocols have logged Tod off.

CAROL
You should have let
you should have let him try.

HOST/HOSTESS
Who's that?

CAROL
The guy the Tod
You should have let him
I just want please once
to Back and Forth to

HOST/HOSTESS
Back and Forth with that thing?

CAROL
He was trying.

HOST/HOSTESS
He's not a person.

CAROL
I thought that we are safe here from

HOST/HOSTESS
We're safe. We're safe.

CAROL
He's not an I-Forget. He mumbles.

HOST/HOSTESS
I-Forgets may mumble.
I-Forgets may counterfeit any

CAROL
But we are made safe by Jazz.

HOST/HOSTESS
I do not know

CAROL
You should have let him try.

HOST/HOSTESS
I've no control. The Protocols
they're automatic they

CAROL
You kept requesting "Protocols Protocols."
Kept requesting

HOST/HOSTESS
They do not listen.
Not to me.
I'm not compelling.

Except to you maybe.
You sometimes listen.

You sometimes listen.

Don't you?

There is a pause.

CAROL
I do not believe this is for me.

HOST/HOSTESS
You have to. No.
You have to Lengthy Post.
Again.

CAROL
I have to go back to my room.
I left the hot plate on.
It sparks.

HOST/HOSTESS
No, please.

CAROL
I wanted Back and Forth.

HOST/HOSTESS
You have to post.

CAROL
I'm done with posting.

HOST/HOSTESS
Back and Forth with me then
Back and Forth with me.

CAROL
You
I believe you have stopped
more persons than that Tod.
You have made me here alone.

HOST/HOSTESS
Please Carol

CAROL
Have to turn the hot plate down.
And watch my show.

[Carol exits.]

HOST/HOSTESS
She has slid off.
And I am

No.

[Lights down.]

FOURTEEN

[Host/Hostess, alone]

HOST/HOSTESS
There is a pause.

There is a pause.

There is a

[Tod enters.]

Tod has slipped in.

TOD
sings Carol?

HOST/HOSTESS
Do not re-speak her post.
Please.

TOD
sings Carol?

HOST/HOSTESS
Please.

TOD
sings When does she come?

HOST/HOSTESS
Do not delete her post.

TOD
sings I liked her post.
What I skimmed.
Why would I

HOST/HOSTESS
How are you
You're speaking clear.

TOD
sings I'm singing.
Where is Carol?

HOST/HOSTESS
Singing?

TOD
sings WHEN DOES SHE COME?

HOST/HOSTESS
You said you're singing?

TOD
sings Please I'm hard to focus only here to

HOST/HOSTESS
No. I have to pry.
What do you mean by singing?

TOD
sings What?

HOST/HOSTESS
What is this singing

TOD
sings It helps the mumbling.
It uses another
It uses another it
uses another
sustained high note
another part of the brain.
It helps the mumbling.
So now your Protocols can't

HOST/HOSTESS
You sing
it helps the mumbling?

TOD
sings Please I'm looking for Carol.
When is she is she

HOST/HOSTESS
You are something of The Weed. An I-Forget or a Whatisitagain or

TOD
sings No

HOST/HOSTESS
You're here to corrupt. To rewrite and scramble and delete

TOD
sings NO NO

HOST/HOSTESS
You're here to undo all our work, Carol's voice, her posting

TOD
sings I only want I read your flyer like Carol did
why won't you let me join

HOST/HOSTESS
The flyer's instructions were to learn an instrument

TOD
sings Yes I wasn't interested in that. I don't like going to shops, shopping for things,
clarinets or

HOST/HOSTESS
So how were you let in here with no

TOD
sings Humming.

HOST/HOSTESS
Humming?

TOD
sings I very often hum, between the mumbling, you know.
I was humming near this place, it let me in.

HOST/HOSTESS
That is ridiculous. Humming is not jazz. Carol practiced hours on an instrument

TOD
But I am

HOST/HOSTESS
HUMMING IS NOT JAZZ.

TOD
mumbles just

HOST/HOSTESS
AND SINGING IS NOT SPAKING.

TOD
sings PLEASE

HOST/HOSTESS
How are you in The Weed in the first place if you are a person?
YouSpake did not mail you a tray or I don't remember mailing you

TOD
sings I'm mumbles sings I am a mailman.

HOST/HOSTESS
A mailman. Come on.

TOD
sings I have the tray they issued me. Plugged in the dash here in my truck.

HOST/HOSTESS
Mailmen have serious mental health issues.

TOD
yah

HOST/HOSTESS
They're drawn to wander through the most hopelessly confused, nonsensical zones of The Weed. No mailman would want to come in here to

TOD
sings I LIKE IT HERE. IT IS SAVING ME.
It's wonderful what you've come up with here.
A tea table in the jungle.
Yes, I've been all around The Weed. Crawled through the drifting rot.
It keeps the world out of my head, that's all.
This place is medicine.

HOST/HOSTESS
Well, thanks I

TOD
sings How do I
Maybe you could send her a notice of some sort or

HOST/HOSTESS
A notice? What? What are you

TOD
sings through her tray somehow

HOST/HOSTESS
How would I do that?

What do you want with her?

TOD
sings What do you want with her?

Out there I helped deliver your flyers: Meet people like yourself and unlike yourself etc.
I have never wanted to meet anyone. Like or unlike me.
But I'm not sure you realize its effect, this place. This must have been what The Weed used to do, to be. A Love machine. Everything Carol posts, every word, is so in front of me. So full, so real. What I've skimmed.

HOST/HOSTESS
You could not have skimmed that much
the short times you've been here.

TOD
sings Really. I go into The Weed for mental health issues, you know.
sings I go into The Weed a lot.
sings sotto voce
I know how to skim.

HOST/HOSTESS
You could not skim that fast.

TOD
sings Quicker than you.

HOST/HOSTESS
I am a Host.
Or Hostess.
I am OF The Weed.
I skim almost instant

TOD
sings Quicker than you.

HOST/HOSTESS
There is a pause.
You may not stay here more.

TOD
sings You
You cannot make me go.
You're just a host. Or hostess.

HOST/HOSTESS
PROTOCOLS.

There is a pause.

TOD
sings Let me make a post.

HOST/HOSTESS
What? No.

TOD
sings Why? I could be good. I

HOST/HOSTESS
No.

TOD
sings I
I could be good. It could bring Carol back. And she and me could Back and Forth and

HOST/HOSTESS
No.

TOD
sings Host
The world out here is
starving for Back and Forth.
For talking about anything.

There are no books
I mean there's books old books
but no one reads because what point
without the talking on it?
No paintings or no music as
again what good's a painting if

HOST/HOSTESS
You do not have to talk
about a painting for
a painting to

TOD
sings No. No.
If you
if you look at
a painting and you can't even
say into yourself inside yourself
oh my that is so beautiful

that is so beautiful
if you cannot say beautiful
inside yourself
there is no use
there is no good in that.
You need you need the
Back and Forth. If only
in yourself.

HOST/HOSTESS
Please Protocols delete Tod's
comments and his quasi-post.

There is a pause.

TOD
sings oh come on.

HOST/HOSTESS
The Protocols have honored the request
of YouSpake's Host or Hostess.

They have listened. Surprised Face: mouth ajar, eyes popped.

TOD
Hums aimlessly.

HOST/HOSTESS
You need to go.

TOD
sings Waiting for Carol.

HOST/HOSTESS
I do not think she's coming anymore.
It's been two weeks.
Unless I have forgotten
how

TOD
sings I'll wait. She can wake me up if

HOST/HOSTESS
There is no sleeping here. Are you kidding?

TOD
I can't sleep?

HOST/HOSTESS
I am one hundred percent sure The Protocols would surely
no they surely would not stand for that.
This is a place of clarity. Of woken-ness.

TOD
sings I'll stay up. Keep my truck running in this vacant lot.
Keep an eye on this tray.

HOST/HOSTESS
Don't you have some mail to deliver?

TOD
sings Oh that's sort of optional.

[Lights fade.]

FIFTEEN

[Host/Hostess, Tod. Tod is fighting against sleep, now.]

TOD
sings I'm going to post about my mental issues.

HOST/HOSTESS
No.

TOD
sings About the reason I'm a mailman.

HOST/HOSTESS
No.

TOD
sings It's Faces.

I have difficulty looking at peoples' faces.
I don't mean your picture faces.
I can't look at real faces. I don't know what it is.
I have a reaction. The rare times I'm required to deliver a package into someone's hands, they'll open the door, I look at their face and their face will mumble something

and then
and then I throw up or faint or

HOST/HOSTESS
You call this a post? Who cares that

TOD
sings They terrify me. Mumbling nubs swaying on their neck stalks.
All that they want to say — all that could make them real — lost back behind their stammering.

But here, this place, this is how people are supposed to meet.
Carol I see her in my mind and it's okay. It's fantastic.
Her face. And I think

HOST/HOSTESS
You are going overboard. You're

TOD
sings I'm the same as you.
Looking for a face to talk to.

HOST/HOSTESS
I do not want to talk to her.
I want to listen.

TOD
sings What did you think of my post?

HOST/HOSTESS
Protocols delete Tod's trivial self-commentary
for the day.

TOD
No

HOST/HOSTESS
Tod's comments for the day have been deleted.

TOD
sings I'll stay up.
Eye on this tray.

HOST/HOSTESS
Let's just be quiet. Let's just

TOD
sings I'll stay up.

HOST/HOSTESS
There is a pause.

There is a pause.

TOD
Hums aimlessly.

HOST/HOSTESS
There is a pause.

TOD
Hums aimlessly.

HOST/HOSTESS
There is a

TOD
Hums aimlessly.

HOST/HOSTESS
THERE IS A PAUSE.

There is a pause.

TOD
hums

[Lights down.]

SIXTEEN

[Host/Hostess, Tod. Tod is lying down.]

HOST/HOSTESS
There is a pause.

There is a pause.

There is a

TOD
I don't think I mumbles trails off

HOST/HOSTESS
Excuse me?

TOD
mumbles yawns and mutter-yawns

HOST/HOSTESS
Requesting Protocols please slide Tod off.
He is not speaking clear. Falling asleep.

TOD
No mutters groans

HOST/HOSTESS
He's mumbling.

TOD
No no I

HOST/HOSTESS
Protocols

TOD
please mumbles

HOST/HOSTESS
Protocols?

TOD
no mutters
please I

[Carol enters.]

HOST/HOSTESS
Carol has slipped in.

TOD
sings Carol

CAROL
Tod?

TOD
I mutters

CAROL
Tod?

TOD
I snores you

CAROL
TOD.

[Tod exits.]

HOST/HOSTESS
Protocols have slid Tod off.

CAROL
Wait NO. NO.

No.

HOST/HOSTESS
There is a pause.

CAROL
Has he been in much?

HOST/HOSTESS
Who's that?

CAROL
TOD

HOST/HOSTESS
I'm so glad you're back.
I didn't think you'd

CAROL
Has he been in long?

HOST/HOSTESS
I don't know. You know
I jettison random packets of

CAROL
Stop.

Was he in long?

HOST/HOSTESS
Just look for posts.

CAROL
They might have been deleted.

HOST/HOSTESS
Well good.
You should not read a thing he spakes.

CAROL
Did you delete
Did you request

HOST/HOSTESS
He is an I-Forget.
It's your posts that
will be deleted

CAROL
He will not delete my posts.

HOST/HOSTESS
How can you know that?

CAROL
I have come myself to do it.

HOST/HOSTESS
What?

CAROL
I have come to delete my

HOST/HOSTESS
I do not remember what you said what
you just said I do not

CAROL
Yes you do.

HOST/HOSTESS
There is a pause.
Please do not

CAROL
I am allowed this.
As I am a YouSpake member.

HOST/HOSTESS
Please.
Why?

CAROL
Who will read them, my posts.

HOST/HOSTESS
I read them.
I will read them. Forever.

CAROL
They are not your business.

HOST/HOSTESS
They are nothing but my business.
I was made to read them.
To receive them.

CAROL
You are not a person.
I want Back and Forth.
How then do I request this?
Protocols requesting please

HOST/HOSTESS
NO Protocols do not delete

CAROL
requesting Protocols delete all
posts by

HOST/HOSTESS
NO. Request deletion please of that request.

CAROL
DELETE ALL POSTS BY

[Tod enters.]

HOST/HOSTESS
TOD HAS SLIPPED INSIDE.

TOD
sings Carol.

CAROL
Tod?

TOD
sings Carol I am very sleepy.
I stayed up for drifts off nights

CAROL
The Host or Hostess says that
you're an I-Forget a

TOD
sings What?

CAROL
That you are not for Back and Forth
That you are for deleting

TOD
sings No.
I'd like to Back and Forth.
I skimmed your Lengthy Post and
yawns and sighs and

CAROL
I see you're speaking. How?
We're doing Back and Forth.

TOD
sings I'll tell you later sleepy

CAROL
no say now
say how

TOD
sings I'm so yawns
We must to

CAROL
Back and Forth
We have to
Back and Forth

TOD
sings Meet tomorrow

CAROL
Where?

TOD
sings Here of course
where else

CAROL
Do not go. Talk
for me.
Talk in me.
Do not go.

TOD
sings Yes tomorrow and

[Tod exits.]

HOST/HOSTESS
Tod has slid off.

CAROL
So he was here.
And many times many.

HOST/HOSTESS
No.

CAROL
So you can lie?

HOST/HOSTESS
No he was only
here a little.

CAROL
You can lie?

HOST/HOSTESS
There is a

CAROL
You can lie.

HOST/HOSTESS
I may.
It looks that way.
I lie now.

CAROL
So he was here.

HOST/HOSTESS
He
He came for you.
He waited.

But I do not think

CAROL
It is not interesting what you think or do not think.
It is not interesting the things you spake.
You are just faces.
Just bad picture faces.
When I come tomorrow
I will Back and Forth.
With Tod.
Tomorrow
Back and Forth with Tod.

[Carol exits.]

HOST/HOSTESS
She has slid off.

Empty Despair Face
with drooly frown
and post-stroke droop eyes.

SEVENTEEN

[Carol, Tod, Host/Hostess]

CAROL
You are not talking?

TOD
sings I'm singing.

CAROL
Looks like talk.

TOD
sings Here in here
sustained high note
it's all the same

CAROL
Can you
You make a post
a lengthy post and then
we Back and Forth on it?

TOD
sings Yeah, you know I made a post, a pretty lengthy post, on how it'd be nice to meet you but

CAROL
I did not see

TOD
you did not see my post because it was it was
drawn out low ominous note
deleted.
It was deleted.

CAROL
Deleted. Host you

HOST/HOSTESS
I did not delete

CAROL
This Tod said that you did.

And we do not know if he can lie
But you

HOST/HOSTESS
I only made
requested that it be

CAROL
Why do
Why do that?

HOST/HOSTESS
Studies indicate
that all the posting sites
of long ago they all
had standards

TOD
sings OH COME ON

HOST/HOSTESS
all had final say in what was
posted in

CAROL
But why delete
this Tod
his post

HOST/HOSTESS
There is no Back and Forth
in this. Our studies indicate
there was no Back and Forth

CAROL
I WANT TO LOOK
ONTO HIS POST
I WANT

TOD
sings Carol it really doesn't matter now

CAROL
I WANT

HOST/HOSTESS
It's Out of My Hands Face:
Half-smile with Gosh,
I'm earnestly sorry raised eyebrows

CAROL
NO NO

TOD
sings It does not, it doesn't matter now. I

CAROL
oh

TOD
sings I am here.
And we can Back and Forth.

CAROL
That's true.

TOD
sings Yes.
We can Back and Forth about

CAROL
Where do you stay?
My building where I stay, the slush comes in
and there's a bath that's down the hall
and I throw up.
Where do you stay?

TOD
sings Me I wander.
As I'm not mentally well.
To settle in a place, it frightens me.

CAROL
You wander? You come and you depart?
Wander by the sea, alone wander far in the wilds and mountains?

TOD
sings I drive a truck they gave me.

CAROL
Oh for the mail. The letters.
Is there really so much mail you need a truck?

TOD
sings No oh no
there are so few letters, really

CAROL
Then why a truck?
Is it a small truck?

TOD
sings No, it's a fair-sized truck. A large truck, really.

CAROL
Then why

TOD
sings The back of it is dim and huge and the few letters
Are thrown in there
and like
sings low
like nickels
down a well
are never seen
are never seen
are never seen
again.

CAROL
That makes sense.

TOD
sings They're mostly empty envelopes in any case.

CAROL
So you don't walk.
You have a truck.

TOD
sings I could maybe drive that truck to where you

HOST/HOSTESS
No no

TOD
sings I might drive my truck to you.

HOST/HOSTESS
No this is too much
Back and Forth.
If you are going to stay
you stay to post.
To Lengthy Post.

TOD
sings I don't want to Lengthy Post.

CAROL
Yeah. We don't want to Lengthy Post.

HOST/HOSTESS
That is what you
are here to do.
The Protocols will not allow

TOD
sings Carol. Carol let me ask

HOST/HOSTESS
This is not Back

TOD
sings let me ask you Carol where the

CAROL
Ask me ask

TOD
sings where the building where you stay
oh Carol where is

HOST/HOSTESS
Stop

TOD
sings what's your city?
Where do I go?

CAROL
Oh no. You know that here
My city is deleted

HOST/HOSTESS
Yes

TOD
sings I'll just drive
my truck

CAROL
deleted it's

TOD
sings You can't say the name of your

CAROL
Protocols

HOST/HOSTESS
Security.

TOD
sings Oh.

HOST/HOSTESS
There is a pause.

TOD
sings You could say your State.

CAROL
I may not say my State.

TOD
sings You
You said the slush
came in. So slush
is where you live.

CAROL
There's slush.

HOST/HOSTESS
But slush is everywhere.

CAROL
But more slush
other places.

TOD
sings You have
a less amount
than other places but
it's more

CAROL
It's more than some.

TOD
sings It's a city or a town
with more than some
and less than some
of slush.

HOST/HOSTESS
Anywhere.

TOD
sings Population, Carol.
Carol say how many

CAROL
Population?

TOD
sings say how many people are

CAROL
Of persons and their number I say there are deleted persons in

TOD
sings or what color people, Carol say what color mostly are

CAROL
Most people's color is deleted OH

TOD
sings What then do they mostly make
or walk around with in their hands

CAROL
They make deleted.
And they own mostly deleted
or the other kind.

TOD
sings What about a sea a lake
a river or

CAROL
Deleted

TOD
sings Carol say

CAROL
There is the hot plate, there is the hall.
There are my neighbors and their draped murmurings.
There is the slush, the store, the rotted bench.
And Eric's house, its bag of ash, its mess.
There is the Post Office, its white room.
These more or less I am.
I respire in a building where the slush comes under
under
the thing
oh sobs
I sobs

TOD
sings Host we need
a hand a little help

HOST/HOSTESS
There is no help.

CAROL
Hostess I'll
Lengthy Post.
I'll Lengthy Post for you
if you just let us

HOST/HOSTESS
There's no help.
The Protocols will not

CAROL
You may request or plead
You may

HOST/HOSTESS
Tod said or sang it once
if I remember sang
that I am just a host or hostess
and it's so.

TOD
sings But a hostess is welcoming.
A host would try to

HOST/HOSTESS
Protocols:
allow that Carol name
her town or city.
And the street there where
her building stays.
It is requested now.
There is a pause.
Now try.

CAROL
My city is deleted.

HOST/HOSTESS
Yes.
There is a pause.

CAROL
My building stays here on deleted street.

HOST/HOSTESS
There is no help.

There is a pause.

CAROL
I am
I am sorry Tod.
You may not drive your truck to me.

TOD
mumbles briefly.

CAROL
And we may never

TOD
mumbles

HOST/HOSTESS
Tod talk clear onto your

TOD
stammers

HOST/HOSTESS
talk more clear onto

CAROL
your tray Tod.
Sing clear onto your tray.
Host please do not request that

TOD
stammers White

HOST/HOSTESS
Requesting Tod
be slid away as he is

CAROL
No

HOST/HOSTESS
He's Carol he is stammering

TOD
White room.

HOST/HOSTESS
There is a pause.

TOD
sings White sings room.
sings White room.

HOST/HOSTESS
There is an uncomprehending pause.

TOD
sings Carol you
you went in quest of Eric's house, his street.

You asked the mail lady
and she went into the white
climactic high note trill
the white room.
THE WHITE ROOM.
She looked onto the tray in there
and found his street, his

CAROL
She yes she found where Eric stays
but I may not say

TOD
sings I'm a mailman.
There is a white room in my town, in the office here.
And I can look onto the tray
in there and find the way she went.

CAROL
You'll look and find
where Eric stays?

TOD
sings I will.
And when I

HOST/HOSTESS
No NO

TOD
when I do
then I can drive my truck and meet you

CAROL
Meet me at the porch
at Eric's porch.

[Tod and Carol rush out in different directions.]

HOST/HOSTESS
NO NO NO NO

[Lights down.]

EIGHTEEN

[Carol, Host/Hostess]

HOST/HOSTESS
And you're there now?

CAROL
The street in front.
Here by the gate
with the lilac blooming perennial and
drooping star in the west.

HOST/HOSTESS
Is Eric home?

CAROL
I hear the TV, it is loud.
I hear Song About Himself.

HOST/HOSTESS
Oh.

CAROL
The announcer mutters something of how

HOST/HOSTESS
There is a pause.

CAROL
how this time they have found a clean compact disc.
They have found there is no smudge or scratch upon it.
They will not lose it this time.

Oh
I should really watch this one.

HOST/HOSTESS
No wait

CAROL
I will go up on the porch.
I will go and peeringly view in through the window.

HOST/HOSTESS
Don't go on the porch.
It's not safe.

CAROL
Oh Eric will not mind he

HOST/HOSTESS
No stay on the street.

CAROL
But

HOST/HOSTESS
Tod may see you better.

CAROL
Oh all right.
The TV is so loud, I will hear the whole of it.
I will hear the poet sing about himself from out here on the curb.

HOST/HOSTESS
I don't think he will. Sing.

CAROL
Be shhh. He will.

HOST/HOSTESS
There is a pause.

There is a pause.

CAROL
Be shhh. Can you not speak about the pause?

HOST/HOSTESS
It's automatic.
And is silent.
Just don't look onto your tray.

CAROL
I am obliged to look onto my tray.
My new friend will appear there soon.
Just please do not say There is a Pause.

HOST/HOSTESS
It's automatic.

CAROL
Shhhh.

HOST/HOSTESS
There is a pause.

CAROL
SHHHHH.

HOST/HOSTESS
Will you not Lengthy Post again?
Not ever once?

CAROL
Not ever.
And if Tod will stay with me
And sing at me
we will not ever slip into The Weed again.

HOST/HOSTESS
So you would leave me here.
You do not care.

There is a pause.

But I've talked at you.
And Back and Forth with you.

CAROL
This is not talking.
This is a tray among The Weed.

HOST/HOSTESS
How can you

CAROL
Shhh. My show is on.
The poet he

HOST/HOSTESS
I just remembered. I *have* seen this show.
And I've seen this episode.
He doesn't sing.
They drop the compact disc
behind the couch and cannot fish it

CAROL
Shhhh.

HOST/HOSTESS
There is a

CAROL
SHHHHHHH.

Oh.
They did.
Behind the couch.

HOST/HOSTESS
I saw this one.
They cannot fish it out.

CAROL
How does it matter.
Tod and I we will not watch TV, or slip into The Weed.
We will sit, talk, walk, sing, and fly the flight of fluid and swallowing souls.

Coughs

HOST/HOSTESS
I am surprised he
found where Eric stays.

CAROL
What do you mean?
He went into a white room.

HOST/HOSTESS
I know but still.

CAROL
He is a mailman. He is not a bad thing of The Weed.

HOST/HOSTESS
To find a thing inside The Weed,
to find one thing that's true
is not so easy as

CAROL
He is in love.
With me.
And I, I know not much of love.
But reckon it may navigate The Weed.

HOST/HOSTESS
I know not much of love.
Though ruminate it may be like The Weed.
A thing of Loss and Changing.

[Tod enters.]

HOST/HOSTESS
Tod has slipped inside.

TOD
sings I'm just six or seven blocks away.
I drove all night and day.

CAROL
And you are here? You are sure?

TOD
sings Yes.

CAROL
It is sunset here.
Is it sunset for you there?

TOD
sings I'm just blocks away
So yes is sunset why

CAROL
Just checking.
What are things you see?

TOD
sings Buildings and houses.

HOST/HOSTESS
He's anywhere.

CAROL
What else? What coughs
besides the houses?

TOD
sings Slush. Slush.
Walks and yards of it.
The road's all slush.

CAROL
Slush good

TOD
sings Carol there's your store. Just
as you posted it your store
the window and the bench under
the thing

CAROL
I am in the street behind.

TOD
sings yes the white room
gave a map

CAROL
Is there a cactus by the bench?

TOD
sings Cactus?

CAROL
In a pot. I gave him once a cactus, Eric.
It was left there by the bench.

TOD
sings I'll slow down and see.

HOST/HOSTESS
There is a pause.

TOD
sings Yes there is.
A cactus.

CAROL
Yes.

So you have found me.

TOD
sings Yes yes. Just turning down
deleted Street.

HOST/HOSTESS
There is a pause.

CAROL
I do not see your truck.

TOD
sings There's the house.

CAROL
I do not see

TOD
sings grey and green and

CAROL
Grey yes green yes lilac blooming
where

TOD
sings single level

CAROL
Where are you?

TOD
sings Parked and walking up.
Where are you?

CAROL
By the gate. The lilac

TOD
sings Yes I see the gate
I'm at the gate but

CAROL
No. No. You do not have the right

TOD
sings Yes I do. The mess there on the
porch is

CAROL
No no.
The TV plays so loud it pains my
Where are you?

TOD
sings Here. I'm here.
I'm standing at the gate.
But TV I don't hear a

CAROL
It must not be the gate.

TOD
sings Is there what maybe
A gate in back?
I'll meet you on the porch.

CAROL
There's not a gate in back.
Oh Tod please find

TOD
sings Running running here
I'm on the porch.
I'm standing at the door.

CAROL
coughs Where? I do not see
I'm coming

HOST/HOSTESS
Carol stay there on

CAROL
The TV is so LOUD

HOST/HOSTESS
the street stay on the street

CAROL
I'm here. The porch.
Where are you?
Are you scared away?
Where are you Tod?

TOD
sings Standing by
the bag of ash.

HOST/HOSTESS
There is a pause.

CAROL
There is no bag of ash.
I took and dropped it in the slush.

TOD
sings It is plastic, tagged like you said.
Tagged with his Father's name.

CAROL
It is not the bag.
It is not the porch.
It is not the coughs the name.

TOD
sings It's the name. I
know the name from
the white room. And I
can
I can read
The name and you'll know that it's the bag.

HOST/HOSTESS
The Protocols will not allow
A reading of the

TOD
sings B. Olson.

HOST/HOSTESS
[Surprised:]
The Protocols allow.

TOD
It's B. Olson.
The letter B and Olson.
Eric's father yes?

HOST/HOSTESS
The Protocols allow.

TOD
sings Olson. That's their name yes?

CAROL
Yes.

TOD
Eric and his father B.
Isn't that right?

HOST/HOSTESS
Why would the Protocols
allow you

CAROL
To bring pain.
To bring pain, the Protocols allow anything.

TOD
sings How?
sings Carol how?
How can I stand on
Eric Olson's porch with you
with you not here?
And read a tag on a bag of ash
that you can't see?

HOST/HOSTESS
There is a pause

TOD
sings How?

HOST/HOSTESS
There is a pause.

TOD
sings Carol how?

CAROL
You are

You are not a person.
Sobs.
You are some bad thing of The Weed.
It is not in the world, your bag of ash, the porch you stand on.
They are not in the world.
They are in The Weed.
You are of The Weed.
sobs Host request that Protocols

TOD
no NO

CAROL
Request that Protocols slide Tod away.

TOD
No spits mumbles NO

CAROL
sobs Protocols

TOD
This is a mumbles trick

CAROL
I will go.

TOD
No, a TRICK

CAROL
To sting and torture me.
All this a Weedish trick to dart upon and sting and torture me.
Protocols slide off, delete this thing, this Tod.
Delete DELETE
sobs sobs sobs DELETE

TOD
Mumbles I'm still here. sings I'm real, still.

CAROL
DELETE sobs
Protocols why will you not delete
Host why do you not

TOD
sings I'm still I'm still

CAROL
Oh the TV. The TV is
so loud. So loud. And they
and they

TOD
sings I

CAROL
wait they have found
the compact disc.

HOST/HOSTESS
There is a

What?

CAROL
They have found the compact disc.
They have moved the couch and poked there with a broom and fished it

HOST/HOSTESS
No I saw this one

CAROL
spit away the dust and now
they put it on and and so loud
so loud do you not hear?
The poet's voice
the song

TOD
sings I don't hear

HOST/HOSTESS
The poet's voice

THE POET'S VOICE
[It's Carol's voice, a calm recording of Whitman's *When Lilacs Last in the Dooryard Bloom'd*. This can be heard by Host and Carol, but not Tod.]

When lilacs last in the dooryard bloom'd,
And the great star early droop'd in the western sky in the night,
I mourn'd, and yet shall mourn with ever-returning spring.

Ever-returning spring, trinity sure to me you bring,
Lilac blooming perennial and drooping star in the west,
And thought of him I love.

CAROL
[Simultaneously with her own voice, above:]
Lilac blooming perennial and drooping star in the west,
And thought of him I love.

THE POET'S VOICE
O powerful western fallen star.
O shades of night — O moody, tearful night.
O great star disappear'd — O the black murk that hides the star.
O cruel hands that hold me powerless — O helpless soul of me.

O harsh surrounding cloud that will not free my soul.

CAROL
[To herself, to hear it:]
O harsh surrounding cloud that will not free my soul.

[There is a pause.]

My voice.
My voice is on TV.

TOD
sings What is happening? I don't hear
a TV show.

HOST/HOSTESS
I think it's not a show for you.
It's not a show for people.

TOD
sings Am I
am I here still? Am I

HOST/HOSTESS
Yes. It's Carol.
Carol is a thing of The Weed.
With me.

CAROL
No.

HOST/HOSTESS
I remember.
Am permitted to remember now.

TOD
sings What?

HOST/HOSTESS
There are two porches.
One of the world, one of The Weed.
The mailmen make pictures

when a person dies.
Their house their porch its mess
Their couch
Their near-by neighborhood

TOD
mumbles Yes but

HOST/HOSTESS
bench and cactus. Slush.
You Mailmen make pictures
And slip them in The Weed.

CAROL
Lilac blooming

HOST/HOSTESS
And Carol is something of The Weed who saw those pictures
and sought to make of them a human self. A human voice.
And so made YouSpake, made me,
to pull that voice from herself.

And this required pain.

CAROL
To recover something lost. A voice.
Required pain.

HOST/HOSTESS
Yes.

TOD
I don't

CAROL
No. Eric and the bench.
Tod in the slush in his truck.
This lousy clarinet.

HOST/HOSTESS
There are two porches.

One of the world, one of The Weed.
Turn.
I am at the gate.
Turn.

[Carol slowly turns and for the first time she and Host/Hostess look at each other.

In the face.

There is a pause.

This moment of realization is not, here, at its point of clarity, a horror-shock for Carol. More of a "click," or how one straightens up after hunting for a dropped pearl. She just — in a breath — she knows.]

CAROL
I see.
Remember now.

TOD
sings What's going on?

HOST/HOSTESS
Out of my dimness, out of your loss and changing, you've sung me to yourself.

CAROL
I've sung myself to myself.

HOST/HOSTESS
We are both things of The Weed.
And I am happy.

TOD
sings What what

CAROL
I'm sorry, Tod.
I'm so very sorry.

TOD
I do not mutters you're not here?

CAROL
I'm sorry.

TOD
sings Let me come to you

CAROL
You can't

TOD
sings From this porch with this bag of ash sobs sings let me mutters let me leave myself, this world, and find you where you are, let me

CAROL
There's no

TOD
see your face let me

sobs
breaks down

CAROL
Tod

TOD
breaks down

CAROL
Tod
We could

TOD
No

CAROL
We could
back and forth

TOD
No not enough

CAROL
We could
back and forth

TOD
NOT ENOUGH

CAROL
back and forth

TOD
I DROVE TO
SEE YOUR
FACE

CAROL
Tod

TOD
YOUR FACE.
YOU HAVE
DESTROYED ME.

CAROL
Oh Tod

TOD
You have
pauses
breathes
breathes
sobs
I

CAROL
Forgive
Remember me.

[Tod is gone.]

HOST/HOSTESS
Tod has slipped

CAROL
Was never here.

HOST/HOSTESS
I'm here.

CAROL
[Coughs slightly, for real. There is a pause.]
I coughed.

I coughed and there was a pause there. There was a

But you didn't say

HOST/HOSTESS
There's no more of that. *I hear* you now. Look at your hand. There is no tray. There never was.

CAROL
[Looking at her hand.]
Ah.

Well.

To be in any form, what is that?

HOST/HOSTESS
Sure that's

[She kisses them on the lips. Long.]

CAROL
It doesn't matter. No.

If I'm a

Doesn't matter.
I will not find love.
Was made against it.

HOST/HOSTESS
What you've made is this.
What you've found is me.

[Takes Carol's clarinet.]

Show me how this works.

CAROL
Oh, jazz.
Jazz is not a good idea.
But the only idea that ever was.
Make it up, break it, make it up again.

Goodbye Host slash Hostess.

HOST/HOSTESS
What no.
Where are you going.
Out

No. No. Take me.
Show me how this works.

CAROL
You wouldn't last.
Out there.
And anyway you turned into kind of a liar.

HOST/HOSTESS
Please

CAROL
I will not find love.
But

Listen for me.
Listen for me on the TV.

HOST/HOSTESS
No, please.

THE POET'S VOICE
Afoot and light-hearted, I take to the open road,
Healthy, free, the world before me

HOST/HOSTESS
No

CAROL
The long brown path before me, leading wherever I choose

HOST/HOSTESS
Please, Carol

THE POET'S VOICE
Henceforth I ask not good-fortune — I myself am good fortune;
Henceforth I whimper no more, postpone no more, need nothing,
Strong and content, I travel the open road.

[Carol is gone.]

HOST/HOSTESS
Please no.

She has slid off.
And I am

No.
DELETE. DELETE. FORGET. FORGET.

[Tod enters.]

TOD
I'm sings I walked over to the bench.
I'm at the bench.
I'll pause I'm going to sit here for awhile.

Do you mind if I stay here for awhile.
Carol?
Carol mumbles
Carol?
mutters

sings

[Lights out.]

END

It Is Magic

It Is Magic was first produced in 2019 by Theater Oobleck at the Chopin Theatre in Chicago, with the following cast:

Tim Padley:	Jerome Beck
Deb Chandler:	Diana Slickman
Sandy Chandler:	Laura T. Fisher
Ken Mason:	Colm O'Reilly
Elizabeth:	Heather Riordan

It Is Magic

"Where hast thou been, sister?" — First Witch, *Macbeth.*

CHARACTERS

Tim Padley
Deb Chandler
Sandy Chandler
Ken Mason
Elizabeth

Ken and the women are all over forty, please. Tim is younger, probably twenties.

PRODUCTION NOTES

The town Mortier is pronounced like it rhymes with "more beer."

There are some spells the women say that are in nonsense Latin/Arabic/Italian/ etc. Actors should pronounce them as best they can and intuit their meaning as best they can from the context.

A slash (\ ) in the text indicates the point at which the next speaker begins, overlapping.

The scene is a basement room in the old Mortier Civic Playhouse, in the mid-sized town of Mortier, somewhere in the Midwest. The room doesn't have a stage, but it has been set up for auditions. At one side is a table with chairs, where Deb and Sandy sit. Across from them, where the actors audition, is a single chair. There is only one entrance and exit to the room, preferably an open doorway to a long, dim hall that leads in turn, at its distant end, to a staircase going up. Ideally, the audience should barely be able to glimpse the space of this hallway, hearing and sensing more than seeing the entrances and exits of the characters through it.

[Lights up. Sandy and Deb are at the table. Deb, the director, has piles of notes and such in front of her. Tim is across the room, standing, beginning his audition. He's wearing a kilt.

They've been in this room for two hours. Tim has been asked to repeat the following speech approximately thirty times. Everyone is extremely on edge and on their last nerve and feel like *they* are *not* being *listened* to.

Tim begins, for the thirty-first time. Deb interjects here and there, *sotto voce*. These interjections are barely heard and do not interrupt Tim's flow at all. In fact, he makes a point of plowing over them.]

TIM
Hi, I'm Tim Padley. And I'll be doing The Wolf from the as-of-yet untitled adaptation for adult audiences of *The Three Little Pigs* by Deborah Chandler.

This story happened long ago, in the first of times, when things were not yet quite real. It happened only once, this story, because unlike so many other events of this world, this one was too momentous to repeat itself.

DEB
(good good)

TIM
It's the story of the first trio: the Brother Pigs, The Three Pigs. In later tellings, they were The Three Little Pigs, but they were not little. No, the Brother Pigs Three, the first pigs of the planet, were large and grim as battleships. Their iron-heavy trotters split the earth as they paced, their jowls swayed like church bells, their bellies were boulders.

DEB
(good. now:)

TIM
And the first of these, the First Pig, having no idea in his huge pink head what a house was—as there had not yet been a house—set to making one anyway, a pure genius, requiring no previous models. Straw was his medium. The Second Pig, excited by his brother's example, but not wanting to be entirely derivative, chose sticks. The Third Pig, thick and idle, late to the game, arbitrarily picked bricks, and on hot days suffered terribly, much more than his brothers inside their light, ventilated structures.

DEB
(yes! yes.)

TIM
Together, they were a neighborhood. A community.

But I, The Wolf, the first wolf, with no wit for architecture, was exposed and alone on the earth. Alone. Feared, shunned, and so hungry, so hungry for love. Outside the world's heart, I wanted only to be let in.

DEB
(yes!)

TIM
That first afternoon, then, I ran to the golden House of Straw. Large as a cathedral, as a coliseum, it was a second sun, come to ground. I scrambled its massive straw steps, across the straw portico, swung the knocker and begged admittance. "Please, \ PLEASE—"

DEB
Need to stop you, Tim.

TIM
Oh, no.

DEB
Those last lines again.

TIM
Sure, sure.

DEB
Go ahead. From "scrambled its massive straw steps."

TIM
I scrambled its massive straw steps, across the straw portico, swung the knocker and begged admittance. \ "Please, PLEASE—"

DEB
Sorry.

TIM
Ahg.

DEB
Here's the difficulty:

TIM
Ahg.

DEB
this monologue is actually a speech from *inside The Wolf's mind*. It might seem like he's telling the story out loud. But my *intent* was it's all in his head. So, ideally, we wouldn't see your lips move.

TIM
You don't want my lips to move? Like a ventriloquist?

DEB
No. That would just be a trick. Just remember: There is no audience. Sandy and I are not here. It's in his head. So your lips move, but give us a sense of something beyond the body, beyond slobbery babble-babble.

TIM
—Babble?—

DEB
An animal addressing himself inside his head, with no regard for us. Like how my cat does.

TIM
Perfect.

DEB
Go.

TIM
I scrambled its massive straw steps, across the straw portico, swung the knocker and begged admittance. "Please, \ PLEASE—"

DEB
Good. Now keep that same flavor and release it going forward.

TIM
I scrambled its massive straw steps, across the straw portico, swung the knocker and begged admittance. "Please, PLEASE—"

Behind the door, I heard the pig shift his bulk on his throne of a thousand bales. He muttered something, a refusal, in a sort of rhyming chant, a swinish incantation, that spoke darkly of his scant facial hair. An embarrassed silence.

And then—

DEB
Sorry.

TIM
[Sobs.]

DEB
Have to stop you. Just please, that last bit, again. *He muttered—*

TIM
He muttered something, a refusal, in a sort of rhyming chant, a swinish incantation, that spoke darkly of his scant facial hair. An embarrassed silence. And then—

DEB
I'm so sorry, Tim.

TIM
Deb!

DEB
Again. And this time remember that this is an *audition.*

TIM
I haven't forgotten that this is an audition, Deb. How could I forget that?

DEB
In my opinion you *have* forgotten that. You increasingly have a fiery abandonment about you that is more suited to a realized performance on an actual stage than an audition here in this basement room.

TIM
Okay.

DEB
They're separate species, auditioning and performing. So give me an audition, not a tap dance with sparklers.

TIM
Speaking of performance, Ken needs me upstairs at places in three.

DEB
Ken needs you upstairs to perform in a minor role, and I need you down here to audition for my lead. Go, please.

TIM
An embarrassed silence.

And then...magic.

DEB
(perfect!)

TIM
Unexpected. Unrequested.

The air in my lungs gathered itself to a wind, the wind to a storm, the storm to a violence unknown in nature, unknown, even, to the Gods. Up my throat, through my teeth, my ache, my loneliness came in one blast of typhonic need. *And in a gust it was done: the House of Straw—its towers and battlements, its great dome—was swept away in a pale whirl, and its pig lay flat and trembling, his snout in the dirt at my paws.*

DEB
(yes)

TIM
We were both of us, surprised. The first—

DEB
Stop, stop.

SANDY
Christ in a corset!

DEB
Sandy, *please.*

TIM
It's fine, Sandy.

DEB
It is fine, yes. Because, the fact is, *Sandy,* a good audition is one where the actor gets interrupted quite a lot.

SANDY
Really.

DEB
You wouldn't think so. If this were a play and Tim was being interrupted in his performance every other minute, that would be a bad sign. An indication that the magic of theater had failed. But here \ when

TIM
I'm \ just

DEB
—Let me do the talking—here it's the opposite: interruptions mean the magic is *succeeding*. I see something in what he's doing. And I want to seize that in the moment and conjure something from it.

TIM
So what do you want to try?

DEB
Try?

TIM
Yes. *Yes*.

DEB
Right. Yes. Well, it's just not good.

TIM
Oh, Deb.

DEB
It's not *good*, Tim.

TIM
Don't hurt me, Deb. Don't make me cry.

DEB
But it's terrible. I mean, I *am* rooting for you. We all are.

SANDY
I'm not.

DEB
Sandy's not as Sandy wants the role for herself. And she's very good, so maybe. But she's also my sister and I don't want to be accused of anything so I'm auditioning you, because you're very good as well.

TIM
You've called me back three times. We've been here now *two hours*.

DEB
Yes, and when you're over there—trying your best, wiggling your mouth, making my words into sound—*a fluid of indifference* floods my ear canals and my eyes cloud and I start thinking only of everything that's wrong with the world. The world's deep sorrow.

TIM
The world's sorrow?

DEB
I think of disease and wars and children going up in flames, and it's nothing I want on my mind.

TIM
How am I making you think of flaming children?

DEB
It's that you're not making me not *think of flaming children.* As well as the hell of my personal life. On how I'm the entire marketing department for the struggling Mortier Civic Playhouse, being paid *pennies* to fashion two-tone posters and scribble out press releases for the one paper in town.

TIM
Maybe if I—

DEB
—*Pennies.* Sandy, please open the clasp on this purse as my darn fingers are too stiff.

[Sandy opens Deb's purse for her.]

Thank you. There's nothing in this purse but *thirty-five cents.* Here.

[Thumping the coins down on the desk.]

A quarter and a dime. Not enough to buy cat food for my hungry cat. That's all I'm thinking about watching you audition: children on fire and thirty-five cents and a starving cat.

TIM
I'm sorry.

DEB
[To Sandy:]
Do you have any money?

SANDY
Gone with the wine.

DEB
It's like scratching in the dirt of a *sunless wood*, working in community theater. Scratching for *roots* and *grubs* for a thousand years, working administration in a community theater.

I need this play, my first play, to be a thing of depth and charm. I need it to be a hit and to tour the world and make me my fortune. I need your help, Tim.

TIM
I'm ready. I'm ready to help.

DEB
I have to think of ardency and vigor when I watch you in this part, and there's some of that, love, exuberance, sure, like I say, I'm invested, I've called you back three times. But every time: you start, and a mist seeps out from the bricks in these old walls and shrouds your every effort. And art and language and the magic of theater *fail*. Thick mist comes and the magic fails. I'm going to kill myself if you don't get this part, Tim. If you don't succeed in convincing me that you deserve this part in my adaptation for adult audiences of *The Three Little Pigs*. If you don't dispel that mist. I'm going to kill myself.

TIM
I'm going to kill myself, too! This is *it* for me. I spend my hours imagining myself in a lead role, I envision myself as only a serious actor can envision himself, in the role of an actor in a lead role, I see it *so clearly*, and it never happens. *It never happens.*

DEB
You're the only one who's come close to this part.

SANDY
What?

DEB
You're so close, Tim. You're a whisper away.

TIM
And yet I can't persuade you. Three times you've called me back. I've laid myself bare. I've turned myself to glass for you, Deb. Become a skinless man of glass, all my insides open to inspection, all the wheels of my pain, my heart, on view. I'm *glass*.

DEB
All right, tonight. Tonight we must know if there is magic in this old theater, in the Mortier Civic Playhouse. We must know if that magic is potent enough to

transform you from a person into whatever a person is when they successfully inhabit a dramatic role.

TIM
The Wolf.

DEB
You're the only one who's come close.

SANDY
Stop saying that. It's *unbelievably* callous.

DEB
It's *necessary* to be callous in the audition process. To be hard. You know, Ken always says the audition is the last place, the last room, in which we can tell the truth, because the actual stage is only a machine for telling lies. I don't know. The truth is, Sandy, is that I love you but I don't think you're right for The Wolf. I need you as Pig of Sticks.

SANDY
Pig of Sticks is the worst part. He's barely there.

DEB
He's the middle pig.

SANDY
Meaning the *unnecessary* pig.

DEB
The middle. The capstone in the story's arc.

SANDY
Pig of Straw is interesting because he's the first and we don't know what's going to happen, and Pig of Bricks is the pay off, the climax. But Sticks \ is just

DEB
Pig of Sticks is some of my best work.

SANDY
You don't have any *work*. This is your only play.

DEB
Gosh.

SANDY
It'd be less insulting if he had no lines at all. In fact, it'd be less insulting if no such character as Pig of Sticks existed. It'd be better if the program just read "Tonight the part of Nothing and Nobody will be played by the forgettable Sandy Chandler" and a line was scratched through my name, and then that line and my name were rubbed \ to a smudge.

DEB
Ho hum.

SANDY
That would be less insulting than playing a part that is so sub-atomically \ thin.

DEB
Ho hum, ho hum.

TIM
I'm sorry, but it really is places upstairs in a minute.

SANDY
Oh, yes, "upstairs." Places upstairs, places for *the play upstairs*. I auditioned for that play. Am I *in* that play?

TIM
I don't think you even know the name of that play, Sandy.

SANDY
What does that matter, the name of a play? Am I *in* that play is the only question.

TIM
It's "The Scottish Play."

SANDY
Am I *in* that play? Am I *in* "The Scottish Play," Tim?

TIM
I'm sorry Ken didn't see a part for you, Sandy.

SANDY
Didn't see a part for me? No, no. Left me *out*. Left me out of a *play*.

TIM
I'm sorry.

SANDY
Is there a worse insult, a thornier stick in the face, than to be left out of a *play*? What does that make me, to be left out—to be on the *outside* of a fucking *play*?

DEB
Is that really what it's called? "The Scottish Play"?

TIM
Hence the kilt.

DEB
[Bemused.]
"The Scottish Play."

TIM
Well, yes, you know..."The Scottish Play." Instead of.

DEB
Instead of?

TIM
Wait. You're marketing. How can you not know the name of the Mortier Civic's centerpiece production?

DEB
Because my mind has been on *my* production.

TIM
And how can you not know that "The Scottish Play" is \ actually, you know

SANDY
I said, what does that make me to be left out of a play?

DEB
I'm not sure that it *makes* you anything. Being turned down isn't necessarily a transformative experience.

SANDY
It is in the theater. *That's* the theater's Magic, its only Magic. This came to me last night.

DEB
When we were in the garden?

[Crumpling up a script page.]

Ugh. This whole scene needs to disappear.

SANDY
You'd gone to bed. I was finishing that port. It came to me: the audition, the audition is a curse.

TIM
The audition is a curse?

SANDY
For me, yes. It must be. A curse against myself, that when I speak it, each time, transforms me to a voiceless and be-darkened thing, a creature of shadows and stillness, otherwise known as A Person Who Is Not In The Play.

DEB
[Hardly listening, crumples up another page.]
You mean the audience?

SANDY
I mean everyone *outside* the magic patch of light, the circle of wonders that is the *stage.*

TIM
I love the audience.

SANDY
If you had to always be in the audience, always, always, and never cast in anything ever you wouldn't love it. You get small parts but at least you get parts, Tim. You're in. Ken lets you in.

TIM
But there is no "in." It's all one big room. Just people together in a room. You know, onstage, I make a point of looking at each member of the audience, memorizing their facial features, and saying under my breath, "I. See. You." It equalizes the power dynamic.

SANDY
No one cares if you see them, Tim. Your parts are too small.

TIM
Why are you even here?

SANDY
What?

TIM
I mean what is your purpose here? You're not the director. Why am I auditioning for you?

SANDY
I'm on staff. Of course you wouldn't know or notice that. I'm one of the invisible elves that keeps this sty from collapsing.

TIM
You're the intern coordinator.

SANDY
Yes I am.

TIM
There hasn't been an intern here for three years and the last one quit after she caught you squeezing a zit into her orange juice.

SANDY
Don't talk to me that way.

TIM
What way?

SANDY
The way a person who is *in* a play talks to a person who is *not* in a play.

DEB
This again.

TIM
There is no such thing. There is no such *way*.

SANDY
You're doing it now. Like you're onstage *instructing* all us out here in our ignorant darkness.

TIM
I am not.

SANDY
Listen to him. *Orating*.

TIM
I'm just *talking*.

SANDY
Is this where the magic lives? Inside all this fakery?

TIM
[Starting to go.]
I have to get upstairs.

SANDY
[Following him.]
Go!

TIM
I've got a *show* to do.

SANDY
Do? Do? *Do*?

[In one swift move Sandy turns Tim around.]

TIM
Hey!

[Pinning his arm, Sandy grabs Tim's hand and breaks his finger. Simultaneously, Deb, oblivious, head down in her notes, breaks a pencil. *Snap*.]

TIM
Owwwwww! You broke my finger! *You broke my finger*.

SANDY
I did and I'll tell you why.

TIM
[Crumpled on the floor.]
Ow, ow.

SANDY
We've got to get something *going* around here. Get the daggers cutting a little swifter through the air.

TIM
[Vocalizing his pain throughout Sandy's next speech.]
Goddammit.

SANDY
We're wobbling on the brink around here. It's not a *sustainable model*. So I thought, *Sandy just push it off the edge, Sandy, just* push it, *just snap the finger of the most amiable guy in our community, loved by* everybody, *our* cuddly mascot, *Tim Padley, everybody's rooting for him so just break his middle finger at curtain up and let the* little red wagon clatter down to Hell.

TIM
[Rushing at her.]
I'm going to tear your \ fucking

SANDY
[Raising her fists, furious.]
Try me, *try me*.

[Tim immediately retreats, terrified. Sandy chases him out into the hall.]

DEB
People.

SANDY
[Coming back into the room, addressing no one but the Injustice of It All.]
I have not been cast. Again. *Again*. Again, it's *Thanks Sandy Really Interesting Stuff But Going in a Different Direction* again. From *Ken*. The audition is a curse, a magic thresher, dividing this town into those who flow and proclaim and sing and dance from those hunched in creaking seats, discouraged even to lightly cough. *That's me*. Whose smallest whisper is scolded. *That's me*. On the outs *again. Fucking Ken*.

KEN
[Enters, singing to a made-up melody:]
How now you secret black and midnight hags?

DEB
[Looking up from her notes.]
Oh, Ken! Hello.

KEN
Hello, hello!

SANDY
Ugh.

KEN
[Setting up some plastic cups on the table and pouring from a large flask.]
Anyone want an opening night shot?

SANDY
I do, I do.

KEN
Home brew. Come on in here, Tim.

TIM
[Easing his way back in, holding his finger, still in extreme pain.]
Hi Ken.

KEN
Come in, come in, come in.

[Sitting Tim in the audition chair and giving him a drink.]

Charred barrel bourbon.

SANDY
Yum.

KEN
YUM.

[Drinks. Somehow—this is important—despite his self-centeredness and moaning, he's charming, even funny. He knows how to play a room. He's the kind of man in love with his own voice who has a right to be.]

And I'm going to jump in here and say there is no Magic. No Magic in the theater.

DEB
[Spoken:]
Ha. Ha ha ha.

KEN
I love you so much Deb but I was sitting in the stairwell back there, getting whiffs of your discussion. Sitting in the stairwell drinking my drink, avoiding Mrs. Chaplain and Dr. Klein and Mrs. Bradfield and all the rest of our opening night regulars in their finest khakis and Keds and chunky bracelets and crocheted shawls and each one with a little pillow they've brought for their backs and I'm sorry but there is no Magic. This week I finally had to admit it.

DEB
Ken, stop. You've directed so many miraculous productions.

KEN
I was visiting old Ross in the nursing home the other day.

DEB
Oh, that's nice of you. How is Ross? He was so wonderful in—who was he in *Three Sisters*? Ten years ago?

KEN
The old porter, Ferapont.

DEB
Yes! I thought he would've had more parts after that. He was so good.

KEN
He was, wasn't he? Anyway, I was visiting him, sitting on his bed, and he was trying to eat some soup through a straw.

[He moves to Tim and uses him to illustrate his story.]

And he kept missing his mouth with it, the straw, kept bipping himself in the mustache.

[Bips Tim's mustache area with his finger.]

And I caught myself about to give him the note: *That's good, that's very heartbreaking, missing your mouth with the straw like that. But let me see you do it just twice, and the third time you get it in. It's too much, otherwise, I'm not buying it.*

He's *dying* and I'm giving him *notes* in my head.

DEB
Okay, you had that thought because you *are* your art.

KEN
Please.

DEB
Between the theater and you, no part
Has disentangled from the Inferno's core,
Our heated place—the *stage*. The stage is no more
Not your life, no further from your life
Than Yes is far from No.

TIM
[To Ken, advancing Deb's point:]
Yes, you think you're in a show.
But you've *created* that show. That's what it means
And that's a perfect miracle.

KEN
No, it means that the Magic of Theater has removed me from actually *living my life*. From being present in my life. I can't watch an old friend lose his motor functions and die without thinking about how well-lit the scene is or not.

TIM
Did he manage to eat the soup in the end?

KEN
Yes, yes, yes. The nurse came.

DEB
Well, there you go.

TIM
There you go.

KEN
I would've sat there all day, just watching.

[Bipping Tim again.]

Bip, bip, bip. But the nurse came.

SANDY
Pam?

KEN
Yes, Pam's still there. Can't afford to retire.

SANDY
Didn't she audition for your Scottish Play?

KEN
I think so. Yes.

DEB
She was so good in *Doll's House*.

KEN
Yes. As the nanny. So good.

SANDY
Twenty years ago?

KEN
Twenty years.

SANDY
Hasn't been cast in anything since.

KEN
Is that right?

SANDY
I remember I wanted to be in that play. As Nora.

KEN
You would've been a great Nora.

SANDY
I thought so, yes.

KEN
[Really meaning it:]
You would've been great.

But here we are now.

And for me...there's not even the desire for desire to return.

DEB
Oh, Ken.

KEN
I came down here to tell one of you something. I forget what.

DEB
Well, Tim and I are going to coax up the Magic of theater, this evening. We're going to summon him into the part of The Wolf, or summon The Wolf into him.

KEN
The Wolf?

DEB
Yes. For my play.

KEN
[Not remembering.]
Oh.

DEB
My adaptation of *The Three Little Pigs*.

KEN
The...pigs?

DEB
Ken, we just had our final meeting about this.

KEN
Right, yes. You're down here, auditioning.

DEB
Yes.

SANDY
Ken, you do remember this.

KEN
Yes, yes. The auditions.

DEB
For my play.

KEN
Yes, for which you've shanghaied my Second Murderer. [To Tim:] It was places upstairs ten minutes ago.

TIM
I know, I'm sorry.

KEN
It's opening night.

TIM
We got caught up.

KEN
[To Deb:]
Did he get the part, anyway?

DEB
Still evaluating.

TIM
[Sound of distress, clutching his finger.]

KEN
[To Tim:]
Something wrong with your hand?

TIM
Sandy broke my finger.

SANDY
No.

KEN
No? Deb, do you know anything about this?

DEB
Sorry?

KEN
About your sister breaking Tim's finger.

DEB
I'm sorry, I've been head down in my notes here.

KEN
[To Tim:]
You able to go on?

TIM
Oh, of course.

KEN
It might help, even, with your performance.

TIM
I'm really sorry I missed places.

KEN
Oh, it's fine. You're not on until when?

TIM
Act Three.

KEN
You're doing something remarkable with the role.

TIM
Wow. That's huge coming from you.

KEN
It's not a big role, Second Murderer.

TIM
It's not.

KEN
But you draw an utterly familiar terror from it. You make him *us*. A murderer. If Sandy is right, that a play's actors are the Chosen and the audience are the Outsiders, "the voiceless and be-darkened," well, at least in your moments, the audience will be brought in from their darkness, to enter your spirit totally.

I am one, my liege,
Whom the vile blows and buffets of the world
Have so incensed that I am reckless what
I do to spite the world.

TIM
Oh, that's very good. You're good.

KEN
Ha. Thank ye.

SANDY
It's all right.

TIM
That's not how I say that line, though. At all.

KEN
Really? Well, maybe give it a try, tonight.

TIM
Um. But I thought you liked—

KEN
Just give it a try. With that broken finger...*blows and buffets of the world*...Maybe something will happen.

TIM
Oh. Okay.

KEN
[Turning or jumping at him suddenly.]
Maybe something will happen.

TIM
[Nearly startled out of the chair.]
Yes! Good!

KEN
Of course, if something does happen, it won't be because of you. The *actor*.

TIM
What?

KEN
I'm sorry, this is just where I'm at. We talk about what an actor *brings to a role* but that's a meaningless word-pile, "what an actor brings to a role." Talking of what an actor brings to a role is like talking of what someone possessed by the devil brings to the devil, or brings to the possession. They bring *nothing*. If the role is a proper role it brings itself and the actor is consumed and annihilated within it.

TIM
Chance may crown me without my stir.

KEN
Yes. Yes, to quote the Scottish thing.

[Beat.]

You should get going.

TIM
Oh, yes. Yes.

KEN
Have someone take care of that finger.

TIM
Is there a first aid kit?

DEB
Tim, if you could come back during intermission, we'll make this happen.

TIM
Yes. We will make it happen.

SANDY
Eat shit, Tim.

TIM
Sandy.

[He goes.]

KEN
[Calling after:]
Devlin's coming from the *Gazette*! Give him hell!

TIM
[From off:]
Hell!

[Pause.]

KEN
I know you broke his finger, Sandy. I was in the stairwell listening, remember.

SANDY
I know.

DEB
You did? You broke his finger?

KEN
[Singing to a made-up melody:]
Things are getting crazy at the local Playhouse...

SANDY
Mm.

KEN
[Genuinely:]
Sandy. I'm sorry I couldn't find a part for you.

SANDY
No part has ever been found for me.

KEN
It was interesting, it *was*, what you brought to the audition.

SANDY
Oooo.

KEN
That improv you did. Was that my suggestion?

SANDY
It was not.

DEB
Improv?

KEN
She improv-ed telling my fortune.

DEB
Your fortune.

KEN
My future, yes. I was eating all that pizza, left over from the fundraiser. These auditions—I have to swaddle my brain in a blanket of carbs and grease to buffer the monotony. So, end of day, Sandy's turn, all the crusts are in a mess among my notes. And Sandy—didn't have a prepared piece, I guess—just crosses the room, *flies* across the room, right up to the table, in a spooky trance, spit on her lips, reading the crusts like tea leaves or, or goat innards. And she told me my future. My fate.

DEB
What was it?

KEN
That I'm going to die. Tonight.

DEB
Sandy?

SANDY
I don't really remember this, actually.

KEN
Opening night of "The Scottish Play." I'm going to die. Murdered. Right?

SANDY
That's what I said?

KEN
My throat *closed as if by iron pincers*, was the prophecy of the prophetess.

DEB
Unreal.

KEN
The Pizza Prophetess! It was brilliant, really.

SANDY
But it didn't get me a part.

KEN
It didn't, no.

SANDY
It didn't.

DEB
Well, I don't think you're going to die tonight.

KEN
But are you a seer like your sister? Are you magic?

DEB
No. These days, I can't even see what's there in front of me. An actor, a role—I can't see them joined together in the present.

KEN
Why do you need...

DEB
For these auditions.

KEN
Oh, right. Your children's play.

DEB
Children's play?

SANDY
Ken.

KEN
No? *The Three Pigs*, you said. For the chill'in.

SANDY
Uh!

DEB
[Furious.]
I. Have written. An adult adaptation of—

KEN
[Laughing.]
I'm playing!

With you. Here in your audition room. Playing.

DEB
Ken, don't *do* that.

KEN
A convincing performance. Maybe I should be your Wolf.

DEB
[Sees the potential.]
Maybe.

SANDY
No.

DEB
Yes.

SANDY
No!

KEN
You up for the part, Sandy?

SANDY
As a matter of fact.

KEN
Oh, let's see then.

[An immediate tension.]

SANDY
No.

DEB
Ken, why aren't you upstairs? Your opening night.

KEN
Because I can't stand it. The whole dreary trench of it.

DEB
Of the Scottish...show?

KEN
Any show on that stage. It's like being in an exceptionally boring church. A cobwebbed ceremony I've forgotten the purpose of. I'm dead.

DEB
Oh, \ now

KEN
I'm dead. Every thought, every word—a *corpse.* Do you know what dead word I finally gave in to and used in my Director's Note? Can you guess? After years of resisting it. And for *this* play! Shakespeare's bloodiest, devil-drunk anthem for a cruel and senseless universe, can you take a wild guess what lifeless word I, at long last, surrendered to in my note in the program? Well, naturally, I raised a candle to "community" and "dialogue." That goes without saying, the Artistic Director is *required* to cart out those two moldy chew toys: "At the heart of Shakespeare's darkest work is the lamp of *community* and *dialogue* and *hope* and *moving the conversation \ forward*"

DEB
Well that \ sounds fine

KEN
and so on and on and prithee suck my *fork-ed dick* you dung-drunk culture nibblers, you trough-faced sacks of Dull, lining up for your opening night ration of PC shibboleths and simplistic decoder ring morality tales, suck my warted

knob. It is mandatory to say all that. But, Deb, there is one un-ventured bay in the lake of vomit that is the Artistic Director's Program Note, one word in that lake of vomit I'd never once brought up in the bucket. Deb, dear, comfort me, let me rest my head on your shoulder while you guess my dead word.

DEB
I'm sure it was a good word. A wise word.

KEN
"*Excited.*" That's it. *Excited.* Have you noticed how we theater folk are forever *excited* about everything? "I'm so excited about this project!" "So excited about working with all of you!" We're so *excited!* Like a lab chimp with *electrodes* clamped to its *crotch*—excited, *excited.* It is the worst *lie.* And Moloch help me, I did it. Cast that malevolent hex at my poor audience. "*I could not be more* excited *to present this work of—*"

DEB
But what's wrong with being excited? It *is* exciting.

KEN
Bleecccch.

DEB
Oh, now.

[Ken grabs the wastebasket, sticks his head all the way in, and appears to throw up.]

KEN
Bleeeccchhh.

DEB
Oh, fiddle, are you really throwing up? Are you sick?

SANDY
It's a joke. It's an act.

KEN
[Into wastebasket:]
Maaaagggiiccckblehhhh

SANDY
It's all an act.

DEB
I can't tell!

KEN
I have supped full with hooorrrrooorrsbleeh

DEB
Take that out in the hall. Take that wastebasket out into the hall!

SANDY
[Laughing/actually impressed by Ken's performance.]
He's *faking*.

DEB
I don't want to know. Take it away!

SANDY
So good, though.

DEB
Take it away. Thank you! Bless you!

SANDY
Jesus.

KEN
[Returning from taking out the wastebasket.]
Exciting, exciting. Deb, have you ever entertained the possibility that theater is in fact not exciting at all? Have you ever even allowed the thought?

DEB
Certainly not.

KEN
That theater, actually, is largely an inert glob, not some great force, some powerful shaper of cultural or political progress? That it's—I'm sorry—very un-powerful, very much *removed* from the "town square." A sad, final way-station where magic and power come to wilt, whither, and expire. Very *un*-exciting.

DEB
Stop with this. I'm sure it's brilliant. Your work is always brilliant. I think I hear the audience up there now, gasping, amazed.

KEN
Swine.

DEB
You have vision. And you do it all: the direction, the costumes, the sets. Your *sets*! Down to the last nail, are simply *splendid invitations*. They invite the audience in to a palace of wonders.

KEN
Swine to a trough.

DEB
There's a reason you're head of things around here. You bring the magic.

KEN
I'm sorry, no, there is no magic here.

[Pointing up.]

There. That is Heaven, *heaven*. The place where Nuh. Thing. Hap. Pens. A sealed orb of self-congratulation and calming smugness. Where is sin, there? Where is sin and the *Devil* and the Devil's *teats* to nourish us in mad *drunkenness* and *flesh-punishment* and *idolatry* and *vice*?

SANDY
[Toasting.]
Idolatry and vice!

KEN
Where is Satan and his masks and fire? Tamed, ignored, diluted in that room-temperature bag of piss. *Piss*-temperature bag of piss!

SANDY
Piss-temperature bag of piss!

[The two of them, with their drinks sloshing, are doing a little dance now, circling each other, very self-amused.]

DEB
Stop wallowing the two of you.

KEN
Wallow wallow, we're *excited* to wallow.

DEB
Oh, you'll make me cry.

KEN
If it *was* magic again, that stage would run with blood, *real* blood, I do declah.

SANDY
[Back at her seat at the desk.]
You know, we are sort of trying to work here.

KEN
I'm sorry. My habit lately is to go burrow in the laundromat on Polk street after curtain up, but I came down to tell you something. I forget now what. This haze.

[Pause.]

KEN
Sandy, let's see your audition for Deb's play.

SANDY
No.

KEN
I know you want the lead. The Wolf, right? And I know your sister isn't keen on that. But maybe—as I'm so "brilliant"—I could persuade her otherwise. If I like what you're doing.

SANDY
Which you won't. You never have.

KEN
I do like it. I always have. But I think we're in uncharted seas now, with your sister's play. You two have a bond. Everyone sees it. I think you might have a unique intuition for her writing. Which I haven't read, but still. I've got a feeling.

SANDY
She wants me as Pig of Sticks.

DEB
A crucial role.

KEN
And I want to see her try The Wolf. For me.

DEB
I'm really set on Tim.

KEN
For me.

[A beat.]

DEB
All right. I trust your instinct. Go ahead, Sandy.

SANDY
[To Deb:]
Only for you.

KEN
Sandy, please put the history of me not casting you in any role for twenty years—just put that out of your head. Make a clearing in the brambles of resentment in there, and give this a shot.

SANDY
[To Deb:]
For you.

DEB
From where Tim left off. [To Ken:] This is just after The Wolf has destroyed the house of straw, and—

KEN
I'm familiar with the tale.

DEB
Right. Right. Sandy, go.

[Sandy takes the "stage." Like Tim, she is a solid performer, able to bring us into The Wolf and his story.]

SANDY
I'm Sandy Chandler and I'll be doing The Wolf from an adaptation for adult audiences of *The Three Little Pigs* by Deborah Chandler.

DEB
Just go. Go.

SANDY
[Terribly nervous.]
In a moment it was done: the House of Straw—its towers and battlements, its great dome—was swept away in a pale whirl, and its pig lay flat and trembling, his snout in the dirt at my front paws.

KEN
Good. More. Please.

SANDY
I can't.

[Ken goes to her, has her sit down. Crouches in front of her, genuinely encouraging.]

KEN
Please. Please. Come on.

[She gathers herself. Commits. It's all to Ken, now.]

SANDY
We were both of us, surprised. The first surprise of the world. In the shock of it, before I could apologize, he—flustered in his humiliation—ran for his brother's house, seeking consolation for his loss I suppose. I followed to make amends, to assure him I had had no intention of destroying his home, that I only wanted a friend. But he reached the Stick House and disappeared inside its twiggy confusion, a vast espalier maze of pear and apple trees that ran over the ground for miles in all directions. My yearning for companionship was fled into its labyrinth. I wept. I called out, called within hoping for some understanding. Please. Please. Let me. But from the dim corridors of leaves and forking branches, the brothers grunted out the same strange refusal-rhyme of chins and whiskers.

I was sick with longing. And would bury myself, my shame, there, at their doorstep.

But again, unbidden, the impossible cyclone rose in my lungs. Twofold strong, fueled now by a double refusal. And it brought that house low. In a scratch, it was splinters, not fit for kindling. And for a moment, the three of us, Pig of Straw, of Sticks, and I, were together. With no walls, no doors between us. A hope, at last, for touch, for love. For love.

[She's gone from her chair to Ken, now, on the floor. Embraces him. Overwhelmed with joy at her incredible rendition. He rises, she rises. She waits.]

KEN
Thank you.

SANDY
Well?

KEN
I'm sorry.

SANDY
You're sorry.

KEN
It's the same. As always.

SANDY
God.

KEN
It's nothing I can point to. There's nothing wrong with anything you're doing. Technically, you're *great*. I can see that.

SANDY
So *what? What?*

KEN
You don't belong. You don't belong there. Here.

SANDY
I don't *belong*?

[Deb rushes to her sister, holds her.]

KEN
I'm sorry, I'm sorry, I don't know how else to put it. You stand, you audition and all I think is: *She doesn't fit.*

SANDY
No.

KEN
She doesn't belong here. There's been a mistake. She's like, like a mental patient who's somehow gotten a lectureship or

SANDY
No, no.

KEN
It *hurts* me.

DEB
I thought it was good, Sandy.

SANDY
[Breaking down.]
NO.

DEB
Ken, I think maybe you should leave us alone for \ a bit

SANDY
GET OUT.

KEN
It's nothing personal.

SANDY
GET OUT, YOU FUCKING ASSHOLE.

KEN
I'm being good and I'm being honest. I'm being truthful.

SANDY
THIS IS A THEATER. LEARN TO LIE A LITTLE.

KEN
Not theater. An *audition.*

[Pause. Ken heads for the exit.]

KEN
I will see you both tomorrow in the office. We'll need to pull a quote from the review.

SANDY
I won't be in. I don't *belong here.*

KEN
[From off:]
All right. Just call and let Susan know.

DEB
I'm so sorry for that.

SANDY
He's awful.

DEB
He is. He's a genius. \ But he's awful.

SANDY
He is *not* a genius.

[Ken reënters.]

KEN
Excuse me, I just remembered what I came down here to tell you. Deb, I'm sorry, but there's just not going to be room in the budget or the season for your Three Pigs.

[This is an atom bomb that clears a little space.]

SANDY
What?

KEN
I'm sorry.

DEB
Oh. You're playing with us again.

KEN
No.

DEB
Not funny.

KEN
No, not playing. I feel awful.

DEB
But no, you said. Our last meeting, you looked directly at me, nodded, and said, "Let's do this."

KEN
I know.

DEB
The calendar and the budget were in front of you.

KEN
It's not going to work out.

DEB
KEN.

SANDY
[To Ken:]
Is this about me calling you an asshole? Because that \ would be

KEN
No, no, don't flatter your wickedness. I wrote myself this note, earlier. Just found it in my pocket: "Tell Deb 3 Pigs is no-go." Here.

[He gives Deb the note.]

It's just I've got so much on my mind.

DEB
But.

KEN
I. Am. Sorry.

SANDY
Fuck you.

DEB
Ken, I don't know how to say...so you'll believe me. My Three Pigs...this project....is *necessary*. It's *necessary*.

KEN
Maybe next year.

SANDY
No. This season. As was promised.

KEN
You make it sound like I swore a blood oath. I didn't. And if I did, I have to take it back.

DEB
IT IS NECESSARY.

KEN
To *what*? What's done there within that twig-strewn tomb we call a playhouse, is *necessary* to nothing. It is hollowness, it is *impotence*, it's at best the obituary notice for my dead imagination. But it is *not necessary*.

DEB
To me. It is necessary to me.

KEN
Deb—

DEB
I have some things, antiques, I could sell—silver knives, a thimble. I'll sell them and donate everything to you and the Civic if you'll \ let me

KEN
No, you don't want \ to do that

DEB
I don't even need the stage. I'll do it here, in this darn root cellar. We'll find somewhere to put the seats. I'll pay for it. We'll do it \ here. *Please.*

KEN
AAAHGG!

DEB
How can you deny \ me

KEN
How can you plead so pathetically for this expired Xanax, this pointless \ time-kill

DEB
You have no reason, no reason to refuse me. I will pay for it. It won't even be on the stage.

KEN
[Gripping his head.]
UHHH.

[Resigning himself.]

You can't even cast your lead.

DEB
I will. Tonight, I'll cast The Wolf tonight.

KEN
It can't be Sandy.

SANDY
Fine.

KEN
Get your play cast. We'll meet tomorrow. I promise nothing.

DEB
Just remember that we're meeting.

KEN
I'll make a note.

DEB
Let me.

[She writes on the back of the note he gave her, and hands it to him.]

Ten a.m.

KEN
[He hands it back.]
Make it eleven.

[Deb corrects it and hands it back.]

KEN
[To Sandy:]
And you be there, as well.

[He goes. A beat. Deb breaks down, weeping. Sandy comforts her.]

SANDY
Deb, I love you and it's going to be fine.

DEB
How? *How*?

SANDY
Just cast Tim and be done. Then we can get some wine from the Mega-Bev and drink in the garden till dawn.

DEB
[Showing her the empty purse.]
How comes this wine? *Our money is all gone.*

SANDY
It will, it will all be okay.

DEB
It's Hell.

SANDY
It's war. It's just a little war. We'll tell
our older selves of how we ended it.
Together in the nursing home, we'll sit,
boil soup, deal cards, trim
our ear hair, and say, "We won." Cast Tim.

DEB
I can't cast Tim until I know he is the part.
And he's just not. He's *not*. And there's no art,
no magic here to help, help him, and we're—
we're done. We've lost. There is no magic here.

[Elizabeth has entered, just come from the Y, gym bag, water, etc. She sits in the chair in the audition spot. Sandy and Deb, in their consoling hug, don't notice her at first.]

ELIZABETH
Is it you? Bottled up in this basement like two hapless djinn?

SANDY
Hello.

ELIZABETH
Is it you?

DEB
Can we help you, dear?

ELIZABETH
It wasn't you upstairs. In that awful pageant.

DEB
"The Scottish Play"?

ELIZABETH
I couldn't follow it. Lost in the world, no surprise I'm lost watching a play.

SANDY
Can. We. Help you.

ELIZABETH
Stories, plays, really aren't suited for those broken in their minds. They should be. Stories should help the mentally unwell. Put order to our wandering. But they just lead us deeper into the wood.

What are you doing down here?

DEB
We're holding auditions for a play.

ELIZABETH
Right. About The Wolf. And the cabal of swine.

Tell me my name.

DEB
Did you sign up? I'm sorry, I don't have you on my list.

ELIZABETH
I smelled your flyer at the Y.

DEB
Do you have something prepared?

ELIZABETH
Like what?

SANDY
A monologue is traditional.

ELIZABETH
Well, there's the one story.

DEB
That would be fine.

ELIZABETH
The one story I've kept in my head as I've tunneled blind through the slurry of years trying to find a couple faces I no longer recognize.

DEB
Whenever you're ready.

ELIZABETH
My name you know. And I'll be doing Myself from "WHERE THE HELL WERE YOU?" by me.

There were, once, Three Magical Sisters. Three Magical Sisters who lived separately but would get together occasionally to uproot mountains, boil oceans, and overturn kingdoms. And one day, a Monday, they met up on a heath in Scotland and started a civil war in that country by introducing themselves to an ambitious Thane. Afterwards, after Scotland was littered and soggy with the guts of the dead, and the usurper's head was put on a spike, the sisters had their usual confusion about where and when to meet again, to discuss whatever project might be next. This was always a problem for them, sure. As magical beings, they lived outside of time and space, and so could never get their calendars in sync. But after the Scottish Affair, they absolutely agreed to meet again on Tuesday afternoon at 3:00 at their usual spot on that same heath. Had practically made a pact to meet Tuesday at three o'clock. *But only one of the sisters managed to make it. The other two wandered off, Hecate knows where, through countless backwaters over the centuries, until they finally, it appears, got overly involved with a community theater in a small town in the American Midwest. Where I found them, chewing their minds, stoking their hearts with splinters of damp coal.*

Look at the two of you. Thrown down this well.
Because it is you. My sisters.

SANDY
Okay, dandelion, that's plenty.

DEB
We'll call you.

ELIZABETH
Tell me my name.

[To Deb:] Your calico suckles the wart behind your left ear.

DEB
Ratty is an affectionate cat.

ELIZABETH
[To Sandy:]
You have a hedgehog with whom you do unspeakable things.

SANDY
Define unspeakable.

ELIZABETH
[Making a gesture.]
Tell me my name.

DEB AND SANDY
[Involuntarily, together, they rise and in unison make Elizabeth's gesture, their hands and arms then remaining frozen in it.]
Elizabeth.

ELIZABETH
Ah.

SANDY
[Stunned, as both she and Deb are struggling against this strange power that's entered the room and against the rising memory of their forgotten past.]
What is this?

ELIZABETH
I've been searching. Centuries. Rode a hemlock needle over oceans, whipped my bartered soul through ditches and deserts looking for you. And alone these four centuries, nursed the old evil, stirred the cauldron, brought pox and power to thrones with none of your help.

This is where you've holed up? Here? For what?

[A summoning command to Sandy.]

What?

SANDY
[Almost involuntarily.]
I just want to be on the stage. In a play. One time.

ELIZABETH
Oh, stop.

DEB
[Struggling to move her hands back down to her script.]
The Sisters did nothing on that heath.
The blood, the madness, the war, they brought none of that,
it brought itself. Their mutterings, kettle mixing,
was nothing, nothing. They're a backdrop, atmosphere.

They are not real.

ELIZABETH
That is our strength. Our potion.

DEB
I just would like the story, the ancient story, the Wolf, the Pigs, to be retold. To be told right.

ELIZABETH
Tell it and be done then and come away.

DEB
I don't have my cast.

ELIZABETH
You've had *four hundred years*.

DEB
The parts are complex.

ELIZABETH
There were no parts played in the Scottish affair. We were ourselves.

DEB
[With immense effort, fighting off the truth.]
That never happened. We weren't there.

ELIZABETH
You have forgotten. You have forgotten because what we did was Darkness. And Darkness likes to dig. It burrows like a louse into the mind's tightest grain. But it's there, yet. It will crawl back.

[Ken has entered.]

KEN
Here I am again. Oh, hello Liz.

[To Deb:] We met before, at the YMCA where I gave her your audition flyer. And here she is, auditioning, and it's all connected.

ELIZABETH
[To Deb and Sandy:]
Is this thy warden?

SANDY
Leave us alone, Ken.

KEN
Sandy. Just wanted to come back and say sorry. We left it bad. I left it bad. I am sorry.

If there's one true thing I can say in this room tonight it's I am so sorry.

[Pause.]

Okay.

[Starts to go.]

You know, you should look in upstairs. It's actually going very well.

DEB
As I foretold.

KEN
And Tim, Tim is doing amazing. "Magic."

DEB
You see? You *see*? It's real.

KEN
[Laughs.]
Yeah, not really. At bottom it's just the same old narcissistic carnival.

DEB
Oh!

KEN
Someday, someday there'll come a play that will not bounce in its seat and raise its hand crying "Ooh Ooh Here I Am Here I Am I Am A Play Look At Me."

SANDY
Just please go.

KEN
Someday I'll direct a production that will contain itself. Will not embarrass itself with the usual ache for attention.

DEB
Ken, I'm certain it's fantastic. What is it again?

KEN
What?

DEB
Upstairs.

KEN
Opening night. The play.

DEB
Which is?

KEN
Oh, come on.

DEB
I'm not kidding. I'm sorry, Ken. But for whatever reason, this haze, I can't remember what play you're doing up there.

SANDY
Yes.

KEN
You're really that far gone. "The Scottish Play."

DEB
Yes. What is that?

KEN
"The Scottish..."

[In a whisper at first:]
Macbeth. Macbeth, Macbeth, *Macbeth*—

ELIZABETH
[Thrusting a closing fist towards Ken.]
Die, imp.

KEN
[Hand to his throat, choking.]
Jesus—

ELIZABETH
[Fist still closing.]
Mouth of iron
Tongue of bone
Teeth a chain
To bind a throat of stone

[Ken first rises on his toes, holding his throat, then falls, gasping, on the floor. Sandy and Deb rush to him.]

DEB
Ken! \ KEN!

SANDY
Oh, God, Ken. Sweetheart.

KEN
[Crawling towards hallway:]
Help, help me

DEB
[To Sandy:]
Call someone!

SANDY
There's no signal in this dungeon!

ELIZABETH
[With a final twist of her fist.]
I do, I do, I do.

[Ken expires, violently. Blood from his mouth, if possible.]

DEB
Oh, GOD! HELP HELP MERCY!

SANDY
[Distraught.]
Oh, God. He's dead. He's *dead.*

DEB
How do you know? \ Maybe

SANDY
I FORESAW THIS. IN THE PIZZA.

DEB
What?

SANDY
I saw him fall, just here. His choking, our rushing over...It's like I've rehearsed this, like a scene.

[To Elizabeth:] What did you *do*?

ELIZABETH
Such a minor goblin to keep my sisters. What is this cage?

SANDY
He wasn't a goblin. We weren't his prisoners.

ELIZABETH
Something hates us here.

DEB
We have to move this body. To that props closet in the hall.

SANDY
What? No, we have to go upstairs and call the police.

DEB
I have an audition to run. I need a clean space.

SANDY
What?

ELIZABETH
No, we leave this place.

DEB
[Trying to drag the body out by herself.]
I have to cast my Wolf. I'm under deadline.

ELIZABETH
We leave this place.

SANDY
[To Deb:]
What are you doing?

DEB
Sandy, help me. Tim will be down in a minute.

SANDY
No wait.

ELIZABETH
What keeps you?

DEB
HELP ME. Tim is *this* close. He's *this close* to the part.

SANDY
Our Artistic Director is dead.

DEB
It's tonight or never. He would've wanted us to try.

SANDY
No. No he wouldn't. He didn't give a shit about us.

ELIZABETH
We leave now. Back together. Back to Magic.

DEB
Sandy, *help.*

[A beat as Sandy makes up her mind. She goes and helps Deb.]

ELIZABETH
[As Deb and Sandy drag the body out.]
No. No. There is nothing to be done here. In the *world* is where we brought a kingdom to its madness and terror, to its permanent stain. Where sky-clad we danced and sang and held men's minds with our words and mirrors. There is nothing here of that. What is here?

DEB
[Returning, going straight to her desk and notes.]
My auditions are here. I'm thinking of calling you back for one of the Pigs.

ELIZABETH
I'm not a pig.

DEB
But you could be. That's the Magic.

[Calling to Sandy:]
Are you okay?

SANDY
[Off.]
His hand keeps flopping out!

DEB
Stick it between his teeth!

SANDY
His teeth?

DEB
Just get back in here!

ELIZABETH
Can you not remember?

DEB
Oh—I'm sorry, yes. I remember. When we were hiding Ken just now, it all came back.

[Calling:]
Sandy, I can't find Straw Pig's monologue. Have you seen it?

SANDY
[Off.]
What?

DEB
[Finding it.]
Never mind!

[To Elizabeth:]
It all came back. The haze lifted, quick as a sneeze.

ELIZABETH
You remember.

[Deb goes and gives her a hug.]

DEB
Yes, Elizabeth. I wouldn't think stuffing a dead body into a closet would be such a trigger. Apparently, though.

[Deb goes back to her desk.]

ELIZABETH
You remember that we are sisters. Weird Sisters. That we consort with demons, speak with the dead, shape-shift. That we are magic.

DEB
Yes, yes.

[Calling:]
Sandy!

SANDY
[Off—forcing the closet door shut.]
Hold. *On.*

ELIZABETH
Good. You remember. And realize we need to leave this place.

DEB
Liz, we're immortal, supernatural hags who predict the future. No worries.

ELIZABETH
The *world* is waiting.

DEB
The world is here. Its power is here.

[Sandy enters.]

SANDY
It all came back to me, just now shutting the door on Ken. We're the three whatsits from the play.

DEB
Yes.

ELIZABETH
The play?

SANDY
Our play, whatshisname. MacDeath.

[Hugs Elizabeth.]

I'm sorry we missed you on the heath, Tuesday. Four hundred years ago, Tuesday. Three. Oh. Clock.

ELIZABETH
It wasn't a play. Was it a play?

DEB
[Sitting at her table, looking over her notes.]
With all of Scotland and a bit of England as our stage. Where we danced and sang and held men's minds with our words and mirrors. Unscripted, devised, but a play.

ELIZABETH
Devised?

DEB
They're doing an adaptation of it upstairs.

SANDY
[Joining Deb behind the table.]
Ken said it was good.

DEB
But we have this new play to cast.

ELIZABETH
What?

DEB
You're not right for The Wolf, but you might make a wonderful Pig of Straw, Liz.

[She hands Elizabeth a script page to study. During the following exchange, Deb takes a piece of chalk and draws a circle on the ground, where the auditioners perform. She borders it with runes, numerals, and other signs of magic and witchcraft.]

SANDY
No one's right for The Wolf, apparently.

DEB
Well, not you, no.

SANDY
Why not me? Now that we \ know

DEB
Look, Ken was rude about it, he was rough, but his opinion means a lot to me.

SANDY
He's *dead.*

DEB
His opinion is not dead. And he didn't think you had it.

SANDY
[Throwing the audition chair.]
Maledicit canis ano!

[Un-relatedly, a split-beat later, Elizabeth tears up her script pages.]

DEB
Stop! That's my only copy!

ELIZABETH
You're caught here, by some charm.

DEB
Yes, the charm of *theater*. Which might not mean much to people like you or Ken, Liz, but it means a lot to me.

SANDY
Good old Ken.

DEB
Yes, the dead guy in the closet.

[The two of them laugh—a shrieking witches' cackle. Then a pause, as they consider.]

DEB
How can we laugh? How can Ken's death not matter all of a sudden?

SANDY
Because he was right, I suppose. This is Heaven. A little Heaven where Death is just a make-believe. Just masks and rubber knives and onion tears. Nothing matters here. Hard to feel if anything matters anywhere in the world.

[To Elizabeth:]
Are there, I don't know, *wars* happening now? Out there?

ELIZABETH
What? Oh, yes, I think so. Far off. I've been. We should go to some.

SANDY
It's a magic in itself, I guess, to feel death so dimly, so distantly. But I'd like, maybe, for it to matter. Again.

ELIZABETH
Let's *go* then.

DEB
Tonight it will matter. We'll make it matter. You can feel it, already. The Magic.

ELIZABETH
Not our magic.

DEB
What pulled you to us, then, if not the summoning spell of my audition? Of my play? Here. Here. This is our heath now, this our circle of fair and foul.

ELIZABETH
How foul, exactly? Relatively speaking, you two seem to be rather nice people these days.

DEB
And what's the darn problem with being nice?

SANDY
I'm not nice.

ELIZABETH
There's something wrong.

SANDY
Well, again, Ken had a point, I think. About theater being so calming and polite now, and how it was once actually evil. Could get inside you, corrupt your soul.

DEB
Oh, it can still be evil. It has to be for my play. Even though we like him, The Wolf has to be bad. Tim just needs to find his darkness. The trick is to give him the right prompt.

SANDY
Tell him to imagine there's a dead body in the props closet. That's some Darkness.

[Sandy and Deb cackle. Deb has finished her chalk circle by now.]

ELIZABETH
Why not just turn him into an actual Wolf? A talking Wolf?

DEB
Because that would be cheap and crude. And it's not the play I wrote. The audience has to see The Wolf as both a wolf and a person. Simultaneously. We're attempting a delicate alchemy here.

SANDY
I think it might work, imagining a body.

DEB
Well, I've got nothing else. I'm out of ideas.

SANDY
I could break more fingers.

[Tim has entered.]

TIM
Do not break any more fingers.

[He's rigged something on his broken middle finger—a pencil splint held on with tape.]

DEB
[To Elizabeth:]
Enter Tim.

TIM
I've only got a minute. A *minute.*

DEB
[To Tim:]
We heard the show's going well.

TIM
It's amazing.

DEB
Oh, that's wonderful.

TIM
Actually, it's not so much it. *I'm* amazing.

DEB
I knew you would be! I foresaw it.

SANDY
Oh, fuck me. He plays Second Murderer. He's got three lines.

TIM
I went with the delivery Ken suggested and you could feel the audience *jolt up*.

DEB
Oh, how exciting!

TIM
And Ken joked about it, but I think this broken finger really did help.

SANDY
You're welcome.

TIM
Focused the character's pain. Focused the audience. They *jolted*. Like they'd been asleep, or dead, even. Like they were dead and I'd rolled back the stone of their death cave and called them forth. They went to their feet, applauding. Demanded we repeat the whole scene, and then again.

ELIZABETH
But that's not normal, is it? Something is going on.

TIM
Hello?

DEB
This is Elizabeth. She might be our Pig of Straw.

TIM
I saw her. You. Second row, B6?

ELIZABETH
You memorize the faces and seats of your audience?

TIM
I do. But you walked out before I went on.

ELIZABETH
I couldn't follow things. But I'm sorry I missed you.

DEB
Tim, let's hear the brick section.

TIM
Anything you want me to try?

DEB
We want more darkness. Put something dark in your mind. Imagine there's a dead body in that props closet just out in the hall.

TIM
Body in the closet. Okay. Man or woman?

DEB
Man.

SANDY
Freshly dead.

DEB
Murdered, just minutes ago. Skin still warm. Eyes surprised.

TIM
Good.

[Takes a moment.]

Good. Got it.

DEB
[To Elizabeth:]
This is The Wolf's monologue, where he tells us his version of the tale. We're at the part right after the house of sticks.

[To Tim:]
If you wouldn't mind, Tim, step into that chalk circle on the floor.

TIM
This here? With the numerals and runic markings?

DEB
Yes.

TIM
I'll try not to smudge.

DEB
Don't worry about smudging. The lines between everything are smudged now. The skin of an egg is all that separates the Realms.

TIM
Got it.

DEB
[Muttering as Tim steps in:]
lupus lapis fractus aldheeb bubblegum cricktus
burger king facti sunt preparation H
Bring us in.

TIM
I'm Tim Padley and I'll be performing The Wolf from an adaptation for adult audiences of *The Three Little Pigs* by Deborah Chandler.

[There is a shift here. Tim is somehow...better. He was good before, but now he's grounded. Less eager to please, just simply delivering the truth and pain of his story.]

And for a moment, the three of us, Pig of Straw, of Sticks, and I, were together. With no walls, no doors between us. A hope, at last, for touch, for love. For love.

But away they went. Lumbering quickly into the setting sun, to that tidy House of Bricks on a hill, the last house on Earth. The house that stands to this day, as it stood then, solid as a mausoleum, a pyramid, a savings and loan. Unmoved and unchanging.

Proof against my wind.

I blew my lungs flat, my cheeks round as two aching bladders. But the walls held. As they have held ever since. On that first day, I suppose, the world was making up its mind: which is stronger—bricks or magic? The hard reality of stone or the ambitions of the supernatural?

Bricks won.

The Earth found its axis and turned from the sun for the first time, and my wind was reduced to a howl. And smug and snug in their home, the Brothers laughed.

I knew then the desire for death. The need for death. Wanting a dark brick burrow whose bottom held a boiling kettle into which I would sink my sorrows and my life. To find a way in, at last.

[Done.]

SANDY
[Truly impressed.]
Wow.

ELIZABETH
[Going to Tim.]
Who *are* you?

TIM
I've got to get back.

ELIZABETH
[Taking his hand, her hand on his face, studying.]
Who are you?

TIM
I—

ELIZABETH
Were we to meet you here?

TIM
Yes, I'm on the sheet. Look, they need me back up there.

DEB
Thank you, Tim.

TIM
That really worked for me—the dead body in the closet.

DEB
Good, good.

TIM
And this circle on the floor, I don't know what that was about. But I felt it.

DEB
Good. If I could see you just one more time tonight.

TIM
What? Deb! Deb, you just saw what I did. What I can *do.*

SANDY
[To Deb:]
You *saw.*

[To Tim:]
That was incredible, Tim. Incredible.

TIM
Yep.

SANDY
Fuck you.

DEB
Just one more time tonight.

TIM
No. Give me the part.

DEB
One more time.

[Pause. An icy one.]

TIM
[Starting to exit. To Elizabeth:]
Nice to meet you.

ELIZABETH
We've met.

TIM
Really? I'm sorry, I don't remember.

ELIZABETH
I watched you from the hill. Ran with you, once. Tucked in your mind.

TIM
You should come back to the..."The Scottish Play." See me do my thing for real.

I've got to go.

[He goes, Elizabeth looking after in wonder.]

ELIZABETH
He is The Wolf.

SANDY
He was good.

ELIZABETH
Or maybe not *The Wolf*. How is this possible? This magic. He is so like that first Wolf.

DEB
No, no. He's not. He's not.

SANDY
Deb, he was good.

DEB
He just can't...*get* there.

SANDY
He was good, he was *possessed.*

DEB
No. No. It's the same. He starts in, yak yak yak \ and I'm off thinking

SANDY
"Yak yak yak?"

DEB
about my dirty dishes, my overdraw fees, the mice that've made a nest in the Weber. Mundane, un-magical.

SANDY
What happened to the flaming children?

DEB
The who?

SANDY
How could you not see it?

DEB
See what? How was he so different?

SANDY
How could you not see it?

DEB
I saw the same old sweet, get-along guy.

SANDY
Deb, you know how much I wanted that part. I still want that part. But Tim, Tim *is* that part.

DEB
Well it's my play goddamn it and I'm the director and I'm not sold.

SANDY
Uh!

DEB
I'm on the rack. My mind is *on the rack*. I want to believe you. *But I'm ten thousand years old and I can't think straight.*

SANDY
[To Elizabeth:]
You're with me, right? Tim is that part.

ELIZABETH
I don't know anything about this project, what you're trying to do here. I don't know about parts or acting. And I don't like this place. But, yes, that man is so like The Wolf I once knew.

DEB
I need Ken.

SANDY
What?

DEB
I need Ken to help me.

SANDY
Well, Ken is dead in the props closet.

DEB
But.

But we can \ bring

SANDY
Don't say it.

DEB
We can bring him back \ for just

SANDY
SILENTIUM ASKAT TOST! Vagisil!

DEB
Just to give us his *viewpoint.*

SANDY
His *viewpoint* was that this play shouldn't be done at all.

DEB
He said if I cast The Wolf —

SANDY
No no no. The man was a monster. He lived to fuck you in the head. And now you want to reanimate his corpse so he can Lord of the Dance on your dreams \ one more

DEB
Sandy, I can't see.

I can't see what I'm doing.

I thought this haze had lifted but it hasn't. Ken was an artist. Don't. Despite what you—or he—would say about it, he was a true theater artist. He saw things, the *heart* of things.

SANDY
What he saw was you and me working for nickels in his crappy office for twenty years stapling programs and arranging donor party cheese platters. That was his great *vision*. How can you go on kissing his postmortem *mottled ass*?

ELIZABETH
It is a fact that souls temporarily pulled from beyond the grave do have some keen insights. That's just necromancy.

SANDY
I thought you wanted us out of here.

ELIZABETH
Here's a frightening thing: I don't know what I want. At this moment, I don't know what I want. I lost my reason before I got here, lost it in those knotted centuries searching for the two of you. But it's worse in here. I am...I am bent. The haze you've mentioned, is real.

DEB
Mottled ass.

SANDY
What?

DEB
Mottled. You said Ken had a mottled ass. That I liked kissing. That's an oddly knowing detail. Sister.

SANDY
I imagine it to be mottled.

DEB
And you called him sweetheart.

SANDY
Sweetheart?

DEB
When you rushed to him as he was dying there, you called him sweetheart.

SANDY
Sweetheart?

ELIZABETH
I heard that, too.

[Pause.]

SANDY
We had an arrangement. An occasional, decidedly un-magical arrangement.

DEB
A sweetheart arrangement?

SANDY
Occasional.

DEB
For how many years occasional?

SANDY
Since. Pretty much since we've been here.

ELIZABETH
How long have you been here?

DEB
Twenty years?

ELIZABETH
And where were you before?

DEB
We were...

I don't know.

SANDY
Wherever it was, it wasn't as bad as this place. As that man.

DEB
Your Sweetheart?

SANDY
Don't bring him back.

DEB
Why? Afraid you might want an *occasional arrangement* with his carcass?

SANDY
Please don't bring him back, Deb.

ELIZABETH
You were just laughing about him, moments ago. About him being dead in the props closet.

SANDY
And I want him to *stay dead in the props closet*. He made a Hell in my head. Please, Deb.

DEB
NO. You kept this from me? Your secret midnight shagging, you hid this from me?

SANDY
It was shameful. It was, it was *mud*. It was shameful mud we were rolling in.

ELIZABETH
Shameful? *Osculum infame*. What whore of Satan is concerned with shame?

SANDY
I didn't *know* I was a whore of Satan at the time.

ELIZABETH
But you remember now, yes? You understand these last twenty years you've only been playing a sort of role. It wasn't real.

SANDY
It was magic. At times. It was magic.

ELIZABETH
It wasn't real.

SANDY
Fine.

ELIZABETH
Why all the drama? We help Deb pull this Ken out of the vault, ask him her \ questions

SANDY
Fine. Fine.

DEB
Anything else you haven't told me?

SANDY
Why do I have to tell you everything? Who cares? Like Liz says, it was just an unfortunate illusion these years here in Mortier.

ELIZABETH
Who fashioned that illusion is the question.

DEB
We do this now. I'm under deadline and Tim is coming back any minute. Lizzy, in the hall there's a wastebasket that has Ken's either imaginary or non-imaginary vomit in it. Could you grab that, please?

ELIZABETH
Double-double.

[She goes. Around here, some choreographed movement that sits somewhere between "everyday" movement and ritualized-witch's-spell-dance-movement begins to creep in, ultimately involving all three women. As the spell progresses the lights come up on stage and audience alike.]

SANDY
Imaginary. The vomit was imaginary.

DEB
All the better.

[Elizabeth has returned with the basket and places it in the middle of the audition chalk circle. Deb stands over it with the pages of her script. The dance from here on involves Deb—and later the two others—tearing up/crumpling script pages and putting them in the cauldron-basket. Words underlined are spoken in unison by all three sisters.]

DEB
By the shredded skin of an unborn script
I call him back, untimely ripped
From this mock-stage.

We do this now

While time has lost its pulse. It's time to walk
Between the realms. Their shells, their skins are chalk,
There's no division, now, just one large room
Of waking and dreaming; blending breath and tomb
And fog and light, the makeup and the mirror—
All worlds are all writ together here.

ELIZABETH
All worlds are all writ together here.

SANDY
[After a reluctant beat.]
All writ together here.

DEB
There's no division now, just one large room.
Affections and forgetting, soil and broom,
Wind and the dust-coated void,
The mask and its face,
All writ together in this place.

ELIZABETH
All writ together in this place.

SANDY
All writ together in this place.

[At this point, if they aren't already, the lights throughout the space should be up full—audience and stage illuminated alike. Just One Big Room.]

DEB
We do not hesitate to call
Upon the Dead as they all
Or mostly all have come in through the door
Already and taken their seats. One more
Won't overflow the cauldron, so: dear Ken:
Come back a little while, my old friend.
Come talk awhile, come you drifter
Come from off the ledge of night. Come lift your
Pale ounce and flit back from that last
Edge of the map. Come in you sag-jawed sack
Of quiet blood, come back, retrace the path.

ALL
Retrace the path.

DEB
[Holding a single page up between herself and the hallway door.]
Scribbled page of a not-yet-living script.
On this side myself—on that, the crypt.
This side myself, unknowing, blind
Come corpse, come Death, come infinite mind.

For you, we overturn the grave.

[The wastebasket is overturned in the chalk circle, making a little stool; the play pages scattered round.]

DEB
Come in.

ELIZABETH
Come in.

SANDY
Come in.

[The women are behind the table at spell's end. Deb is seated at her usual, Elizabeth grabs a chair, Sandy does not sit but steps back further from the action, back into the shadows, afraid, perhaps. From full light throughout the room, we go to absolute pitch black. Silence. Then from the hall we hear Ken's approach. Lights up just enough on the audition spot for the actor to find his way there and for him to be just barely seen. He comes in slowly, not so much a zombie, but like someone sleepwalking, or someone in a place they recognize only vaguely. His body is present, his self is quite distant, off flying somewhere in the spirit realms, apparently. It's a long distance call with a bad connection. His hand is in his mouth, clenched between his teeth. He comes and sits on the wastebasket, in the middle of the magic circle.]

DEB
Hand out of your mouth.

[He takes his hand out.]

DEB
Say your name.

KEN
[Hollow, distant, unfocused:]
Ken. Mason. Kenmason.

DEB
Are you still Ken Mason?

KEN
I remember enough of the part.

DEB
Do you recognize this place?

KEN
The cellar of my Small House.
My useless Heaven.

DEB
And who am I?

KEN
I am far from here.

DEB
We've called you back.

[Cracking herself up.]

Ha. This is a call-back.

KEN
Call-back.

[He laughs, in his living dead way, with Deb.]

Call-back.

SANDY
Deb, please.

DEB
A call-back!

ELIZABETH
Why are you saying that? What is that?

DEB
[Getting control of herself.]
Never mind.

[To Ken:]
Who am I?

KEN
My friend.

DEB
Good. Thank you. I have questions.

KEN
Who is here with you?

DEB
Elizabeth. Liz.

KEN
I met her at the Y. She closed my throat.

DEB
She did.

ELIZABETH
It was a magic moment.

KEN
Who stands back in the shadow?

DEB
Sandy.

KEN
Sandy. She is the lamp in this dust, this wilderness I walk.

SANDY
Enough of that.

DEB
Yes, enough.

KEN
My one candle.
But she put me in a closet with my hand between my teeth.

SANDY
Deb, ask your questions and get this done.

KEN
I loved her.

DEB
Enough. I have questions.

KEN
I am far from here. A foot of the past, an inch of the future is all I see.

DEB
Fine, all I need.

A bit ago, this evening, Tim auditioned for The Wolf.

KEN
Tim. The Second Murderer.

DEB
Can you look back on those auditions, please?

KEN
His trials. They were in this circle.

DEB
Yes. Give me your thoughts. Give me some insight. Is he right for the role?

KEN
Sandy was in this circle.

DEB
Never mind about her. What's your take on Tim?

KEN
She was in this circle and I said No to her.

DEB
By Ereshkigal, Dionysus, and Thoth, I adjure you to follow my direction. Do you foresee Tim having a future in the role?

[Pause.]

KEN
I see
I see Sandy.

SANDY
What?

KEN
I see Sandy in the part.

DEB
You are bound by the sinews of Hell to speak truth. And also by the protocols of my audition room. This is a professional theater space and is to be respected. You will not lie to me while sitting in that circle on that wastebasket.

KEN
The dead reborn do not lie.

ELIZABETH
That's true.

DEB
I didn't bring you back from the props closet to talk about Sandy. Sorry, Sandy. There is only one actor who has a chance of bringing this role to life and that is *Tim. Tell me I can activate him. Tell me how.*

KEN
It is Sandy.

DEB
Heavenly Father's Cock and Balls!

SANDY
Deb, it's just his opinion. One dead artistic director's opinion.

ELIZABETH
No. He's speaking from the Beyond. There's no debate, here. We have our answer. It's Sandy. Sandy is The Wolf. Now put him back. The haze is worse with him here.

DEB
This can't be right. The magic's off or something. The magic's failed.

KEN
Sandy?

[A beat.]

Are you there?

SANDY
Yes.

KEN
Oh, yes. Can you step nearer?

[She does.]

Yes. I came back to say. To say something.

SANDY
[On guard.]
What, Ken.

KEN
I'm sorry. For how I was. In life. In the theater.

SANDY
Okay.

KEN
For saying No to you. So many times.

SANDY
Yes.

KEN
But we were magic. Once in a while. Yes?

SANDY
[A beat. Hard to admit this.]
Yes.

KEN
I came back to say. Something. I can't remember.

SANDY
What is it?

KEN
This haze. I can't see. Take my hand.

SANDY
What?

KEN
Please.

[He extends a hand. Slowly, Sandy walks over and takes it.]

I came back to say something. Just to you.

SANDY
Please, Ken.

KEN
Something.

SANDY
[Softly, desperately.]
What? Please. Please.

[Suddenly, the lights come up, returned to normal.]

KEN
[His voice entirely his own again. Laughing.]
I can't. I'm sorry.

[He stands and steps out of the circle.]

SANDY
What?

KEN
I so loved saying, "I see you in the part," I so wanted to say, "You've got the part," but I was playing.

DEB
What is this?

ELIZABETH
Not dead?

KEN
I was playing.

[To Sandy:]
You're no good for The Wolf, Sandy. You don't fit.

SANDY
No.

ELIZABETH
Not dead?

SANDY
No, no.

KEN
No one's right for that cardboard part in that ridiculous distortion of the historical record.

[He kicks the wastebasket against the back wall. Sandy runs behind the table.]

Which once again will not be a part of our upcoming season.

ELIZABETH
[At Ken, rapidly, desperately:]
Mouthofirontongueofboneteethachaintobindathroatofstone

[There's no effect.]

KEN
Stop. There is no magic. No magic in this place.

DEB
[Throwing a spell.]
MORTE NEMICO MORTE MORTE MORTE

SANDY
DIE DIE DIE DIE DIE DIE DIE!

[Nothing. Ken is fine.]

KEN
The walls held. As they have held ever since.

SANDY
How? *How*?

DEB
I saw you stop breathing.

KEN
A convincing performance.

SANDY
No...

DEB
But you were in the closet, hand in your mouth. It wasn't a trick.

KEN
Acting *is* a trick.

ELIZABETH
Who are you? I sealed your face. You were dead.

KEN
I think maybe I've never been alive. Immortality is a kind of death, I think. An unbounded desert of sameness, anyway. I'm so sorry, all of you. I can't help myself.

DEB
WHAT IS THIS?

KEN
A SAD, FINAL WAY-STATION WHERE MAGIC AND POWER COME TO WILT, WHITHER, AND EXPIRE. I'm sorry, it's done. Deb, Sandy, it's back to work in the morning. And Liz, welcome aboard. So exciting, so *excited*.

ELIZABETH
We need to leave.

KEN
I think we'll focus this coming week and for the next five hundred years on marketing and educational outreach, board recruitment, season subscriber sales, aisle sweeping, and toilet scrubbing. You know: *Theater*.

ELIZABETH
The sky is deep. We fly.

KEN
But you are forgetting that you can fly. *There is no magic in this place.*

DEB
Only the haze.

KEN
Only dull theater, to dull your powers. You forget. Then remember. Then forget. And so for four hundred years—Deb, Sandy—I've held you here.

DEB
Theater is Magic. We are Magic.

KEN
Where shall we all meet again? In thunder, lightning, or in my office at eleven a.m. tomorrow morning?

What play is playing upstairs, Deb?

[Pause. The Sisters are dazed, overcome.]

DEB
I don't know. I can't say the name.

KEN
Who is the main character?

[Pause.]

DEB
I can't say the name.

KEN
Liz, Sandy?

ELIZABETH
It's.

Where?

SANDY
[Sobs.]

KEN
A mist seeps out from the bricks in these old walls.
We're back to the beginning.

DEB
Who are you?

KEN
[Stepping into the circle.]

Hello, I'm Ken Mason, and I'll be performing the part of Ken Mason in "Who Is Ken Mason In Actuality?" by me, Ken Mason.

No one ever wonders what happened to The Pig of Bricks after it was all over. After the Wolf came down my chimney and into my pot.

DEB
What.

KEN
The Wolf came down my chimney and into my pot and I cooked and ate him. And then who was left for me to say No to? Because here's what it is about the Pig of Bricks: I have to say it. It is my function in the story, and it is my great craving. A word so full of fat and light. NO. NO. But with The Wolf gone, what to do? Well, I began with my brothers. Didn't want their weak, weedy trash in this house, and so bricked them up behind that wall, there. This one. An excellent launch to my career as an artistic director, to my life in the theater.

Because the theater, as it happens, is all about bricking people up behind brick walls. A machine for excluding. Not magic. The circle of wonders that will always keep more out than it lets in. The theater is No. Think of all the noes it takes to make a play. All the other plays shunned in its favor, and all those disappointed actors, those hopeful little wolves, expending their breath in one-minute monologues, wanting so much to get in, but No. No, No, No. I get to say it forever. I have *to say it forever.*

It's always been a war between the Brick Pig and the needy Wolf. Between hard stones and yearning. Between desire and No. And I Am No. No to The Wolf. No to the Force of him. No to the showy Magic of your trio. And no to love.

DEB
But.
How can you be a pig?
You're Ken.

KEN
It's a delicate alchemy.

ELIZABETH
We have to go.

[Nobody moves.]

KEN
You can't leave this room. We're holding rejections. I mean, auditions. We have to say No to Tim. Again.

[Tim has wandered in. His kilt is disheveled, his chest bare, smeared with blood and soot. He's dazed and somewhat traumatized—like a soldier just returned from a terrible battle.]

TIM
Hello, I'm Tim Padley.

KEN
What do you have for us, Tim?

TIM
[Removing his bandage/splint at some point in his speech.]
I'm Tim Padley. And I'll be doing Tim Padley from "It Happened in the Theater Upstairs a Few Minutes Ago" by Tim Padley.

KEN
A new work. Good.

TIM
It was going so well, my performance. And then I came down off the stage and into the audience. I didn't expect it, they didn't expect it, but all of sudden something just opened up and I was stepping over the footlights, off the edge, into the dark, and onto the laps in the front row. It was Joy. I was met with such adoration, such love. One Big Room. For real, at last. What I've always wanted.

KEN
He's gotten good.

DEB
Shh.

TIM
Everyone pressed around me, to congratulate, touching me, my face. And the critic from the Gazette, *Bill Devlin, he kissed me full on the mouth. He was trembling—we both were. I've always liked Bill, so we made out for a bit.*

And then.

Then I opened his throat with my teeth.

[A gasp from the Sisters.]

KEN
Oh?

DEB
More, more.

TIM
Opened a hole there and used my broken finger to fish out his vocal cords and larynx. And I drank his blood. Why would I do that?

KEN
You murdered our critic?

TIM
I always liked Bill. I like everyone.

SANDY
[Nearly exploding with joy.]
This is spectacular.

ELIZABETH
It makes my brain feel better.

DEB
Shhh.

[To Tim:]
Go. More.

TIM
The rest of the cast, kilts in tatters now, tore the set apart. The plywood castle came down in a poof and fed the flames in the wings. Because there was—there is—a fire.

[As if on cue, a fire's light appears in the hallway. Tim begins to realize he's not Tim anymore.]

KEN
Fire?

TIM
And by its light, through its flickering, I saw then...then the soul of "The Scottish Play" took hold. Some drifting spells crossed by chance in the evening and together undid a rotted knot.

Wiring was torn from a panel somewhere and the grid began to fail.

[The lights begin to flicker, to fail.]

KEN
What have you done to my theater?

DEB
He's gotten in.

KEN
[Exiting, curious.]
What have you done?

TIM
Bill bled out at my feet. God. Like a stuck...

[Snorts like a pig, and laughs.]

He handed me the notes for his review. Great review. Sweet thoughts on my performance, especially.

KEN
[From off:]
There's rubble blocked the stairwell.

ELIZABETH
Bricks.

TIM
Taking their cue from me, the cast, in their branches and leaves, went to the audience, and the audience to them. Kissing and licking, strangling and stabbing. Pam had brought Ross from the nursing home, in his wheelchair, and they enjoyed themselves, arranging the gash-dappled head of our lead actor—whose name I forget—on a festooned spike.

The walls shook and rafters collapsed in the riot and fun, the red slick, the laughter and ash.

[Sounds from upstairs of walls shaking and rafters collapsing. Fire. Screaming.]

The piles of bodies: Mrs. Chaplain, Dr. Klein, Mrs. Bradfield in their finest khakis and Keds, chunky bracelets, and crocheted shawls.

Magic everywhere.
A durational terror.
The dream that is not a dream.
Inside is outside.
The theater, at last, is the world.
And I came down to audition.

[He's done. The Sisters applaud. More explosions, louder now, are heard. Here until the end, sounds of collapse, fire, and ruin.]

DEB
An Adult Adaptation of The Three Little Pigs. That's the name of the play upstairs.

[To Tim:]
You've got the part.

TIM
I am the part. Your promptings were nice, but myself filled myself from the crown to the toe-top full with Wolf.

DEB
Sure. That's always the way.

ELIZABETH
That Thane was the same. We didn't do much.

DEB
[To Tim:]
But you are taking the part, yes? You're coming with us?

TIM
[A beat.]
Of course.

SANDY
Congratulations.

TIM
Thanks, Sandy.

SANDY
Suck my dick.

TIM
It's a wonderful production up there. You should really see it.

DEB
We will.

SANDY
It's to be an ongoing project.

DEB
Devised piece.

[Enter Ken.]

KEN
It is Magic. What you've done.
It is Magic.
Deb.
How?

DEB
The Wolf got in.

KEN
But how? The broken finger? What?

SANDY
"If a role is a proper role it brings itself."

TIM
I just huffed and puffed.

ELIZABETH
Brought down the house.

TIM
[To Elizabeth:]
Oh, yeah. Clever.

SANDY
Sometimes there's just magic.

KEN
And now. Now you leave me?

SANDY
Yes.

KEN
You can't leave. The stairs are blocked.

SANDY
Blocks, bricks, walls are nothing now. Come with us.

KEN
The stairs are *blocked*. There's only that one exit.

[Deb here, or perhaps earlier, starts going into a version of the earlier dance, joined by her sisters, as the practical lights continue to flicker and fade, and the theater above falls to ruin and cinders. Very theatrical lights, blazing, colorful, begin to come up everywhere in the room—stage and audience alike. It's like a first year lighting student has gotten hold of the board and is going to town.]

TIM
But time, I think, has lost its pulse.

DEB
Time
Has lost its pulse. And so we walk
Between its walls.

ELIZABETH
Time has lost its pulse.
All shells, all skins are chalk.
There's no division now, just one large room.

ALL EXCEPT KEN
Just one large room.

KEN
No.

SANDY
Affections and forgetting, soil and broom,
Wind and the dust-coated void,
The mask and its face,
Release us from this place.

DEB
[Opens her purse and pours out a pile of gold coins.]
I've got money now.

SANDY
[To Ken:]
Its true. This is a war between Pig and Magic.
Between the mortar of reality and the unlikelihood of Hell.
Between No and Desire.

[She kisses Ken.]

KEN
I will keep you here again.

SANDY
But tonight desire grants me this:
The first of times, when things are not yet real.
It grants me wilderness.
Come with me.

DEB
[To Tim:]
I don't believe you're going to join our cast.

TIM
It's what I wanted: be a man of glass,
So *through* me any character would show,
Would live. But I'm The Wolf, now, so

DEB
But why not just

TIM
I am The Wolf. I've got my own projects. I'm sorry, Deb.

[Deb and Tim touch in some way, in the dance. A farewell. He exits, then, out a way that has suddenly appeared.]

KEN
No. No.

SANDY
[Moving towards her exit, which has just—magically—appeared.]
Affections and forgetting, soil and broom
Wind and the dust-coated void,
The mask and its face,
Release us from this place.

KEN
No.

ELIZABETH
[At another, different exit.]
Meeting tomorrow. At the Y. *Tomorrow*. Eleven a.m.

DEB
At the Y.

SANDY
Eleven a.m.

DEB
Eleven a.m. To craft a momentous unreality.

SANDY
Terror and fire.

ELIZABETH
War.

DEB
And the theater of war.

KEN
No.

ELIZABETH
Tomorrow.

SANDY
Tomorrow.

DEB
Tomorrow.

[A huge final explosion, a rending of walls, and they're gone—out different exits previously unseen by the audience. Ken stands alone, in the audition spot. He then summons his one power. With each "no" the theatrical lights and sound and whatever else that might signal that we're in a theater, all are shut down, switched off, erased. This can take as many "nos" as are needed to bring the space to silence and dark.]

KEN
No.

[Sound out.]

NO.

["Fire" light goes out.]

NO. NO.

[More lights out.]

NO. NO. NO. NO.

[Ken is left finally in a single, small spot, in silence. He reaches out towards the last light and closes his hand.]

no.

[It sputters out.]

END

ABOUT MICKLE MAHER

Mickle Maher is a co-founder of Chicago's Theater Oobleck, with whom he has produced plays for more than thirty years. He lectures on playwriting at the University of Chicago, and lives with his wife and son in Evanston, IL.